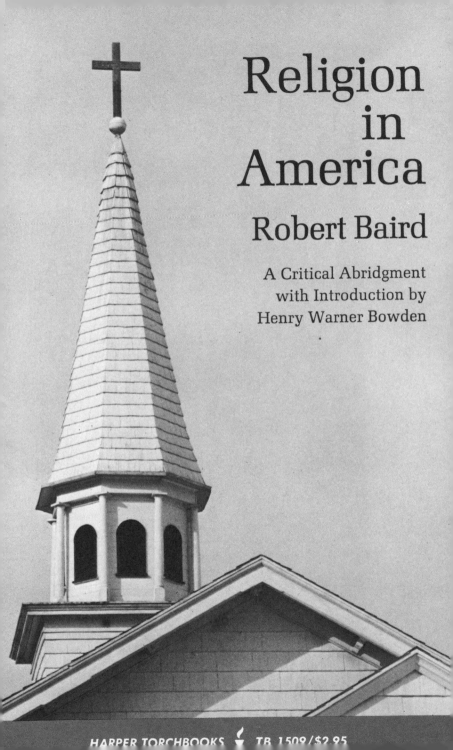

Religion
in
America

Robert Baird

A Critical Abridgment
with Introduction by
Henry Warner Bowden

Religion in America

Religion
in America

Robert Baird

A Critical Abridgment
with Introduction by
Henry Warner Bowden

Harper Torchbooks
Harper & Row, Publishers
New York, Evanston, and London

RELIGION IN AMERICA

Copyright © 1970 by Henry Warner Bowden.

This book was originally published in unabridged form in 1856 by Harper & Brothers, Publishers, New York.

First HARPER TORCHBOOK edition published 1970

LIBRARY OF CONGRESS CATALOG CARD NUMBER: 75-114093

Contents

v

BOOK III

THE NATIONAL ERA

BOOK IV

THE VOLUNTARY PRINCIPLE IN AMERICA; ITS ACTION AND INFLUENCE

BOOK V

THE CHURCH AND THE PULPIT IN AMERICA

BOOK VI

THE EVANGELICAL CHURCHES IN AMERICA

BOOK VII

NON-EVANGELICAL DENOMINATIONS IN AMERICA

Introduction

There are few accessible primary sources on American religious activity in the first half of the nineteenth century, so the publication of this volume meets a real need. The writings of Robert Baird (1798–1863) are particularly relevant to this need because they include a history of religion from the earliest colonization, a survey of contemporary activities and speculations about future prospects. *Religion in America* offers a manual of accurate historical information upon which modern students can rely, but in addition to that it captures the perspective from which Baird wrote and demonstrates the axiom that it is not as much the facts of the case but the presentation of them that gives prominence to a piece of writing. Whether the subject concerns past struggles for religious liberty, present activities to amalgamate Christian virtues and society at large, or plans to spread the Gospel even wider in the future—all discussions bear the stamp of their author. Studying Baird affords the reader both a wealth of specific historical information and access to one of the most balanced and penetrating analysts of religion in his day.

Robert Baird was a missionary agent of the American and Foreign Christian Union, making his initial voyage to Europe in February of 1835.* During a sixteen-year period he crossed the Atlantic eighteen times and covered the Continent from France to Russia, Italy to Sweden, traveling over three hundred thousand miles in efforts to promote Protestant evangelicalism, Sunday School organization, Bible distribution, and temperance reform. In

* Henry M. Baird, *The Life of the Rev. Robert Baird, D.D.* (New York: Anson D. F. Randolph, 1866), pp. 88, 166, 169, 253. Those pages document various changes in the name of the association, but the intent of the organization remained substantially the same.

Portions of this introduction have appeared in the *Journal of Presbyterian History*, 47, 2 (June, 1969), pp. 149–72. They are used here by permission of the *Journal*.

the course of those endeavors he met individuals who were interested in the new patterns of religious life reported to be flourishing in the United States.* Much of his response to this interest about American religion took the form of public addresses and publications, the most comprehensive of which began to take shape in a series of lectures at Stockholm in 1841. Urged by the enthusiasm of his audiences as well as by the sojourner's habit of comparing European practices with those of earlier experience, Baird began amassing notes for a volume which turned out to be a classic in its field. *Religion in America; or, An Account of the Origin, Relation to the State, and Present Condition of the Evangelical Churches in the United States, with Notices of the Unevangelical Denominations* was written in the summer of 1842 at Geneva, published in Scotland, 1843, reprinted in the United States, 1844, and put out in a revised edition in 1856. In the original volume, references to the United States were consistently made with a European reading public in mind. By 1856 a significant American audience had emerged, and the second edition was revised in language directed primarily to the latter group. But some of the new paragraphs were interspersed with older ones written in a different idiom. The confusing result was a text which referred sporadically to "this country" and then "that country" while meaning the United States all the time.

Baird must have felt gratified that his text quickly found its way into French, German, Swedish, and Dutch translations, because he thought his work useful to Europeans who were interested in the "religious economy" of a land they had never visited. Originally he had no thought of distributing the volume in his homeland. It

---

* Other than the present volume, his publications in this area included: *Histoire des Sociétés de Tempérance des États-Unis d'Amérique* (Paris, 1836); *L'Union de l'Église et de l'État dans la Nouvelle Angleterre, considérée dans ses effets sur la Religion aux Etats-Unis* (Paris, 1837); *The Progress and Prospects of Christianity in the United States of America, with Remarks on the Subject of Slavery in America, and on the Intercourse between British and American Churches* (London, 1851); papers read at the Evangelical Alliance entitled "On the History, Present State and Prospects of the Evangelical Alliance Cause in the United States" (1851), "The Progress and Propsects of Christianity in the United States of America" (1851), and "The Influence of Civil and Religious Liberty on Roman Catholicism in the United States of America" (1861).

appeared in 1844 with no changes because Baird thought too many of his countrymen confronted their religious heritage with the same ignorance as nonresidents. Indeed, it was long acclaimed as the standard reference work narrating and evaluating the achievements of American Christianity up to 1855. Its pages comprised the best historical summary of major denominations and the most judicious assessment of the distinctive features of religious life in the New World. Baird's work follows an obvious parallel with that of Philip Schaff, who produced volumes each time *Religion in America* appeared: *The Principle of Protestantism* (1845) and *America* (1855). These men were the only ones at the time who succeeded in comprehending the whole range of religious activity in the United States, and it is the opinion of this writer that Baird's work is more valuable because its use of data and interpretational themes is more comprehensive than Schaff's. Baird's volume was hailed as authentic in historical detail and correct in its choice of salient features.* Its wide acclaim allows us to use it as a source for understanding the dominant image of American Protestantism before the Civil War.† He

---

* A sampling of book reviews in leading denominational journals can give some indication of how Baird's work was received. See *Presbyterian Review and Religious Journal* XVII, 64 (April, 1844), pp. 37–58; *Princeton Review* XVI, 2 (April, 1844), pp. 324–25; *Baptist Magazine* (February, 1844), p. 82; *Methodist Quarterly Review* XXVI, 3rd ser., IV (April, 1844), pp. 322–23; *Biblical Repertory and Princeton Review* (January, 1845), pp. 17–43. For the later edition, see *New Englander* XIV, 4 (November, 1856), pp. 609–14; *Methodist Quarterly Review* XXXVIII, 4th ser., VIII (October, 1856), pp. 641–42; *Church Review and Ecclesiastical Register* IX, 4 (January, 1857), pp. 605–6; *Biblical Repertory and Princeton Review* (October, 1856), pp. 642–54.

† Critical scholarship in this century has not failed to notice the value of Baird's pioneering work. The following selection of recent specialists will lead the student into many of the ways in which the classic volume has benefited modern syntheses. Unfortunately space does not admit quoting their judgments, but see Peter G. Mode, *Source Book and Bibliographical Guide for American Church History* (Menasha, Wis.: George Banta Publishing Co., 1921), p. 3; William W. Sweet, *Religion on the American Frontier, 1783–1840*, vol. *IV, The Methodists, A Collection of Source Materials* (Chicago: University of Chicago Press, 1946), p. 46; Timothy L. Smith, *Revivalism and Social Reform, American Protestantism on the Eve of the Civil War* (New York: Harper & Row, rev. ed., 1965), pp. 10, 45, 89; Nelson R. Burr, *A Critical Bibliography of Religion in America* (Princeton: Princeton University Press, 1961), pp. 60, 169; Winthrop S. Hudson,

embodied most of the leading Protestant assumptions about what constituted evangelical Christianity and how such religion ought, legally and theologically, to function in the lively experiment of American democracy.

Baird depended on the more basic research of other historians for information as to the establishment and growth of ecclesiastical bodies in the United States. A partial list of denominational authors he consulted includes Rufus Babcock on Baptists, Nathan Bangs on Methodists, Samuel Schmucker on Lutherans, R. J. Breckinridge and J. F. Berg (both Protestants) on Roman Catholics, Leonard Bacon and Charles Hodge on Presbyterians. He accepted the word of these denominational annalists and synthesized their data into a narrative embodying the traits of a self-consciously American and ecumenical viewpoint. In Book V, chapter vii (53),* he included a lengthy essay on revivalism, written by another author in 1842, because he knew of no other source "where the whole subject [had] been so well presented in any language." His consultant on the theory and practice of revivals was Chauncey Allen Goodrich, professor of rhetoric and then of pastoral work at Yale from 1817 to 1860. Even though Baird's eclectic type of research did not lead to any significantly different methods of acquiring historical knowledge, his categories of assimilating and presenting that data are far from being outdated. He anticipated every major structural category used by American church historians today, incorporating not only historical sketches of separate denominations but working in addi-

---

Religion in America (New York: Charles Scribner's Sons, 1965), p. 132; Perry Miller (ed.), *America; A Sketch of Its Political, Social, and Religious Character* by Philip Schaff (Cambridge: Belknap Press of Harvard University Press, 1961), p. xxxi; Perry Miller, *The Life of the Mind in America, From the Revolution to the Civil War* (New York: Harcourt, Brace & World, 1965), p. 4 and passim; William A. Clebsch, "A New Historiography of American Religion," *Historical Magazine of the Protestant Episcopal Church* XXXII, 3 (September, 1963), p. 226; and William A. Clebsch, *From Sacred to Profane America: The Role of Religion in American History* (New York: Harper & Row, 1968), p. 5. Finally, see Jerald C. Brauer, "Changing Perspectives on Religion in America," in J. C. Brauer (ed.), *Reinterpretation in American Church History* (Chicago: University of Chicago Press, 1968), pp. 2–3 and passim.

* Chapter numbers used in this volume are given in brackets or parentheses beside the original.

tional themes like sectionalism, immigration, and racial tensions, as well as church-state controversies on federal and state levels. He employed chronological limits to colonial and early national periods which have been accepted as standard; and his attempt to identify the religious foundations of a distinctly American character has continued to interest historical scholars to this day.

The American missionary agent was very clear on the points he wanted readers to remember about the United States and equally forceful about misconceptions to be rejected. He knew his own mind and was able to present the chief characteristics of his nation's religion in a cogent fashion, hoping at the same time to supplant impressions made by migratory flocks of foreign travelers which he considered superficial and misleading. His running battle with Tocqueville on these matters was conducted mainly through extended footnotes (Bk. I, chap. xi; Bk. V, chap. vi [52]; and Bk. VII, chap. x [74]), but it is interesting to see in which areas Americans felt slighted or misunderstood. Some of Baird's interpretations have withstood the test of time, while others have been revised in the light of more critical research. But the point at issue is not how much a volume originally composed in the 1840s contrasts with contemporary scholarship. Later historians may qualify or perhaps contradict Baird's theses, but that does not detract from their usefulness as tracts for the times. The real point of studying this classic is that it represents, in distilled and annotated form, a view of history and a sense of values that once constituted a dominant pattern in American thought.

Baird's work stands as an expression of a confident Protestantism reviewing its accomplishments at mid-century. It allows us a view of how that religious consensus defined itself, what values it deemed significant, and how it thought those ideals had been vindicated in American experience. The book is one of the last expressions of a grand vision that would permeate all facets of life with a religious influence and touch all races, social strata, and ethnic backgrounds with a Protestant ecumenicity.* Such a vision

---

* Robert T. Handy, "The Protestant Quest for a Christian America 1830–1930," *Church History* XXII, 1 (March, 1953), p. 16. See also Sydney E. Ahlstrom (ed.), *Theology in America, The Major Protestant Voices from Puritanism to Neo-Orthodoxy* (Indianapolis: Bobbs-Merrill, 1967), p. 45.

comprised ideas about individualistic approaches to soul-winning, an uncritical and straightforward use of Biblical materials and missionary campaigns for converting the world to democracy, capitalism, and an ethos of hard work, piety, and sober intensity.* Throughout Baird's rich blend of ideas and attitudes, two categories served to bring all subsidiary ideas into an orderly arrangement. The recurring themes of evangelical Protestantism as the core of religious activity in the United States and the voluntary principle as the mainspring of its success lay behind everything else he had to say. Before one starts on the text itself, it might be helpful to clarify the principles of evangelical consensus and voluntaryism as they were understood at mid-century last.

I

Any satisfactory discussion about how the voluntary principle worked in the United States around 1850 presupposes a clear understanding of the basis on which religious groups co-operated in that environment. And it seems natural to define "evangelical churches" before entering into a discussion of their voluntary efforts to build up morality in the nation. Baird did not choose to follow this line of reasoning in his presentation, but this introductory essay shall conform to more recent canons of argument. Following that arrangement, then, the material in Books VI and VII provides necessary information for comprehending Books II, III, and IV. At the outset one must note that Baird, like most of his fellow citizens, did not have an ecclesiology as such. He simply took theological standards that applied essentially to individual conduct and related them to congregations of like-minded individuals. Questions of polity and liturgy were called "points of inferior consequence," and the rigors of a fully systematic theology of the church were reduced to a common denominator of permissive scope. Following traditional categories of Christian witness, evangelical churches were defined along complementary lines of orthodox belief and practical effectiveness in society at large. If

---

* For a good characterization of this frame of mind, see William G. McLoughlin, "Is There a Third Force in Christendom?" *Daedalus, Journal of the American Academy of Arts and Sciences* (Winter, 1967), p. 51.

Baird may be taken as a test case, the common notion in main-stream Protestantism at the end of the Jacksonian period was not that of a self-consciously distinct religious party with intellectual peculiarities or political potential.* A more accurate designation of that loose alliance would be that Protestants considered themselves sufficiently agreed on theological fundamentals to allow for co-operative action toward tangible objectives.† But both aspects of the definition, confessional as well as purposive, were essential to full qualification as a type of evangelical Christianity.

In discussions regarding the doctrinal content of evangelical piety Baird disclosed an inner tension which he never fully resolved. But while at first glance it seems there was hardly anything to hold denominations together other than vague gen-eralities, in the last analysis he held out for a fairly definite content in orthodox Protestantism. Baird emphasized the compatibility of American denominations because he was convinced they were in basic agreement; another factor must have been a patriot's desire to answer European criticisms of increasing pluralism. Thus prompted by data and inclination, he made repeated assertions that "evangelical Christians of the United States exhibit a most remarkable coincidence of views on all important points" (Bk. VI, chap. xviii [65]). He was convinced that all vibrant churches in the New World taught "the doctrines of the Reformers of the sixteenth century, of the apostles, and of the Saviour himself; the sum of which is, that there is salvation only through faith in Jesus Christ . . ." (Bk. VI, chap. vi [61] and Conclusion). Since most churches were agreed on sound doctrine, Baird held that they "ought to be viewed as branches of one great body, even the entire visible Church of Christ in this land" (Bk. VI, chap. xviii [65]). He was ready to admit that there were numerous doctrinal debates,

---

* Charles I. Foster, *An Errand of Mercy, The Evangelical United Front, 1790–1837* (Chapel Hill: University of North Carolina Press, 1960), pp. viii, 178, 273. Foster's useful insights into the British precedents and American usages of the united front are carefully delimited and usually accurate (the best is pp. 123–25). In Baird's view, however, there seems to be no real political consciousness and no appreciation of any disintegration after 1837.

† See Sidney E. Mead, *The Lively Experiment, The Shaping of Christianity in America* (New York: Harper & Row, 1963), pp. 103–4.

but in his view they centered primarily on anthropological questions and the practical problems of making faith relevant to modern man, not on altering that faith. In terms of general tendencies, Baird felt assured that "the progress of religious opinion [was] toward the simplest and most Scriptural views of the Gospel as God's gracious message, which every man may embrace . . . toward the primitive simplicity of Christian truth" (Bk. VII, chap. x [74]). Finally, Baird's comprehensive diplomacy led him to a formula that had become a platitude: he declared evangelical theology simply and uncritically to be "the Christianity of the New Testament" (Bk. VII, chap. x [74]).

At the same time, however, there were definite limits in Baird's mind for regulating theological innovation. He may have taken the view that most religious spokesmen would find it easy to agree on certain basic concepts, but that does not mean he considered all doctrinal differences of secondary importance. Far from being latitudinarian, his discussion of the Campbellites carried the warning that

there is no more certain way of introducing all manner of heresy than by dispensing with all written creeds and formularies of doctrine, and allowing all who profess to believe in the Bible, though attaching any meaning to it they please, to become members of the Church. . . . Before half a century has passed, all manner of error will be found to have entered and nestled in the House of God. (Chap. 62)

When theology was admitted as a significant factor, Baird had difficulty deciding whether the Disciples of Christ, for example, or the Free-Will Baptists should be ranked among the evangelicals. The latter body (numbering 49,809 members in 1855) relied on the Bible to serve as its creed and rules of discipline, a tendency fostering "great danger from Arians and Socinians creeping in among them." As a result, Free-Will Baptists received slight notice in the book, while the Seventh Day Baptists (6,500 members) attracted disproportionate attention, because they were "quite evangelical in the doctrines that relate to the way of salvation." Despite the apparent lack of theological content in evangelical piety, Baird's Princeton education and Presbyterian regard for intellectual precision led him to insist that "creeds are unavoidable, and had better be *definitely expressed* in writing than merely *understood*" (Bk. VI, chap. viii [62]).

No creed was ever specified. Rather than declare in favor of any traditional symbol, Baird posited basic doctrinal guidelines which he thought had to remain constant. In 1841 the American Sunday School Union had asked Charles Hodge, professor of theology at Princeton Seminary, to outline the doctrines held in common by evangelical denominations. Adopting the rubrics of the resulting volume for his own book, Baird advanced seven broad headings— Scripture, sin, justification, faith, repentance, profession of religion, and holy living—as ones necessary and sufficient for classifying a religious perspective as evangelical. At another place in his historical survey Baird constructed a more explicit theology of evangelicalism, six basic points on which he thought all sound ecclesiastical bodies were agreed "in their substantial and real meaning." Those beliefs were formulated in the following manner: the existence of a Trinitarian God, of the same substance and equal in respective attributes; the depravity and condemnation of all mankind; the atonement by the Son of God, "who assumed human nature . . . and by His obedience, suffering, death, and intercession, has procured salvation for men"; the possibility of regeneration by the Holy Spirit with concomitant fruits of faith and repentance; the final judgment of all men; and places accommodating the results of that judgment, everlasting misery for the wicked, blessedness for the righteous (Bk. V, chap. ii [51]).*

In addition to particular points of doctrine, such a consensus had to be held with a conviction derived from personal encounter with God. No merely "historical belief" or general assent to propositions could transform individuals into true believers, even if confessions were accompanied by an outwardly moral life. Baird's

---

* Baird had obviously departed from the influence of Charles Hodge and Princeton Seminary, as witness the criticism leveled against the theology in his book: *Biblical Repertory and Princeton Review* (January, 1845), pp. 34–43; (October, 1856), pp. 642–54. Despite such remonstrances, Baird's warm approval of revival techniques and effects places him much more in line with Nathaniel W. Taylor and New Haven theology than with Princeton. For the best discussion of those camps, see Sydney E. Ahlstrom, "Theology in America: A Historical Survey," in J. W. Smith and A. L. Jameson (eds.), *The Shaping of American Religion,* vol. I (Princeton: Princeton University Press, 1961), pp. 257–59, 263–66.

insistence on a second spiritual birth in the crisis situation of a revival setting is the principle usually taken as characteristic of evangelical groups, but it is important to see that as late as 1855 the general principle could not be separated from a specific doctrinal substratum. Baird had a fundamental grounding in the religious perspective that emphasized gradual growth in the Christian faith. At the same time he was realistic enough to see that revivalism had become a permanent part of the American religious scene, and he was flexible enough to accommodate new approaches. An intellectualized faith, vigorous Calvinism, and an educated ministry sat uneasily with campground enthusiasm and Arminian sympathies, but not to a degree that prevented Baird's adopting elements from both. Taking his discussion as a whole, it seems that Baird did not have a profound appreciation for revivalistic spiritualism. His use of someone else's article on revivalism suggests that he was not a wholehearted advocate of either perspective. One of Baird's strong points was an ability to compromise, and this instance is a good example of such inclusive diplomacy.

It was a bold attempt and an ironic if not scholarly achievement to classify all evangelical bodies into a few easily understood categories. Despite their varied interpretations of points in the doctrinal consensus, Baird thought denominations fell into either a Calvinistic or an Arminian camp. The former group contained such large bodies as Presbyterians, Evangelical Baptists, Episcopalians, Congregationalists, German and Dutch Reformed, while the latter category comprised all branches of Methodists, Lutherans, Cumberland Presbyterians, and United Brethren. He was also able to arrange them handily into three groups according to church government: Episcopalian, Methodist, and Moravian branches held to an episcopal polity; the Presbyterian, Reformed, Lutheran, and Covenanters followed a presbyterian arrangement; while the Congregationalists and Baptists chose congregational autonomy (Bk. VI, chap. i [56]). Baird dealt with basic problems of interpretation in what many will consider too hasty a manner because he minimized their importance. It is particularly interesting to notice in this regard that he made no mention of Baptism or the Lord's Supper as marks of the church, nor did he use liturgy as a means of distinguishing various ecclesiastical groups. While aware that some might be dissatisfied with their place in his classification system, Baird was compelled by an ecumenical desire to reduce as many groups as possible to common denominators and to have them recognize their basic compatibilities. As long as the fundamental tenets of evangelical theology were held in connection with vital, personal commitment, then he was willing to overlook lesser differences and move to the second mark of evangelical legitimacy.

True Christian churches were described as being fully dedicated to doing God's work on earth as a necessary complement to orthodox theological confession. Religious bodies concentrating exclusively on internal growth or quietistic devotionalism fell short of Baird's standard for relevant witness. At a later time he describes what these groups were doing to build up the religious life of the nation, but suffice it now to say that churches were expected to cooperate in such activities. Lutherans, for example, were praised for their similarity to other denominations in this regard; all their more particularistic work, which had no impact on the growth of national character, was left unnoticed. Victories all along the united front of evangelical witness were judged so effective that Baird thought he was privileged to write at a time when religion and culture had become harmonious components of a single way of life. Churches in the United States had been freed from interference by civil magistrates on matters of doctrine, discipline, and polity; yet despite such autonomy, their theology and purposes were so similar that they formed "one great host . . . under the command of one Chief" (Bk. VI, chap. i [56]).*

Confidence in that working harmony led Baird into a discussion of statistics to explicate social effectiveness as the second mark of evangelicalism. The national census of 1855 estimated the total population at 26.5 million; ministers of evangelical churches numbered 29,430; and participating churchmen totaled over 4 million.

---

* Obviously the point about social effectiveness as a second mark of evangelical commitment did not change the minds of European critics who continued to think in the old church-sect typology that was finally crystalized by Ernst Troeltsch. The same sorts of arguments offered by Baird are still necessary, as for example in Franklin H. Littell, *From State Church to Pluralism: A Protestant Interpretation of Religion in American History* (New York: Doubleday and Co., 1962), p. xix.

Such figures provided substance for the image of a Protestant America because they provided a minister for every 900 souls and exhibited "as large a proportion of consistent Christians as . . . other parts of Christendom." Then using an equation which he does not explain, Baird concluded that over 18 million citizens were "more or less under the influence of the evangelical denominations" (Bk. VI, chap. xvii [64]). By mid-century he thought the data proved the churches were at last as faithful to their activist commitment as they always had been on doctrinal matters.*

Baird was one of the first American church historians to utilize a great range of statistics, but some of the conclusions he tried to force out of them strain our credibility and reduce the eminence he might have attained. For one thing, the totals he gives do not always tally with the figures he adds together. Further, one might question the value of stating a ratio between evangelical clergymen and the entire population, when the 1/900 number had little relation to the facts of demography and church affiliation. But one cannot avoid concluding that statistical evidence was distorted when Baird discussed the number of citizens influenced by religion. When dealing with the evangelical churches, Baird expanded church membership by a factor of 4.5 to arrive at the sum total of the population affected by true Christianity. He never explained the origin or the feasibility of that numerical factor; but, to make matters worse, he did not employ the same rationale for unevangelical churches. In that latter category, members of all sorts were found to number approximately 3.4 million, but their influence was judged to extend to no more than 4 or 5 million, not 13.5

---

* Baird never justified his use of the 4.5 equation, but he may have been fairly accurate in using it. Major Protestant denominations made rather strict demands on all intending to be members; consequently, many were interested in attending services but were not willing to have their private lives regulated by church discipline. Such people numbered several times the number of actual members at Sunday services. On the other hand, it is likely that most of those attending a Catholic mass would be members. See T. Scott Miyakawa, *Protestants and Pioneers, Individualism and Conformity on the American Frontier* (Chicago: University of Chicago Press, 1964), pp. 18, 246–47. For a more contemporary reference, see Andrew Reed and James Matheson, *A Narrative of the Visit to the American Churches by the Deputation from the Congregational Union of England and Wales* (New York: Harper & Bros., 1835), Vol. I, p. 132.

million as one might expect. Baird never explained why he thought
every evangelical Christian influenced 4.5 citizens in society, while
unevangelicals affected a maximum of 1.5 persons. The discrep-
ancy indicates Baird's eagerness to place evangelical religion in the
best possible light and concurrently restrict the prospects of unevangelicals. From his treatment of the material, one would not
derive an accurate impression of the relative strength of denominations across the board. After perusing Baird's statistical tables, it
would be surprising to discover that by 1850,

the Roman Catholic Church, which at the close of the Revolution was
tenth in point of size and everywhere except in Pennsylvania laboring
under some civil restrictions, was the largest. Second in size were the
Methodists, followed by the Baptists, Presbyterians, Congregationalists,
and Lutherans. Seventh in size were the Disciples—an upstart group
less than twenty years old. The Protestant Episcopal Church had
fallen to eighth place, while, perhaps most amazing of all, Joseph
Smith's Mormons were ninth.*

Questions regarding the legitimate and equitable use of statistics
raise problems about their lasting value in this book.

Just as there was a twofold criterion for defining evangelical
alignment, there were similar grounds for judging religious bodies
which did not belong. The outsiders could be further divided into
unevangelical Christians, who merited some favorable comment,
and non-Christian sects which neither thought nor acted correctly
(Bk. VII, chap. x [74]). Non-Christian bodies comprised the
Jews, Rappites, Shakers, Mormons, all types of deistic "infidelity,"
and all forms of "socialism." Baird denounced them in uncompromising terms, and they were summarily dismissed as playing no
real part in the major trends of American life. The list of unevangelicals included Roman Catholics, Unitarians, Universalists,
Hicksite Quakers, Christ-ians and Swedenborgians, but Baird
thought only Catholics and Unitarians actually deserved serious
consideration. Those two denominations pointed up once again the
tension and consistency in the historian's judgmental structure.

---

* Sidney E. Mead, *The Lively Experiment*, p. 107; see also William W.
Sweet, *The American Churches, An Interpretation* (New York: Abingdon-
Cokesbury Press, 1948), p. 42.

Beginning again on the confessional side of the ledger, he placed unevangelical groups in a separate column because they were not viewed as churches "whose religion is the Bible, the whole Bible, and nothing but the Bible . . ." (Bk. VII, chap. i [67]). Baird was careful to point out that, in the main, Roman Catholics did "hold those doctrines on which true believers in all ages have rested their hopes for eternal life," and he never confused them with those who openly rejected sound theology. But at the same time he thought Catholics had buried the truth "amid the rubbish . . . of human tradition and inventions" to a degree that compromised their allegiance to orthodoxy and vitiated their full implementation of civic virtues. Unitarians presented the reverse problem. They had often been in the forefront of battles for reform and seemed to improve all of society by their adherence to a sense of common human decency. But their underlying theology was judged insufficient because it contradicted major tenets of the basic framework for evangelical action. So the cohesiveness of orthodoxy and activism as Baird's twin marks of evangelicalism withstood attempts to subordinate one to the other; Catholics and Unitarians, each for a different reason, were found inadequate and lumped together as unevangelical. Even though the combined strength of all those groups affected the lives of an estimated five million people, Baird placed them outside his main concern because they were "sects that either renounce, or fail faithfully to exhibit the fundamental and saving truths of the Gospel."

II

The greater part of Baird's literary effort involved a consideration of how evangelical churches pooled their resources to accomplish tangible common goals in the United States. But before describing ways in which religion freely participated in such collective programs, he included a fairly lengthy historical study of the origins of religious liberty in the New World. That historical material provided a framework for discussing his main interests, the application and prospects of the voluntary principle as America's unique contribution to modern Christian vitality.

As a defender of religious liberty, Baird thought it necessary to meet charges made against it and assess the dangers pluralism was thought to embody. The first criticism he took up was the notion that no religion at all is better than a false one. While admitting that most members of unevangelical sects would remain indifferent to an established church, he argued that their experimentation in theology was a positive sign because, once men's minds were questing for religious truth, they would be more open to a faithful representation of the Gospel. Instead of being dismayed by the proliferation of sects and erroneous opinions, Baird viewed the increase of denominations as a sign of healthy diversification, a natural process in a democratic state that prevented both the institutionalization of dogmatism and polarized opposition. He also employed the standard defense of American pluralism by showing that "there is scarcely an evangelical communion . . . which is not the mere extension by emigration of a similar body in Europe." After tracing the historical roots of major ecclesiastical groups back to European soil and proving that New World freedom had nothing to do with their origin, he took up a more contemporary train of thought and argued against the enthusiasm for merging denominations into a single, nationwide institution. Baird was realistic enough to see that men will always differ on points of doctrine and church order, and so he defended a pluralism that preserved good will against the prospects of conformity won through Procrustean tactics. His command of facts as well as his love of democracy gave force to his laconic demurrer: "The world has already seen what sort of union and brotherhood can be produced by all being brought into one immense Church, that admits of no deviation from the decrees of its councils. . . ." (Bk. VII, chap. xix [66]).

If there was such a happy congruence of motive and mission among evangelical churches, why did European visitors continually identify a contentious spirit as characteristic of religious sects in the New World? In Baird's view the strife among sects had been misunderstood and magnified out of proportion; the hostility between evangelical churches and unevangelical groups was real and justifiable. His conception of a great theological consensus permitted slight and passing quarrels among Christian bodies on secondary points, but such minor disputes did not deserve the stigma attached to them. Sectarianism, or more delicately, "uncharitableness," came to the surface only when evangelicals were "contending for saving truth" and refused "to hold fellowship with errors of vital moment." That latter activity, contending for right views and righteous living, was what foreign visitors simultaneously declared lacking in the United States and then deplored when they discovered it actually in force. The effective churches of mainstream Protestantism united, then, internally on theological and purposive compatibility and externally on opposition to "the errors of Rome, and . . . other aberrations from the true Gospel . . ." (Bk. VI, Chap. xix [66]).

It was the dominant opinion among European observers that the "American plan of religious freedom" had no rational foundation but was largely the result of environmental circumstances. They thought that since early religious groups had confronted no state churches, no institutions defended by habit, antiquity, or sentimental prejudice, it had been relatively easy to place all denominations on a common level and tolerate them with equanimity. Baird's first task, then, was to correct this erroneous impression by reviewing the facts of religious establishments and explicating the arguments used for 150 years in their behalf. He pointed out that in every section of the country there had been good men who "made no secret of their fears that the cause of religion would . . . be ruined [by disestablishment]; that the churches would be forsaken by the people, whose unaided efforts would prove unequal to the expense of maintaining them . . ." (Bk. I, chap. xiv). In addition to concerned citizens, churchmen were prone to equate preservation of established churches with zeal for the cause of God. Under that combined influence, 10 out of the 13 original colonies provided governmental support for religious institutions from the very beginning. Only a brave minority, "those who first . . . had learned it in the school of persecution," were willing to accept the principle of religious toleration. Rhode Island, Pennsylvania, and, for a brief period, Maryland and Delaware were the limited areas fostering genuine religious liberty. In most cases, however, the right of individual conscience had to overcome a solid wall of opinion and precedent.

Baird's treatment of the ideas and circumstances leading to a separation of religious organizations and civil authority did not contain any theological arguments to favor that end.* His view was that legislative support for both Episcopal and Congregational establishments had simply proved detrimental to the cause of religion, and in their characteristically pragmatic way American leaders agreed that voluntary support was ultimately the best policy. Taking Massachusetts as a paradigmatic case, Baird tried to show how state churches unwittingly worked against themselves. Even though the original plan tried to furnish new towns with ministers as soon as they were chartered, keep political power in the more trustworthy hands of church members, and exclude would-be settlers of questionable virtue, the laws made to secure those advantages provided for decay rather than growth. For one thing, the plan could not deal humanely with dissent. Whippings, fines, banishment for Williams and Hutchinson, death for Anabaptists, Quakers, and those accused of witchcraft, all these were judged excessive penalties by American religionists of 1855. Theological norms and enforced conduct had relaxed to a degree, it seemed obvious that

so absurd a spectacle would never have taken place among so enlightened a people as the colonists of Massachusetts . . . had not the union of the Church and the State led the government so often to act on grounds purely religious, and to take cognizance of subjects which no political government is capable of deciding upon. (Bk. II, chap. xix [21])

Other disadvantages of the New England way had their effect more exclusively within churches. The close correlation between church membership and citizenship made it necessary to introduce the Half Way Covenant and thus lower standards of religious truth and practice. With churches of diluted quality, it was more difficult to maintain sound doctrine because members chose ministers who

---

* In 1965 John F. Wilson wrote a thought-provoking essay to introduce his critical selection of documents entitled *Church and State in American History* (Boston: D. C. Heath & Co., 1965). On pp. ix–xi, xiii, and xv of that introduction he gave cogent arguments why the words "church" and "state" should not be applied to the history of religious groups in the United States, especially after 1785. With the conviction that European terminology does not apply, I have avoided it except where Baird's explicit words are used.

spoke what was pleasing to the majority. Baird was convinced that Unitarianism gained a foothold in the New World under the protection of a state establishment, and, without broaching the question of the actual causes of Unitarianism, "but for this law, no such societies or preachers would ever have existed." Finally, all franchised citizens, rather than those few who attended services, were allowed to choose pastors of local churches; and as a result orthodoxy suffered total exclusion in many districts. State support of religion thus proved itself incapable of maintaining a satisfactory standard of belief or conduct. Experience in the southern colonies added another lesson: compulsory uniformity tended to produce lassitude among those favorable to the system and created resentment among those opposed (Bk. II, chap. xx [22]).

Just as Baird was not interested in marshaling theological tenets to defend the line of separation between religious institutions and civil governments,* he was equally indisposed to recount any participation of religious groups in the American Revolution. There was no mention of the "black regiment" which preached in favor of the rebellion, nor a consideration of religious grounds for resisting tyranny, an item which has become commonplace in literature since the 1850s. In Baird's view the revolutionary period had disastrous effects on the cause of evangelical religion, and he quickly passed over the era, pausing only to mention the legal transactions that made for greater religious freedom. Since Virginia seemed to set the tone for other states, considerable space was used to explain its dissolution of church-state ties. The narrative of similar events in other states followed a rather schematic line that included little factual data. In the Old Dominion, however, Baird dealt very carefully with all important factors because he wanted to convey the proper interpretation to his readers and help them assess accurately the roles of agents involved. Most

---

* Sidney E. Mead, "Neither Church nor State: Reflections on James Madison's 'Line of Separation,'" *A Journal of Church and State* X, 3 (Autumn, 1968), pp. 349–63, continues the line of reasoning that the terminology regarding religious groups and civil magistrates in this country must be employed in a manner congruent with historical fact. Instead of the old, inadequate terms, "religious institutions" and "civil authority" seem more appropriate.

Europeans were accustomed to thinking that action separating church and state had been primarily the work of Thomas Jefferson, but Baird tried to reject that view and provide one more amenable to mid-nineteenth-century Protestants. He was unwilling to admit that Jefferson played an effectual part in creating an atmosphere beneficial to religion because he knew the nation's third president had been a deist, an "arch-infidel" who harbored nothing but debased reasons for dragging Christian groups down to the same level as other religions of the world (Bk. III, chap. iii [26]). Baird was unable to see that conditions might have changed between 1785 and 1855. Thus he placed a priority on the activities of those who eventually benefited from disestablishment and used those circumstances to build strong sects of active Protestantism.* Presbyterians, especially those of the Hanover Presbytery, Baptists, and Quakers were designated the true pioneers of American religious liberty. Left-wing churches, not deist partisans like Jefferson, had been the true fathers of the "American Plan" because they balanced their opposition to conformity with a sincere dedication to the success of true faith in men's hearts. Their activity had been constructive and stemmed from positive motives, and in Baird's view those evangelical activists merited greater recognition than one who could not have been pleased by a flourishing network of free churches.

What was really involved in practicing religion on a voluntary basis? If churches could not find adequate support by legislative enactment, then religion would rely "under God, upon the efforts of its friends, acting from their own free will" (Bk. IV, chap. i [33]). For all of Baird's concentration on voluntaryism as the distinguishing characteristic of religion in America, he did not credit environment with being the cause of its vitality. His selection of the voluntary principle was sound in the sense that he chose one of the features which set American practice apart from other

---

* Sidney E. Mead, *The Lively Experiment,* p. 38 and fn. 2 on p. 192, has shown how pietists recognized their incompatibility with deists only after the war and their joint victory of attaining the separation of church and state. Mead's significant essay long ago recognized how Baird stood for the latter-day view of Protestants who had forgotten their erstwhile alliance with deism.

nations; but when he described the most basic factors involved in religious progress, he spoke of elements familiair to Christian ministers from London to Berlin. The true causes of religious vitality in the United States were: conscientious preaching of God's Word, attention to Christian nurture through Sunday schools and Bible classes, distribution of Bibles, and voluntary support of educated ministers to lead men to understand Biblical truth. It is clear that mid-century Protestants did not consider their success an inevitable or accidental consequence following the nation's policy of religious toleration; that was "only the occasion . . . not the means, by which the Church of Christ has made so great advances" (Conclusion). For men such as Baird the numerical strength and cultural influence of pan-American Protestantism was taken as a vindication of its essential truth.

Discussion of how the voluntary principle applied to American life actually comprised three different ways in which evangelical churches pursued activities they considered proper to their witness. The first and most important activity was to extend knowledge of the Gospel; then churches joined forces to attack and destroy existing evils in society; or, failing that, to co-operate on benevolent and humane grounds to alleviate such suffering as they could. In treating the activity of churches along these three levels Baird confined himself primarily to statistical data, implying that, since the legitimacy of their goals was beyond question, the burden of his proof lay in explicating the scope of problems overcome. His account of the work of innumerable voluntary associations hammered away at a single conclusion: American churches had been equal to the tasks before them.

On the level of evangelizing a growing and mobile nation, ministers faced odds that would probably have daunted their European brethren because by 1855 the population exceeded twenty-seven million and was increasing at a rate unparalleled in history. In Baird's view the task for Protestants in facing that burgeoning populace was simply one of supplying people with the basic elements of religious instruction. His book included lengthy descriptions of the American Home Missionary Society and five other missionary boards directed by specific denominations, together with lists of expenditures and personnel involved, all calculated to prove that the investment was profitable and demands were being met. Religious interests were also instrumental in improving primary education, grammar schools, and colleges, not because religious mentors wished to proselytize children, "but rather that at these schools the youth of the nation may be qualified for receiving religious instruction effectually elsewhere" (Bk. IV, chap. xi [39]). The Education Aid Society provided means to educate men who felt called to preach, and thirty-seven theological seminaries were available to train them for service. The American Sunday School Union, American Bible Society, American Tract Society, and various other agencies aided the process of Christian nurture by providing the means of understanding God's plan of salvation. Throughout his long discourse Baird preferred not to linger on the religious and social values preached by this united evangelical front. He disclosed instead a Yankee admiration for efficient machinery and a fascination with statistics which he probably considered unanswerable proof of the enterprise.

The second type of voluntary co-operation was directed toward changing some of the deplorable practices in society at large. Men from various Christian persuasions joined forces to improve conditions in prisons, promote a more thoroughgoing observance of the Sabbath, establish peace, and introduce more temperate use of alcoholic beverages. Baird also mentioned various antislavery societies (not abolitionists) in this category, indicating that their cause had become respectable enough to find a place on religion's list of essential activities. The beneficent institutions, dedicated to relieving man's temporal needs, were not essential to the prime objective of evangelical churches. Men of humane sentiments could work to alleviate poverty and disease, build hospitals, almshouses, orphanages, and asylums for the insane, blind, deaf, and dumb, but relief work as such was not considered germane to spreading the Gospel (Bk. IV, chap xxvi [48]). Another interesting aspect of this treatment of voluntary co-operation was the place of foreign missions because it further illustrates the limits in Baird's perspective. The work of the American Board of Commissioners for Foreign Missions, similar efforts of seven other denominations, the American and Foreign and Christian Union, and even the American Colonization Society were put in a separate section of the book. If that conception is representative of majority opinion at the time, then Protestants thought the evangelization of their own land, first through preaching and second through social reform, was more important than "the propagation of the Gospel in pagan countries."

While churches pursued goals pertinent to their spiritual vocation, at the same time they were convinced they contributed to the special qualities of democratic life. Christianity and the American character appeared as constituent elements of a single fabric, each reinforcing the strengths of the other.* On one side religious freedom necessitated active self-reliance and an application of industry and energy that helped produce citizens of solid reliability. The voluntary principle was judged a good school for citizens because "men are so constituted as to derive happiness from the cultivation of an independent, energetic and benevolent spirit, in being co-workers with God in promoting His glory, and the true welfare of their fellow-men" (Bk. IV, chap. xxx [49]). Earlier in the book he had stated that it was a thorough acquaintance with the Bible that fitted men for responsible freedom. By studying Scripture "they learned to look upon all men as children of the same heavenly Father. . . . They saw no reason, therefore, why one man should lord it over another. . . . And they learned from the Bible that obedience is due to rulers, not because they are different in blood or rank from other men, but because government is 'an ordinance of God.' " This exhausts his theoretical defense of democracy.

More with an eye toward his European readers, Baird raised the question of how civil governments affected religious practice in the New World. Here, too, he tried to calm the fears of those unacquainted with the situation and to prove that democratic society was integral to the growth of American Protestantism. The

---

* For a good treatment of the origin and dating of this concept, see C. I. Foster, *An Errand of Mercy,* p. 185. See also Clifford S. Griffin, *Their Brothers' Keepers, Moral Stewardship in the United States, 1800–1865* (New Brunswick, N.J.: Rutgers University Press, 1960), pp. 45–46, 99; and Jerald C. Brauer, "The Rule of the Saints in American Politics," *Church History* XXVII, 3 (September, 1958), pp. 251–53.

Constitution stated that Congress could not make a law establishing orthodoxy or prohibiting the free exercise of religious views, but that declaration was not taken to imply that legislators should exclude Christianity from national policy altogether. Baird held the view that both federal and state constitutions tacitly accepted the tenets of "sound religion" as part of their structure and openly supported its activities. There were several instances to suggest the national government was favorable to the Christian sympathies of its constituents: courts, customhouses, and public offices were closed on the Sabbath; presidents occasionally proclaimed days of fasting or thanksgiving; chaplains were appointed for the army and navy; in judicial affairs the oaths of atheists were disallowed; public lands were granted for building Christian charitable institutions. All this support came from magistrates who sought not to show favoritism, but simply to recognize that religion was fundamental to the operation of orderly government (Bk. III, chaps. v and vi [28 and 29]).

Another point which indicates the degree to which Baird equated evangelical Christianity and national character was related, ironically, to dissent. While arguing that colonial establishments had been wrong to punish those confessing a faith deviating from the norm, he asserted that by 1855 Protestant Americans were unwilling to grant the right of rejecting religion altogether. Within a broad and generous structure of doctrinal standards, men could fashion their faith as they wished. Yet any dissent from that loose net of orthodoxy cast grave doubts not only on the validity of their spiritual orientation but on their right to hold such an opinion at all. Drawing such a distinction exposed one of the more callous and self-satisfied attitudes found in the system of values dominant at the time:

Rights of conscience are religious rights, that is, rights to entertain and utter religious opinions, and to enjoy public religious worship. Now this expression, even in its widest acceptation, can not include irreligion—opinions contrary to the nature of religion, subversive of the reverence, love, and service due to God, of virtue, morality, and good manners. What rights of conscience can atheism, irreligion, or licentiousness pretend to? . . . They have no right, . . . to come forward and propagate opinions and proselytize. (Bk. III, chap. ix [252-53])

Men who were so sure of themselves, who had successfully blended their ideals with the patterns of national life found it easy to read their success back into history. They understood the planting of colonies and struggles for political independence within a context that envisioned the Kingdom of God as its final goal. And they judged all developments in the light of that standard.

After having reviewed the origins and application of voluntaryism, Baird turned to its prospects in the United States, including both problems to be dealt with and sources of encouragement. As he saw it there were three problems confronting future co-operation among churches and a fruitful interaction between their programs and national character. The immense range of open land and the human rush to occupy it seriously taxed the efforts of voluntary associations to provide churches and an adequate religious influence on the frontier. Slavery was also a great obstacle because it created irreligious attitudes in master and slave that frustrated attempts to rectify the situation. And finally, immigrants of more recent years had brought ignorance, poverty, and moral depravity in their train, posing greater logistic difficulties on the seaboard than those met in the Midwest.

Yet despite these impediments, the cause was advancing, and Baird was confident the trend would be continued. He utilized statistics to indicate how voluntary support was able to recruit and finance an adequate ministry and erect enough new buildings to keep pace with growing membership rolls. He spoke in generalities when dealing with criticisms of the nation's moral condition, but the lack of specific data did not prevent him from forcibly denying that religious freedom contributed to such ills as bank failures, political unrest, race riots, and a high crime rate. Slavery, however, was the one area that gave him pause. While blaming European commerce for its introduction, he could not blink the fact that Americans still exploited or acquiesced in the practice. Baird made no secret of his desire to "efface this dreadful evil," but he relied exclusively on the slow influence of Christian suasion (Conclusion). He saw the achievement of peaceful and equitable manumission as the "greatest and most difficult" task yet to be solved by Protestant churches. And with their long record of victories on other moral battlefields, it is not incomprehensible that Baird, like most religious spokesmen, clung to the futile hope for conversion and reform, a change of heart, and voluntary improvement.

Any attempt at a general analysis of this classic work cannot hope faithfully to reproduce its wealth of topics, detail, and accurate data. It can only give some indication of Baird's theological and historical viewpoint by showing how great quantities of material were synthesized and stamped by that perspective. That distinctive mark affords the reader an opportunity to study the mind of American Protestantism as it was constituted a century before our time. The intervening years have brought drastic reorientations in religious thought, highlighted by debates over science, Biblical criticism, and the relative weight of social issues. They also witnessed a shift in the relationship between Protestant evangelicalism and secular patterns, with religious influences moving from their accustomed pre-eminence to varying degrees of isolation. In view of these later developments, it is rewarding to understand the mind of those who lived in a more confident period when such problems formed a cloud on the horizon no larger than a man's hand.

III

It remains to explain in a few lines the scope and editorial aspects of this edition of Baird's work. The 1856 volume extended to 688 pages, but the present reproduction has been held to one-third that length. And while the original contained a wealth of information on hundreds of topics, it was also encumbered with repetitions that modern readers could be spared. The abridged Baird is smaller and much neater, and it still retains the thrust and emphases of the original as well as most of its pertinent information. The guiding principle for judging material has been that a new edition such as this should provide students of the period with one of the tools of their trade. Recently a critic has reminded us that "the only way to be a historian is to know the sources for [one's] period and to understand the ways of examining and evaluating them."* The deletions and selections have been made in

---

* Richard Luman, book review in *Church History* XXXVII, 4 (December, 1968), p. 455.

hopes that the resulting volume will serve as a concise and accurate reproduction of Baird.

Mechanical devices have been kept to a minimum, and all editorial comments appear within brackets. Whenever sentences, parts of sentences, have been omitted, ellipses are used; wider spacing in the copy indicates that at least one whole paragraph has been omitted. Some chapters have been omitted entirely; their titles are given in brackets in places they are omitted. A few typographical errors in the early text have been silently corrected. Several footnotes of questionable value have been dropped. The last silent device to be mentioned deals with numbers: whereas Baird often wrote out a figure such as "seven hundred thousand, four hundred and twenty-seven," those words have been converted to numerals, in this case 700,427. Other than those minor changes, the present text stands as a reproduction of the early classic. Its cadence, arrangement, punctuation, and rhetoric have been preserved to give the flavor of ante-bellum Yankee opinion. This abridgment can be used as a self-sufficient unit, or it can serve as a window to the larger volume of a century ago, leading students to a more thorough understanding of Baird's life and work.

The main perspective and emphases have already been discussed, but there are several attitudes or idiosyncrasies which bear mentioning because they give more color to the narrative. For example, Baird was very much taken with the notion that Anglo-Saxons were the best people on earth; he claimed that they brought democracy to these shores and gave substance to every national virtue. It is difficult to tell whether there is an air of defensiveness or a WASP smugness behind such an emphasis on race superiority, but it forms a definite part of his views on colonization, immigration, and social stability. In the light of such racial consciousness, Baird was ambivalent in his ideas about American Indians. At times he spoke with a reformer's zeal against unjust treatment at the hands of white men, but most of the time he spoke of them as savages whose ingrained way of life resisted acculturation. The urgings of Christian charity might lead him to decry abuses, but all in all Baird thought the Indian deserved what he got because he spurned the benefits of that religion and civilization destined to cover the continent. His attitudes about the black man were hardly more sympathetic. Negro slaves appeared to be more receptive to Christian teachings and merited more consideration than Indians because of their tractability. But in the last analysis Baird respected the doctrine of states' rights more than he supported strong measures to abolish human misery.

Baird believed that the American commonwealth had received providential favor: the land was a garden kept in reserve until there were Protestant nations to discover and occupy it. A race of sober and religious men had been fostered to build a nation where old vices would not prevail and where the voice of the people could approximate and sustain the voice of God. In many such instances Baird's prose sounds like a theological counterpart to the work of George Bancroft. The volume on religion in America has over fifteen explicit references to, and as many indirect uses of, Bancroft's history. Indeed, the latter's *History of the United States, from the Discovery of the American Continent* . . . provided a fundamental interpretational theme upon which Baird simply made variations. All these opinions supply more features for the rough sketch of Baird made in this Introduction. But they are secondary to his well-grounded convictions, and the reader is best left to form his own conception of what kind of man Baird really was. His main ideas pertained to the past, present, and future of religion in the United States, and the book's prime value rests on them because they subsumed a culture within their limits.

BOOK I

Preliminary Remarks

CHAPTER 1

General Notice of North America

The configuration of the Continent of North America, at first view, presents several remarkable features. Spreading out like a partially opened fan, with its apex toward the south, its coasts, in advancing northward, recede from each other with considerable regularity of proportion and correspondence, until, from being separated by only sixty miles at the Isthmus of Darien, they diverge to the extent of 4,500 miles; the eastern coast pursuing a north-easterly, and the western a north-westerly direction.

. . . the whole portion of North America which is now either occupied or claimed by the people of the United States, was, when first visited by Europeans, and for more than a century afterward, one vast wilderness. The luxuriant vegetation with which it had been clothed year after year, for ages, was destined only to decay and enrich the soil. Thus did the work of preparing it to be the

1

abode of millions of civilized men go silently and steadily on; the earth gathering strength, during this long repose, for the sustentation of nations which were to be born in the distant future. One vast and almost unbroken forest covered the whole continent, imbosoming in its sombre shadows alike the meandering streamlet and the mighty river, the retired bay and the beautiful and tranquil lake. A profound and solemn silence reigned everywhere, save when interrupted by the songs of the birds that sported amid the trees, the natural cries of the beasts which roamed beneath, the articulate sounds of the savage tribes around their wigwams, or their shouts in the chase or in the battle. The work of God, in all its simplicity, and freshness, and grandeur, was seen everywhere; that of man almost nowhere; universal nature rested, and, as it were, kept Sabbath.

Two hundred years more pass away, and how widely different is the scene! Along the coasts, far and wide, tall ships pass and repass. The white sails of brig and sloop are seen in every bay, cove, and estuary. The rivers are covered with boats of every size, propelled by sail or oar. And in every water the steamboat, heedless alike of wind and tide, pursues its resistless way, vomiting forth steam and flame. Commerce flourishes along every stream. Cities are rising in all directions. The forests are giving way to cultivated fields or verdant meadows. Savage life, with its wigwams, its blanket covering, its poverty, and its misery, yields on every side to the arts, the comforts, and even the luxuries of civilization.

CHAPTER 2

The Aborigines of

North America

North America, when discovered by Europeans, was in the occupancy of a great number of uncivilized tribes; some large, but most of them small: and, although differing in some respects from one another, yet exhibiting indubitable evidence of a common origin. Under the belief that the country was a part of the East Indies, to reach which, by pursuing a westerly course, had been the object of their voyage, the companions of Columbus gave the name of Indians to those nations of the Aborigines whom they first saw. Subsequent and more extensive exploration of the coasts of America convinced them of their mistake, but the name thus given to the indigenous tribes has adhered to them to this day.

A striking similarity of organization pervades the tribes of North America.* All have the same dull vermilion, or cinnamon complexion, differing wholly from the white, the olive, and the black varieties of the human family; all have the same dark, glossy hair, coarse, but uniformly straight. Their beards are generally of feeble growth, and instead of being permitted to become long, are almost universally eradicated. The eye is elongated, and has an orbit inclined to a quadrangular shape. The cheek-bones are prominent; the nose broad; the jaws projecting; the lips large and thick, though much less so than those portions of the Ethiopic race.

Yet there are not wanting considerable varieties in the organization and complexion of the Aborigines of North America. Some nations are fairer-skinned, some taller and more slender than others; and even in the same tribe there are often striking contrasts. Their limbs, unrestrained in childhood and youth by the appliances which civilization has invented, are generally better formed than those of the white race. The persons of the males are more erect, but this is not so with the females; these have become bowed down with the heavy burdens which, as slaves, they are habitually compelled to bear.

Poets have sung of the happiness of the "natural," in other words, uncivilized life. But all who know anything of the aboriginal tribes of North America, even in the present times, when those

---

* This may be said also of all the aboriginal tribes of America entire, from the shores of the Northern Ocean to the Island of Terra del Fuego. But there was a vast difference in regard to civilization. The inhabitants of Mexico and Peru, when those countries were visited and conquered by Cortes and Pizarro, were far more civilized than the tribes of the portion of North America which we are considering. No remains of antiquity among the latter can be for a moment compared with those of the kingdoms of Montezuma and Central America.

that border upon the abodes of civilized men live far more comfortably than did their ancestors three hundred years ago, are well aware that their existence is a miserable one. During the excitements of the chase, there is an appearance of enjoyment; but such seasons are not long, and the utter want of occupation, and the consequent tedium of other periods, make the men in many cases wretched. Add to this the want of resources for domestic happiness; the evils resulting from polygamy; the depressions naturally caused by the sickness of friends and relatives without the means of alleviation; the gloomy apprehensions of death: and we can not wonder that the "red man" should be miserable, and seek gratification in games of chance, the revelries of drunkenness, or the excitements of war. I have seen various tribes of Indians; I have traveled among them; I have slept in their poor abodes, and never have I seen them, under any circumstances, without being deeply impressed with the conviction of the misery of those especially who are not yet civilized.

They are not without some notions of a Supreme Power which governs the world, and of an Evil Spirit who is the enemy of mankind. But their theogony and their theology are alike crude and incoherent. They have no notion of a future resurrection of the body. Like children, they can not divest themselves of the idea that the spirit of the deceased still keeps company with the body in the grave, or that it wanders in the immediate vicinity. Some, however, seem to have a confused impression that there is a sort of elysium for the departed "brave," where they will forever enjoy the pleasures of the chase and of war. Even of their own origin they have nothing but a confused tradition, not extending back beyond three or four generations. As they have no calendars, and reckon their years only by the return of certain seasons, so they have no record of time past.

Though hospitable and kind to strangers to a remarkable degree, they are capable of the most diabolical cruelty to their enemies. The well-authenticated accounts of the manner in which they sometimes treat their prisoners would almost make us doubt whether they can belong to the human species. And yet we have only to recall to our minds scenes which have taken place in highly-civilized countries, and almost within our own day, when Christian men have been put to death in its most horrible forms by those who professed to be Christians themselves, to be convinced that, when not restrained by the grace and providence of God, there is nothing too devilish for man to do.

A great deal has been said and written about the gradual wasting away and disappearance of the tribes which once occupied the territories of the United States.

It is not intended to deny that several tribes which figure in the history of the first settlement of the country by Europeans are extinct, and that several more are nearly so. Nor is it denied that this has been partly occasioned by wars waged with them by the white or European population; still more by the introduction of drunkenness and other vices of civilized men, and by the diseases incident to those vices. But while this may be all true, still the correctness of a good deal that has been said on this subject may well be questioned. Nothing can be more certain than that the tribes which once occupied the country now comprised within the United States, were, at the epoch of the first settlement of Europeans on its shores, gradually wasting away, and had long been so, from the destructive wars waged with each other; from the frequent recurrence of famine, and sometimes from cold; and from diseases and pestilences against which they knew not how to protect themselves. If the Europeans introduced some diseases, it is no less certain that they found some formidable ones among the natives. A year or two before the Pilgrim Fathers reached the coast of New England, the very territory on which they settled was swept of almost its entire population by a pestilence. Several of the tribes that existed when the colonists arrived from Europe were but the remnants, as they themselves asserted, of once powerful tribes, which had been almost annihilated by war or by disease. This, as is believed, was the case with the Catawbas, the Uchees, and the Natchez. Many of the branches of the Algonquin race, and some of the Huron-Iroquois, used to speak of the renowned days of their forefathers, when they were a powerful people. It is not easy, indeed, to estimate what was the probable number of the Indians who occupied, at the time of its discovery, the country east of the Mississippi and south of the St. Lawrence, comprising what is still the most settled portion of the United States; and from which the Indian race has disappeared, in consequence of emigration or other causes. But I am inclined to think, with Mr. Bancroft, to whose diligent research in his admirable work on the United States I am greatly indebted on this subject, as well as on many others which are treated in this work, that there may have been in all not far from 180,000 souls.* That a considerable number were slain in the numerous wars carried on between them and the French and English during our colonial days, and in our wars with them after our independence, and that ardent spirits, also, have destroyed many thousands, can not be doubted. But the most fruitful source of destruction to these poor "children of the wood" has been the occasional prevalence of contagious and epidemic diseases, such as the small-pox, which some years since cut off, in a few months, almost the whole tribe of the Mandans, on the Missouri.

It is difficult to estimate, with any thing like absolute precision, the number of Indians that now remain as the descendants of the tribes that once occupied the country of which we have spoken. Without pretending to reckon those who have sought refuge with tribes far in the West, we may safely put it down at 115,000 or 120,000 souls. The entire number of Indians within the present limits of the United States is estimated by the Commissioner of Indian Affairs at 400,764, of whom 123,000 are west of the Rocky Mountains. Of what is doing to save them from physical and moral ruin, I shall speak hereafter.

[Two chapters, "Discovery of That Part of North America Which Is Comprised in the Limits of the United States" and "The Position and Extent of the United States; Nature and Resources of the Country," followed here in the original.]

---

* Bancroft's *History of the United States,* vol. iii, p. 253.

CHAPTER 3

The Colonization of the
Territories Now Constituting
the United States
at Length Accomplished

The first permanent colony planted by the English in America, was Virginia. Even in that instance, what was projected was a factory for trading with the natives, rather than a fixed settlement for persons expatriating themselves with an eye to the future advantage of their offspring, and looking for interests which might reconcile them to it as their home. It was founded in 1607, by a company of noblemen, gentlemen, and merchants in London, by whom it was regarded as an affair of business, prosecuted with a view to pecuniary profit, not from any regard to the welfare of the colonists. These, consisting of forty-eight gentlemen, twelve laborers, and a few mechanics, reached the Chesapeake Bay in April, 1607, and having landed, on the 13th of May, on a peninsula in the James River, there they planted their first settlement, and called it Jamestown, in honor of James I., then the reigning monarch of England—an honor to which his claims were more than doubtful. There had been bestowed upon the company, by royal charter, a zone of land extending from the thirty-fourth to the thirty-eighth degree of north latitude, and from the Atlantic to the Pacific Ocean, together with ample powers for administering the affairs of the colony, but reserving to the king the legislative authority, and a control over appointments; a species of double government, under which few political privileges were enjoyed by the colonists.

What from the wilderness-state of the country, the unfriendliness of the Aborigines, the insalubrity of the climate, the arbitrary conduct of the company, and the unfitness of most of the settlers for their task, the infant colony had to contend with many difficulties. Yet not only did it gain a permanent footing in the country, but, notwithstanding the disastrous wars with the Indians, insurrectionary attempts on the part of turbulent colonists, misunderstandings with the adjacent colony of Maryland, changes in its own charter, and other untoward circumstances, it had become a powerful province long before the establishment of American Independence. . . .

Massachusetts was settled next in the order of time, and owed its rise to more than one original colony. The first planted within the province was that of New Plymouth, founded on the southwest coast of Massachusetts Bay, in 1620; but although it spread by degrees into the adjacent district, yet it never acquired much extent. It originated in a grant of land from the Plymouth Company in England, an incorporation of noblemen, gentlemen, and burgesses, on which King James had bestowed by charter all the territories included within the forty-first and forty-fifth degrees of north latitude, from the Atlantic to the Pacific Ocean. That company having undergone several modifications, much more important settlements were made under its auspices—in 1628 at Salem, and in 1630 at Boston, from which two points colonization spread extensively into the surrounding country, and the province soon became populous and powerful. A colony was planted in New Hampshire in 1631, and some settlements has been made in Maine a year or two earlier; but for a long time the progress of these was slow. In 1636, the celebrated Roger Williams, having been banished from Massachusetts, retired to Narragansett Bay, and by founding there, in 1638, the city of Providence, led to the plantation of a new province, now forming the State of Rhode Island. In 1635, the Rev. Thomas Hooker and John Haynes having led a colony into Connecticut, settled at the spot where the city of Hartford now stands, and rescued the Valley of the Connecticut from the Dutch, who, having invaded it from their province of New Netherlands, had erected the fort called Good Hope on the right bank of the river. Three years thereafter, the colony of New Haven was planted by two Puritan Nonconformists, the Rev. John

Davenport and Theophilus Eaton, who had first retired to Holland on account of their religious principles, and then left that country for Boston in 1637. Thus, with the exception of Vermont, which originated in a settlement of much later date, made chiefly from Massachusetts and New Hampshire, we see the foundation of all the New England States laid within twenty years from the arrival of the Pilgrim Fathers at Plymouth.

Meanwhile, Maryland, so called in honor of Henrietta Maria, daughter of Henry IV. of France, and wife of Charles I., had been colonized. The territory forming the present State of that name, though included in the first charter of Virginia, upon that being canceled and the company dissolved, reverted to the king, and he, to gratify his feelings of personal regard, bestowed the absolute proprietorship of the whole upon Sir Charles Calvert, the first Lord Baltimore, and his legal heirs in succession. Never was there a more liberal charter. The statutes of the colony were to be made with the concurrence of the colonists, thus securing to the people a legislative government of their own. Sir Charles was a Roman Catholic, but his colony was founded on principles of the fullest toleration; and though he died before the charter in his favor had passed the great seal of the kingdom, yet all the royal engagements being made good to his son Cecil, who succeeded to the title and estates, the latter sent out a colony of about two hundred persons, most of who were Roman Catholics, and many of them gentlemen, accompanied by his brother Leonard. Maryland, though subjected to many vicissitudes, proved prosperous upon the whole. Though the Roman Catholics formed at first the decided majority, the Protestants became by far the more numerous body in the end, and, with shame be it said, enacted laws which for a time deprived the Roman Catholics of all political influence in the colony, and tending to prevent their increase.

The first colony in the State of New York was that planted by the Dutch, about the year 1614, on the southern point, it is supposed, of the island where the city of New York now stands. The illustrious English navigator, Hudson, being in the employment of the Dutch at the time of his discovering the river that bears his name, Holland claimed the country bordering upon it, and gradually formed settlements there, the first of which was situated on an island immediately below the present city of Albany. Hudson being supposed to have been the first European that sailed up the Delaware, the Dutch claimed the banks of that river also. But their progress as colonists in America was slow. Though Holland was nominally a republic, yet she did not abound in the materials proper for making good colonists. The country presenting but a limited scope for agriculture, the people were mostly engaged in trade, or in the arts.

Pursuing in the New World the same selfish principles which made the Dutch mercantile aristocracy the worst enemies of their country in the Old, the New Netherlands colonists were allowed little or no share in the government, and accordingly, notwithstanding the greatest natural advantages, the progress of the colony was very slow. . . .

New Jersey was . . . granted to the Duke of York, who, in 1664, handed it over to Lord Berkeley and Sir George Carteret, both proprietors of Carolina. . . . West Jersey was afterward purchased by a company of Friends, or Quakers: and a few years later, in 1680, William Penn, previous to his undertaking to plant a colony on a larger scale in Pennsylvania, purchased East Jersey, with the view of making it an asylum for his persecuted co-religionists. Finally, East and West Jersey being united as one province under the direct control of the crown, obtained a legislature of its own, and enjoyed a gradual and steady prosperity down to the Revolution by which the colonies were severed from England.

Pennsylvania, as indicated by its name, was founded by the distinguished philanthropist we have just mentioned; but he was not the first to colonize it. This was done by a mixture of Swedes, Dutch, and English, who had for years before occupied the right bank of the Delaware, both above the point where Philadelphia now stands, and many miles below. The charter obtained by William Penn from Charles II. dates from 1681. On the 27th of October in the following year, the father of the new colony, having landed on his vast domain in America, immediately set about the framing of a constitution, and began to found a capital, which was destined to become one of the finest cities in the western hemisphere. The government, like that established by the Quakers in New Jersey, was altogether popular. The people were to have their own Legislature, whose acts, however, were not to conflict with the just claims of the proprietor, and were to be subject to the approval of the crown alone. The colony soon became prosperous. The true principles of peace, principles that form so conspicuous a part of the Quaker doctrines, distinguished every transaction in which the Aborigines were concerned. It is the glory of Pennsylvania that it never did an act of injustice to the Indians.

The territory belonging to the State of Delaware, was claimed by Penn and his successors, as included in the domain described in their charter; and for a time formed a part of Pennsylvania, under the title of the Three Lower Counties. But the mixed population of Swedes, Dutch, and English, by which it was occupied, were never reconciled to this arrangement, and having at last obtained a government of its own, Delaware became a separate province.

The settlement of the two Carolinas began with straggling emigrants from Virginia, who sought to better their fortunes in regions further south, and were afterward joined by others from New England, and also from Europe. At length, in 1663, the entire region lying between the thirty-sixth degree of north latitude and the River St. John's in Florida, was granted to a proprietary company in England, which was invested with most extraordinary powers. . . . Their grand object was gain, yet the celebrated John Locke, at once a philosopher and a Christian, was engaged to make "Constitutions," or a form of government, for an empire that was to stretch from the Atlantic to the Pacific. The result of the philosophical law-giver's labors was such as the world had never before seen the like of. . . . These "Constitutions," into the further details of which we can not enter, were attempted to be introduced, but were soon rejected in North Carolina; and after a few years' struggle, were thrown aside also in South Carolina, which had been separated from the Northern province. The colonists adopted for themselves forms of government analogous to those of the other colonies; the proprietary company was after awhile dissolved; the Carolinas fell under the direct control of the crown, but were governed by their own Legislatures. Their prosperity was slow, having been frequently interrupted by serious wars with the native tribes, particularly the Tuscaroras, which, as they were the most powerful, were for a long time also the most hostile.

Last of all the original thirteen provinces, in the order of time, came Georgia, which was settled as late as 1732, by the brave and humane Oglethorpe. The colonists were of mixed origin, but the English race predominated. Although it had difficulties to encounter almost from the first, yet notwithstanding wars with the Spaniards in Florida, hostile attacks for the Indians, and internal divisions, Georgia acquired by degrees a considerable amount of strength. . . .

CHAPTER 4

Interior Colonization

of the Country

. . . It will be observed, that a hundred and twenty-five years elapsed between the foundation of the first and the last of the original thirteen provinces; also, that, with the exception of New York and Delaware, which received their first European inhabitants from Holland and Sweden, they were all originally English; but, eventually, these two were likewise included in English patents, and their Dutch and Swedish inhabitants merged among the English.

All these colonies were of slow growth; ten, even twenty years being required, in several instances, before they could be regarded as permanently established. That of Virginia, the earliest, was more than once on the point of being broken up. Indeed, we may well be surprised that, when the colonists that survived the ravages of disease, and attacks from the Indians, were still further reduced in their number by the return of a part of them to England, the remainder did not become disheartened, and abandon the country in despair. The Plymouth colonists lost, upon the very spot where they settled, half their number within six months after their arrival; and terrible, indeed, must have been the sorrows of the dreary winter of 1620–21, as endured by those desolate yet persevering exiles. But they had a firm faith in God's goodness; they looked to the future; they felt that they had a great and glorious task to accomplish; and that, although they themselves might perish in attempting it, yet their children would enjoy the promised land.

Stout hearts were required for such enterprises. Few of the colonists were wealthy persons, and as those were not the days of steamships, or of fine packets, and large and well-appointed merchant vessels, the voyages had to be made in small and crowded ships. The inconveniences, to say nothing of the sickness that attended them, were but ill calculated to nerve the heart for coming trials; and as the colonists approached the coast, the boundless and solemn forests that stretched before them, the strangeness of every object that filled the scene, the absence of all tillage and cultivation, and of a village or house to give them shelter, and the uncouth and even frightful aspect of the savage inhabitants, must have damped the boldest spirits. In the case of Plymouth and some others, the settlers arrived during winter, when all nature wore her gloomiest attire. The rudest hovels were the only abodes that could be immediately prepared for their reception, and for weeks together there might only be a few days of such weather as would permit their proceeding with the operations required for their comfort. Not only conveniences and luxuries, such as the poorest in the mother-country enjoyed, but even the necessaries of life were often wanting. Years had to be passed before any considerable part of the forest could be cleared, comfortable dwellings erected, and pleasant gardens planted. Meanwhile, disease and death would enter every family; dear friends and companions in the toils and cares of the enterprise would be borne, one after another, to the grave. To these causes of depression there were often added the horrors of savage warfare, by which some of the colonies were repeatedly decimated, and during which the poor settler, for weeks and months together, could not know, on retiring to rest, whether he should not be awakened by the heart-quailing war-whoop of the savages around his house, or by finding the house itself in flames. Ah, what pen can describe the horror that fell upon many a family, in almost all the colonies, not once, but often, when aroused by false or real alarms! Who can depict the scenes in which a father, before he received the fatal blow himself, was compelled to see his wife and children fall by the tomahawk before his eyes, or be dragged into a captivity worse than death! With such depressing circumstances to try the hearts of the colonists—circumstances that can be fully understood by those only who have passed through them, or who have heard them related with the minute fidelity of an eye-witness—who can wonder that the colonies advanced but slowly?

Still, as I have said, they gradually gained strength. At the Revolution of 1688, in England, that is, eighty-one years after the first settlement of Virginia, and sixty-eight after that of Plymouth, the population of the colonies, then twelve in number, was estimated at about 200,000, which might be distributed thus: Massachusetts, including Plymouth and Maine, may have had 44,000; New Hampshire and Rhode Island, including Providence, 6,000 each; Connecticut, from 17,000 to 20,000; making up 75,000 for all New England; New York, not less than 20,000; New Jersey, 10,000; Pennsylvania and Delaware, 12,000; Maryland, 25,000; Virginia, 50,000; and the two Carolinas, which then included Georgia, probably not fewer than 8,000 souls.

After having confined their settlements for many years within a short distance, comparatively speaking, from the coast, the colonists began to penetrate the inland forests, and to settle at different points in the interior of the country, in proportion as they considered themselves strong enough to occupy them safely. Where hostility on the part of the Aborigines was dreaded, these settlers kept together as much as possible, and established themselves in villages. This was particularly the case in New England, where, the soil being less favorable to agriculture, colonization naturally assumed the compact form required for the pursuits of trade and the useful arts, as well as for mutual assistance when exposed to attack. As the New England colonists had all along devoted themselves much to the fisheries and other branches of commerce, their settlements were for a long time to be found chiefly on the coast, and at points affording convenient harbors. But it was much otherwise in the South. In Virginia, particularly, the colonists were induced to settle along the banks of rivers to very considerable distances, their main occupation being the planting of tobacco, and trading to some extent with the Indians. In the Carolinas, again, most hands being employed in the manufacture of tar, turpentine, and rosin, or in the cultivation of rice, indigo, and, eventually, of cotton, the colonial settlements took a considerably range whenever there was peace with the Indians in their vicinity. Where there was little or no commerce, and agricultural pursuits of different kinds were the chief occupation of the people, there could be few towns of much importance; and so much does this hold at the present day, that there is not a city of 40,000 inhabitants in all the five Southern Atlantic States, with the exception of Baltimore in Maryland, Richmond in Virginia, and Charleston in South Carolina.

Even at the commencement of the war of the Revolution, in 1775, the colonies had scarcely penetrated to the Allegheny or Appalachian Mountains in any of the provinces that reached thus far, and their whole population was confined to the strip of land interposed between those mountains and the Atlantic Ocean. . . .

It is now (1856) about seventy-two years since the tide of emigration from the Atlantic States set fairly into the Valley of the Mississippi; and though no great influx took place in any one year during the first half of that period, it has wonderfully increased during the last. When this emigration westward first commenced, all the necessaries that the emigrants required to take with them from the East were to be carried on horseback, no roads for wheeled carriages having been opened through the mountains. On arriving at the last ridge overlooking the plains to the west, a boundless forest lay stretched out before those pioneers of civilization, like an ocean of living green. Into the depths of that forest they had to plunge. Often long years of toil and suffering rolled away before they could establish themselves in comfortable abodes. The climate and the diseases peculiar to the different localities were unknown. Hence, fevers of a stubborn type cut many of them off. They were but partially acquainted with the mighty rivers of that vast region, beyond knowing that their common outlet was in the possession of a foreign nation, which imposed vexatious regulations upon their infant trade. The navigation of those rivers could be carried on only in flat-bottomed boats, keels, and barges. To descend them was not unattended with danger, but to ascend by means of sweeps and oars, by poling, warping, *bush-whacking,** and so forth, was laborious and tedious beyond conception.

This account of the progress of colonization in the great central valley, furnishes a better key to the political, moral, and religious character of the West than any other that can be given. The West, in fact, may be regarded as the counterpart of the East, after allowing for the *exaggeration,* if I may so speak, which a life in the wilderness tends to communicate for a time to manners and character, and even to religion, but which disappears as the population increases, and as the country acquires the stamp of an older civilization. Stragglers may, indeed, be found in all parts of the West from almost all parts of the East; and many emigrants from Europe, too, Germans especially, enter by New Orleans, and from that city find their way by steamboats into Indiana, Illinois, Missouri, Wisconsin, and Iowa. But all these form exceptions that hardly invalidate the general statement.

CHAPTER 5

Peculiar Qualifications

of the Anglo-Saxon Race

for the Work of Colonization

Wholly apart from considerations of a moral and religious character, and the influence of external circumstances, we may remark, that the Anglo-Saxon race possesses qualities peculiarly

---

* The word *bush-whacking* is of Western origin, and signifies a peculiar mode of propelling a boat up the Mississippi, Ohio, or any other river in that region, when the water is very high. It is this: instead of keeping in the middle of the stream, the boat is made to go along close to one of the banks, and the men who guide it, by catching hold of the boughs of the trees which overhang the water, are enabled to drag the boat along. It is an expedient resorted to more by way of change than any thing else. Sometimes it is possible, at certain stages of the rivers, to go along for miles in this way. Even to this day the greater portion of the banks of the rivers of the West are covered with almost uninterrupted forests.

adapted for successful colonization. The characteristic perseverance, the spirit of personal freedom and independence, that have
ever distinguished that race, admirably fit a man for the labor and
isolation necessary to be endured before he can be a successful
colonist. Now, New England, together with the States of New
York, New Jersey, Delaware, and Pennsylvania, with the exception of Dutch and Swedish elements, which were too inconsiderable to affect the general result, were all colonized by people of
Anglo-Saxon origin. And assuredly they have displayed qualities
fitting them for their task, such as the world has never witnessed
before. No sooner have the relations between the colonies and the
Aborigines permitted it to be done with safety (nor has this always
been waited for), than we find individuals and families ready to
penetrate the wilderness, there to choose, each for himself or for
themselves, some fertile spot for a permanent settlement. If friends
could be found to accompany him and settle near him, so much
the better; but if not, the bold emigrant would venture alone far
into the traceless forest, and surmount every obstacle single-
handed, like a fisherman committing himself to the deep, and
passing the live-long day at a distance from the shore. . . .

Living on the lands which they cultivate, the agricultural inhabitants of the New England and Middle States are very much dispersed; the country, far and wide, is dotted over with the dwellings
of the landholders, and those who assist them in the cultivation of
the soil. For almost every landowner tills his property himself,
assisted by his sons, by young men hired for that purpose, or by
tenants who rent from him a cottage and a few acres. Field work in
all those States is performed by men alone; a woman is never seen
handling the plough, the hoe, the axe, the sickle, or the scythe,
unless in the case of foreign emigrants, who have not yet adopted
American usages in this respect.

Take the following case as an illustration of the process that is
continually going on in the frontier settlements. A man removes to
the West, he purchases a piece of ground, builds a house, and
devotes himself to the clearing and tillage of his forest acres. Before long he has rescued a farm from the wilderness, and has
reared a family upon it. He then divides his land among his sons, if
there be enough for a farm for each of them; if not, each receives

money enough to buy one as he comes of age. Some may settle on lands bestowed upon them by their father; others, preferring a change, may dispose of their portion, and proceed, most commonly unmarried, to "the new country," as it is called, that is, to those parts of the West where the public lands are not yet sold. There he chooses out as much as he can conveniently pay for, receiving a title to it from the District Land Office, and proceeds to make for himself a home. This is likely to be in the spring.

Having selected a spot for his dwelling, generally near some fountain, or where water may be had by digging a well, he goes round and makes the acquaintance of his neighbors residing within the distance, it may be, of several miles. A time is fixed for building him a house, upon which those neighbors come and render him such efficient help, that in a single day he will find a log-house constructed, and perhaps covered with clap-boards, and having apertures cut out for the doors, windows, and chimney. He makes his floor at once of rough boards riven from the abundant timber of the surrounding forest, constructs his doors, and erects a chimney. Occupying himself, while interrupted in out-door work by rainy weather, in completing his house, he finds it in a few weeks tolerably comfortable, and during fair weather he clears the underwood from some ten or fifteen acres, kills the large trees by notching them around so as to arrest the rise of the sap, and plants the ground with Indian corn, or maize, as it is called in Europe. He can easily make, buy, or hire a plough, a harrow, and a hoe or two. If he find time, he surrounds his field with a fence. At length, after prolonging his stay until his crop is beyond the risk of serious injury from squirrels and birds, or from the growth of weeds, he shuts up his house, commits it to the care of some neighbor, living perhaps one or two miles distant, and returns to his paternal home, which may be from one to three hundred miles distant from his new settlement. There he stays until the month of September, then marries, and with his young wife, a wagon and pair of horses to carry their effects, a few cattle or sheep, or none, according to circumstances, sets out to settle for life in the wilderness. On arriving at his farm, he sows wheat or rye among his standing Indian corn, then gathers in this last, and prepares for the winter. His wife shares all the cares incident to this humble beginning. Accustomed to every kind of household work, she strives by the diligence of her fingers to avoid the necessity of going to the merchant, who has opened his store at some village among the trees, perhaps some miles off, and there laying out the little money they may have left. With economy and health, they gradually become prosperous. The primitive log-house gives place to a far better mansion, constructed of hewn logs, or of boards, or of brick or stone. Extensive and well-fenced fields spread around, ample barns stored with grain, stalls filled with horses and cattle, flocks of sheep, and herds of hogs, all attest the increasing wealth of the owners. Their children grow up, perhaps to pursue the same course, or, as their inclinations may lead, to choose some other occupation, or to enter one of the learned professions.

This sketch will give the reader some idea of the mode in which colonization advances among the Anglo-Saxon race of the Middle and New England States of America. Less Anglo-Saxon in their origin, and with institutions and customs modified by slavery, the Southern States exhibit colonization advancing in a very different style. When an emigrant from those States removes to the "Far West," he takes with him his wagons, his cattle, his little ones, and a troop of slaves, resembling Abraham when he moved from place to place in Canaan. When he settles in the forest, he clears and cultivates the ground with the labor of his slaves. Every thing goes on heavily. Slaves are too stupid and improvident to make good colonists. The country, under these disadvantages, never assumes the garden-like appearance that it already wears in the New England and Middle States, and which is to be seen in the northern parts of the great Central Valley.

Next to the Anglo-Saxon race from the British shores, the Scotch make the best settlers in the great American forests. The Irish are not so good; they know not how to use the plough, or how to manage the horse and the ox, having had but little experience of either in their native land. None can handle the spade better, nor are they wanting in industry. But when they first arrive they are irresolute, dread the forest, and hang too much about the large towns, looking around for such work as their previous mode of life has not disqualified them for. Such of them as have been bred to mechanical trades might find sufficient employment if they would let ardent spirits alone, but good colonists for the forests they will never be. Their children may do better in that career. The few Welsh to be found in America are much better fitted than the Irish for the life and pursuits of a farmer.

The perseverance and frugality of the German, joined to other good qualities which he' has in common with the Anglo-Saxon race, enable him to succeed tolerably well even in the forest, but he finds it more to his advantage to settle on a farm bought at second-hand and partially cultivated. The Swiss are much the same with the Germans. The French and Italians, on the other hand, are totally unfit for planting colonies in the woods. Nothing could possibly be more alien to the ordinary habits of a Frenchman. The population of France is almost universally collected in cities, towns, villages, and hamlets, and thus, from early habit as well as constitutional disposition, Frenchmen love society, and can not endure the loneliness and isolation of the settlements we have described. When they attempt to form colonies, it is by grouping together in villages, as may be seen along the banks of the St. Lawrence and of the Lower Mississippi. Hence their settlements are seldom either extensive or vigorous. They find themselves happier in the cities and large towns. If resolved to establish themselves in the country, they should go to comparatively well-settled neighborhoods, not to the forests of the Far West.

CHAPTER 6

On the Alleged Want

of National Character

in America

Foreigners who have written about the United States, have often asserted that it is a country without a national character. Were this the mere statement of an opinion, it might be suffered to pass unnoticed, like many other things emanating from authors who undertake to speak about countries which they have had only very partial, and hence very imperfect, opportunities of knowing. But as the allegation has been made with an air of considerable pretension, it becomes necessary that we should submit it to the test of truth.

If oneness of origin be essential to the formation of national character, it is clear that the people of the United States can make no pretension to it. No civilized nation was ever composed of inhabitants derived from such a variety of sources: for in the United States we find the descendants of English, Welsh, Scotch, Irish, Dutch, Germans, Norwegians, Danes, Swedes, Poles, French, Italians, and Spaniards;* and there is even a numerous and distinguished family in which it is admitted, with pride, that the blood of an Indian princess mingles with that of the haughty Norman or Norman-Saxon. Many other nations are of mixed descent, but where shall we find one derived from so many distinct races?

Neither, if national character depends upon the existence of but one language, can the citizens of the United States make any claim to it: for the colonists from whom they are descended brought with them the languages of the different countries whence they came, and these are retained in some instances to the present day. At least eleven of the different languages of Europe have been spoken by settlers in the United States.

But let us examine these two points somewhat more minutely, and we can not fail to be struck with the facts which will be presented to our view.

And in the first place, never has there been witnessed so rapid a blending of people from different countries, and speaking different languages, as may be seen in the United States. Within the last two hundred years, people have been arriving from some eleven or twelve different countries, and distinguished by as many different tongues. Yet so singular a fusion has taken place, that in many localities, where population is at all compact, it would puzzle a stranger to determine the national origin of the people from any

---

* Even China and the islands of the Pacific are furnishing their contingent, also, to California.

peculiarity of physiognomy or dialect, far less of language. . . . Almost the only exceptions to this universal amalgamation and loss of original languages are to be found in the Germans and French; and even in regard to these, had it not been for comparatively recent arrivals of emigrants caused by the French Revolution, the St. Domingo massacres, and various events in Germany, both the French and German languages would have been extinct ere now in the United States. The former is spoken only by a few thousands in the large cities, and some tens of thousands in Louisiana. . . . German, also, spoken although it be by many thousands of emigrants arriving yearly from Europe, is fast disappearing from the older settlements. The children of these Germans almost universally acquire the English tongue in their infancy, and where located, as generally happens, in the neighborhood of settlers who speak English as their mother tongue, learn to speak it well. Indeed, over nearly the whole vast extent of the United States, English is spoken among the well-educated with a degree of purity to which there is no parallel in the British realm. . . .

English literature has an immense circulation in America; a circumstance which may be an advantage in one sense, and a disadvantage in another. We are not wanting, however, in authors of unquestionable merit in every branch of literature, art, and science. Still, if a literature of our own creation be indispensable to the possession of a national character, we must abandon all claim to it.*

It may be added, that we have no fashions of our own. We follow the modes of Paris. But in this respect, Germans, Russians, Italians, and English, without any abatement of their claims to national character, do the same.

Amalgamation takes place, also, by intermarriages, to an extent elsewhere quite unexampled; for though the Anglo-Saxon race has an almost undisputed possession of the soil in New England,

---

* [Ed.—Baird says this despite the fact that later on he gives a lengthy footnote listing most of the authors who constituted a golden age in American letters. See Bk. IV, chap. xxi (46).]

people are everywhere else to be met with in whose veins flows the mingled blood of English, Dutch, German, Irish, and French.

Nor has the assimilation of races and languages been greater than that of manners, customs, religion, and political principles. The manners of the people, in some places less, in others more refined, are essentially characterized by simplicity, sincerity, frankness, and kindness. The religion of the overwhelming majority, and which may therefore be called national, is, in all essential points, what was taught by the great Protestant Reformers of the sixteenth century. With respect to politics, with whatever warmth we may discuss the measures of the government, but one feeling prevails with regard to our political institutions themselves. We are no propagandists: we hold it to be our duty to avoid meddling with the governments of other countries; and though we prefer our own political forms, would by no means insist on others doing so too. That government we believe to be the best for any people, under which they live most happily, and are best protected in their right of person, property, and conscience; and we would have every nation to judge for itself what form of government is best suited to secure for it these great ends.

Assuredly there is no country that possesses a press more free, or where, notwithstanding, public opinion is more powerful; but on these points we shall have more to say in another part of this work.

The American people, taken as a whole, are mainly characterized by perseverance, earnestness, kindness, hospitality, and self-reliance, that is, by a disposition to depend upon their own exertions to the utmost, rather than look to the government for assistance. Hence, there is no country where the government does less, or the people more. In a word, our national character is that of the Anglo-Saxon race, which still predominates among us in consequence of its original preponderancy in the colonization of the country, and of the energy which forms its characteristic distinction.

Has the reader ever heard Haydn's celebrated oratorio of the Creation performed by a full orchestra? If so, he can not have forgotten how chaos is represented at the commencement by all the instruments sounded together without the least attempt at concord. By-and-by, however, something like order begins, and at length the clear notes of the clarionet are heard over all the others, controlling them into harmony. Something like this has been in America the influence of the Anglo-Saxon language, laws, institutions, and CHARACTER.

But if, when it is alleged that we have no national character, it be meant that we have not originated any for ourselves, it may be asked, What nation has? All owe much to those from whom they have sprung; this, too, has been our case, although what we have inherited from our remote ancestors has unquestionably been much modified by the operation of political institutions which we have been led to adopt by new circumstances, and which, probably, were never contemplated by the founders of our country.

CHAPTER 7

The Royal

Charters

. . . The United States have had to struggle with . . . difficulties, originating in the old royal charters. Little regard was paid to the prior claims of the Indians, in the extensive grants made by those charters, directly or indirectly, to the colonists. The pope had set the example of giving away the Aborigines with the lands they occupied, or, rather, of giving away the land from under them; and although, in all the colonies founded by our English ancestors in America, there was a sort of feeling, that the Indians had some claims on the ground of prior occupation, yet these, it was thought, ought to give place to the rights conferred by the royal charters. The colonists were subject to the same blinding influence of selfishness that affects other men, and to this we are to ascribe the importunity with which they urged the removal of the Indians from the lands conveyed by the royal charters, and which they had long been wont to consider and to call their own. In no case, indeed, did the newcomers seize upon the lands of the aboriginal occupants, without some kind of purchase; yet unjustifiable means were often employed to induce the latter to cede their claims to the former, such as excessive importunity, the bribery of the chiefs, and sometimes even threats. Thus, although with the exception of lands obtained by right of conquest in war, I do not believe that any whatever was obtained without something being given in exchange for it, yet I fear that the golden rule was sadly neglected in many of those transactions. In Pennsylvania and New England, unquestionably, greater fairness was shown than in most, if not all the other colonies; yet even there, full justice, according to that rule, was not always practised. Indeed, in many cases, it was difficult to say what exact justice implied. To savages roaming over vast tracts of land which they did not cultivate, and which, even for the purposes of the chase, were often more extensive than necessary,—for them to part with hundreds, or even thousands of square miles, could not be thought a matter of much importance, and thus conscience was quieted. But although our forefathers may not have done full justice to the poor Indians, it is by no means certain that others in the same circumstances would have done better.

The impatience of the colonists to obtain possession of lands which their charters, or arrangements consequent thereon, led them to regard as their own, has at times thrown the General Government into much embarrassment and difficulty. . . .

To rid itself of such embarrassments created by the old charters, the General Government, at the instance of great and good men, adopted, some years ago, the plan of collecting all the tribes still to be found within the confines of any of the States, upon an extensive district to the west of Arkansas and Missouri, claimed by no State, and, therefore, considered as part of the public domain. There it has already collected the Cherokees, the Choctaws, the Chickasaws, the Creeks, and several smaller tribes. Soon territories of all the States will be cleared of them, except in so far as they may choose to remain and become citizens. Nor can I avoid cherishing the hope that the great Indian community now forming, as I have said, west of Missouri and Arkansas, will one day become a State itself, and have its proper representatives in the great council of the nation. . . .

CHAPTER 8

How a Correct Knowledge

of the American People,

the Nature of Their Government,

and of Their National Character

May Best Be Attained

He who would obtain a thorough knowledge of the people of the United States, their national character, the nature of their government, and the spirit of their laws, must go back to the earliest ages of the history of England, and study the character of the various races that from early times have settled there. He must carefully mark the influences they exerted on each other, and upon the civil and political institutions of that country. He must study the Saxon Conquest, followed by the introduction of Saxon institutions, and Saxon laws and usages; the trial of an accused person by his peers; the subdivision of the country into small districts, called townships or hundreds; the political influence of that arrangement; and the establishment of seven or eight petty kingdoms, in which the authority of the king was shared by the people. . . .

To the resistance of the Anglo-Saxon race in England to the domination of the Norman aristocracy, that kingdom was ultimately indebted for the free institutions it now enjoys. The oppressions of the nobility and of the crown were checked by the cities and boroughs, in which the Anglo-Saxon commons became more and more concentrated, with the advance of civilization and population. The nobles themselves, on occasions when they, too, had to contend for their rights and privileges against the sovereign, gave a helping hand to the people; and in later times especially, after the people had established the power of their Commons, or third estate, on an immovable foundation, aided the sovereign against alleged encroachments on the part of the people. Thus the cause of liberty gained ground both among the nobility and the commonalty.

With the progress of the Reformation, the strife between the two races became exasperated: the nobility and gentry desiring little more than the abatement or rejection of the papal usurpation; the Saxon race, led by men whose hearts were more deeply interested in the subject, desiring to see the Church rid of error and superstition of every form. From the discussion of the rights of conscience, the latter went on to examine the nature and foundations of civil government; and being met with violent opposition, they proceeded to lengths they had never dreamed of when they first set out. In the fearful struggle that followed, both the national Church and the Monarchy were for a time completely overthrown.

It was just as this grand opposition of sentiment was drawing on to a direct collision, and when men's minds were engrossed with the important questions which it pressed upon them, that the two colonies destined to exercise a predominant influence in America left the British shores. The first of the two in point of date sought the coasts of southern, the second sailed to those of northern Virginia, as the whole Atlantic slope was then called. The one settled on James River, in the present State of Virginia, and became, in a sense, the ruling colony of the South; the other established itself in New England, there to become the mother of the six Northern States. Both, however, have long since made their influence felt far beyond the coasts of the Atlantic, and are continuing to extend it toward the Pacific, in parallel and clearly-defined lines; and both retain to this day the characteristic features that marked their founders when they left their native land.

If not purely Norman in blood, the Southern colony was entirely Norman in spirit; whereas the Northern was Anglo-Saxon in character, and in the institutions which it took to the New World. Both loved freedom and free institutions, but they differed as to the extent to which the people should enjoy them. The one had sprung from the ranks of those in England who pleaded for the prerogatives of the crown and the privileges of the nobility; the other, from the great party that was contending for popular rights. The one originated with the friends of the Church as left by Queen Elizabeth; the other, with those who desired to see it purified from what they deemed the corruptions of antiquity, and shorn of the exorbitant pretensions of its hierarchy. The one, composed of a company of gentlemen, attended by a few mechanics or laborers, contemplated an extensive traffic with the natives; the other, composed, with a few exceptions of substantial farmers of moderate means, and industrious artisans, contemplated the cultivation of the ground, and the establishment of a state of society in which they might serve God according to His Word. The one had no popular government for some years after its foundation; the other was self-organized and self-governed before it disembarked upon the shores that were to be the scene of its future prosperity. Finally, the religion of the one, though doubtless sincere, and, so far as it went, beneficial in its influence, was a religion that clung to forms, and to an imposing ritual; the religion of the other was at the farthest possible remove from the Church of Rome, both in form and spirit, and professed to be guided by the Scriptures alone.*

[Seven chapters followed here in the original: "How to Obtain a Correct View of the Spirit and Character of the Religious Institutions of the United States," "A Brief Notice of the Form of Government in America," "A Brief Geographical Notice of the United States," and four others on "Obstacles Which the Voluntary System Has Had to Encounter in America."]

---

* [Ed.—Those interested in the ways popular myths can be utilized to sustain almost any preconception should consult *De Bow's Review* XXVIII (January, 1860), pp. 9–14. That magazine used the fashionable distinction between puritan New Englander and cavalier Virginian and reached greatly different conclusions than Baird found with the same premises. One available source is David M. Potter and Thomas G. Manning (eds.), *Nationalism and Sectionalism in America, 1775–1877, Select Problems in Historical Interpretation* (New York: Henry Holt & Co., 1949).]

BOOK II

The Colonial

Era

CHAPTER 9

Religious Character

of the Early Colonists

—Founders of New England

. . . if we would thoroughly understand the religious condition and economy of the United States, we must begin with an attentive survey of the character of the early colonists, and of the causes which brought them to America.

Besides, as has been well observed,* a striking analogy may be traced between natural bodies and bodies politic. Both retain in manhood and old age more or less of the characteristic traits of

---

* See M. de Tocqueville, "Démocratie en Amérique," Première Partie, tome i., chap. i. Also Lang's "Religion and Education in America," chap. i., page 11. [Ed.—For those consulting English translations of Tocqueville, one of the better editions is the revised and corrected version brought together by Philips Bradley and published by Alfred A. Knopf (New York, 1945). In that printing the analogy to which Baird refers is found in vol. I, chap. II, pp. 26–27.]

their infancy and youth. All nations bear some marks of their origin, the circumstances amid which they were born, and which favored their early development, and left an impression that stamps their whole future existence.

We begin our inquiry, therefore, into the religious history and condition of the United States, by portraying, as briefly as possible, the religious character of the first colonists, who may be regarded as the founders of that commonwealth. In doing this, we shall follow neither the chronological nor the geographical order, but shall first speak of the colonists of New England; next, of those of the South; and, finally, of those of the Middle States. This gives us the advantage at once of grouping and of contrast.

[Baird includes here a long historical sketch of the development of Protestantism in sixteenth-century England and the subsequent division of Puritans from more conservative, reform-minded churchmen. In addition to a chronological survey of successive monarchical policies on religious dissent, the author makes a clear and accurate distinction between Nonconformist and Separatist ecclesiastical groups. After furnishing a background essential for an adequate perspective on the temper of the times, Baird moves to a consideration of the pious flock of John Robinson which fled from English persecution to Amsterdam in 1608.]

CHAPTER 10

Religious Character of

the Founders of New England

—Plymouth Colony

[The author traces the movements of exiled Independents to Leyden, recounts their physical hardships and analyzes pertinent factors leading to their eventual decision to leave Holland. Drawing upon earlier works such as Edward Winslow's *Brief Narrative* and William Bradford's *History of Plymouth Plantation,* Baird includes information about negotiations with royal authorities and the Virginia Company; an extended footnote preserves a touching farewell sermon by John Robinson. Agreements were reached, and earnest preparations began for colonizing; after noting that a sister ship, the Speedwell, was forced to return to port, thus further restricting the number of original Pilgrims, the narrative proceeds.]

. . . it was not until the 6th of September that the Mayflower finally sailed with a hundred passengers. The voyage proved long and boisterous. One person died, and a child was born, so that the original number reached the coast of America. On the 11th of November they entered the harbor of Cape Cod, and after having spent fully a month in looking about for a place that seemed suitable for a settlement, they fixed at last on the spot now bearing the name of the town where they had received the last hospitalities of England. There they landed on the 11th of December, old style, or the 22d of December, according to the new; and to this day the very rock on which they first planted their feet at landing is shown to the passing stranger as a cherished memorial of that interesting event. On that rock commenced the colonization of New England.

On the day of the arrival of the Mayflower in Cape Cod harbor, the following document was signed by all the male heads of families, and unmarried men not attached to families represented by their respective heads:

"In the name of God, Amen. We whose names are underwritten, the loyal subjects of our dread sovereign lord, King James, by the grace of God, of Great Britain, France, and Ireland, king, defender of the faith, etc., having undertaken, for the glory of God, and advancement of the Christian faith, and honor of our king and country, a voyage to plant the first colony in the northern parts of Virginia, do, by these presents, solemnly and mutually, in the presence of God and one of another, covenant and combine ourselves together into a civil body politic, for our better ordering and preservation, and furtherance of the ends aforesaid, and by virtue hereof to enact, constitute, and frame such just and equal laws, ordinances, acts, constitutions, and offices, from time to time, as shall be thought most meet and convenient for the general good of the colony; unto which we promise all due submission and obedience. In witness whereof, we have hereunder subscribed our names, at Cape Cod, the 11th of November, in the year of the reign of our sovereign lord, King James, of England, France, and Ireland the eighteenth, and of Scotland the fifty-fourth, Anno Domini 1620."

Here may be said to have been the first attempt made by an American colony to frame a constitution or fundamental law—the seminal principle, as it were, of all that wonderful series of efforts which have been put forth in the New World toward fixing the foundations of independent, voluntary self-government. John Carver was chosen governor of the colony, and to assist him in administering its affairs, a council of five, afterward increased to seven members, was appointed.

After selecting what they considered to be the best spot for a settlement, as the ship's boat could not come close to the water's edge, they suffered much in health by having to wade ashore. The few intervals of good weather they could catch, between snow and rain, they spent in erecting houses; but before the first summer came round, nearly half their number had fallen victims to consumptions and fevers, the natural effects of the hardships to which they had been exposed. What must have been the distress they suffered during that long winter, passed beneath unknown skies, with a gloomy, unbroken forest on the one hand, and the dreary ocean on the other!

But with the return of spring came health, and hope, and courage. The colony took root. The ground it occupied had been cleared for it by the previous destruction of the tribes of Indians which had occupied it by pestilence. Of course, the colonists could not buy land where there was nobody to sell. They soon made the acquaintance of the neighboring tribes, acquired their friendship, and entered into treaty with them. Their numbers were in course of time increased by successive arrivals of emigrants, until, in 1630, they exceeded 300. After the second year they raised grain not only to supply all their own wants, but with a surplus for exportation. They soon had a number of vessels employed at the fisheries. They even planted a colony on the Kennebec, in Maine, and extended their trade to the Connecticut River, before the close of the first ten years of their settlement, and before any other English colony had been formed on the coast of northern Virginia, or of New England, the name given it by Captain Smith in 1614, and by which it was ever after to be distinguished.

The governor and council were chosen every year. At first, and for above eighteen years, "the people" met, as in Athens of old, for the discussion and adoption of laws. But as the colony extended, and towns and villages rose along the coasts and in the interior, the "Democratic" form of government gave place to the "Republican," two delegates being chosen from each township to form "the General Court," or Legislature of the commonwealth.

For some time they had no pastor or preaching elder, but Mr. [William] Brewster led their public devotions until they came to have a regular minister. Their affairs as a church were conducted with the same system and order that marked their civil economy.

Such is a brief account of the founding of Plymouth colony, the earliest of all the colonies that were planted in New England. Placed on a sandy and but moderately productive part of the coast, and commanding a very limited extent of inland territory from which to derive the materials of commerce and wealth, it could not be expected to become a great and important colony, like others of which I have yet to speak. But it was excelled by none in the moral worth of its founders. All professing godliness, they almost without exception, as far as we know, did honor to that profession. True religion was with them the first of all possessions. They feared God, and He walked among them, and dwelt among them, and His blessing rested upon them. The anniversary of their disembarkation at Plymouth has long been regularly celebrated upon the yearly return of the 22d December, in prose and in verse, in oration and in poem: a patriotic and religious duty, to which have been consecrated the highest efforts of many of the noblest and purest minds ever produced by the country to whose colonization they led the way.

CHAPTER 11

Religious Character of

the Early Colonists

—Founders of New England

—Colony of Massachusetts Bay

The first English settlements in America arose . . . from the act of James I., when he invested two Companies, the one formed at London, the other at Bristol and other towns in the west of England, each with a belt of territory extending from the Atlantic to the Pacific Ocean; the one lying between the 34th and 38th, the other between the 41st and 48th degrees of north latitude. Both Companies were formed in a purely commercial spirit; each was to have its own council, but the royal Council was to have the superintendence of their whole colonial system. The London Company was dissolved . . . after an existence of eighteen years. The other accomplished nothing beyond giving encouragement to sundry trading voyages, to the coast of the country made over to it by its charter.

At length, at the repeated instance of Captain Smith, the Western Company sought a renewal of their patent, with additional powers, similar to those of the London Company's second charter in 1609, with the view of attempting an extensive plan of colonization; and, notwithstanding opposition from the Parliament and the country at large, they succeeded in their request. On November 3d, 1620, the King granted a charter to forty of his subjects, among whom were members of his household and government, and some of the wealthiest and most powerful of the English nobility, conveying to them in absolute property, to be disposed of and administered as they might think proper, the whole of that part of North America which stretches from the Atlantic to the Pacific, between the 40th and 48th degrees of north latitude, under the title of "The Council established at Plymouth, in the County of Devon, for the planting, ruling, ordering, and governing New England, in America." Under the auspices of a vast trading corporation, invested with such despotic powers, the colonization of New England commenced. While this charter was in course of being granted, the Pilgrims were fast approaching the American coast. No valid title had, as yet, given them any legal right to set their feet upon it, but this they obtained a few years after from the newly-formed Plymouth Company.

But the most important grant made by the Plymouth Company, often called in history the Council for New England, was one conveying the Massachusetts territory to a body organized in England in 1628, for the purpose at once of providing an asylum for persons suffering for conscience' sake in the Old World, and of extending the kingdom of Christ in the New, by founding a colony on a large scale. With this view, six Dorchester gentlemen bought from the company a belt of land stretching from the Atlantic to the Pacific, between three miles south of Charles River and Massachusetts Bay, and three miles north of every part of the River Merrimac. Of these six, three, namely, Humphrey, Endicot, and Whetcomb, retained their shares; while the other three sold theirs to Winthrop, Dudley, Johnson, Pynchon, Eaton, Saltonstall, and Bellingham, so famous in colonial history, besides many others, men of fortune, and friends to colonial enterprise. Thus strengthened, this new company sent out two hundred colonists under Endicot, a man every way fitted for such an enterprise—courageous, cheerful, and having firmness of purpose and warmth of temper, softened by an austere benevolence. These arrived in Massachusetts Bay in September, 1628, and settled at Salem, where several members of the Plymouth colony had already established themselves.

The news of this event still further augmented the now growing interest felt in England on the subject of colonizing America. In the painful circumstances in which the Puritans were placed, they could not fail to have their attention drawn to the continued prosperity of the Plymouth settlement, and naturally rejoiced to hear of a land toward the setting sun, where they might enjoy a tranquility to which they had long been strangers in the land of their fathers. Such was the interest felt throughout the kingdom, that not only in London, Bristol, and Plymouth, but at Boston, and other inland towns, influential persons were found ready to risk their fortunes in the cause. Efforts were made to procure the royal sanction for the patent granted by the Plymouth Company to that of Massachusetts, and a royal charter in favor of the latter, after much trouble and expense, passed the seals on the 4th of March, 1629.

This charter, bearing the signature of Charles I., was evidently granted under the idea that the persons whom it incorporated were to be rather a trading community than a civil government. They were constituted a body politic, by the name of "The Governor and Company of Massachusetts Bay in New England." The administration of its affairs was committed to a governor, deputy-governor, and thirteen assistants, elected by the shareholders. The freemen were to meet four times a year, or oftener if necessary, and were empowered to pass laws for the regulation of their affairs, without any provision rendering the royal assent indispensable to the validity of their acts. Strictly considered, the patent simply conferred the rights of English subjects, without any enlargement of religious liberty. It empowered, but did not require the governor to administer the oaths of supremacy and allegiance. The persons in whose favor it was granted were still members of the Church of England—not Independents or Separatists—and probably neither the government, nor the first patentees, foresaw how wide a departure from the economy of that Church, would result from the emigration that was about to take place under its provisions.

It is surprising that a charter which conferred unlimited powers on the corporation, and secured no rights to the colonists, should have become the means of establishing the freest of all the colonies. This was partly owing to its empowering the corporation to fix what terms it pleased for the admission of new members. The corporation could increase or change its members with its own consent, and not being obliged to hold its meetings in England, it was possible for it to emigrate, and thus to identify itself with the colony which it was its main object to found. This was actually done. As the corporation was entirely composed of Puritans, it was not difficult, by means of resignations and new elections, to choose the governor, deputy-governor, and assistants, from among such as were willing to leave England as colonists.

The first object of the new company, on obtaining a royal charter, was to re-enforce the party which had gone out with Endicot and had settled at Salem. The re-enforcement consisted of two hundred emigrants, under the pastoral care of the Rev. Francis Higginson, an eminent Nonconformist minister, who was delighted to accept of the invitation to undertake that charge. By their arrival, which happened in June, the colony at Salem was increased to three hundred persons; but diseases and the hardships incident to new settlements cut off, during the following winter, eighty of that number, who died only lamenting that they were not allowed to see the future glories of the colony. Among these was their beloved pastor, Mr. Higginson, whose death was a great loss to the little community.

The year following, namely, 1630, was a glorious one for the colonization of New England. Having first taken every preparatory measure required for self-transportation, the corporation itself embarked, accompanied by a body of eight hundred to nine hundred emigrants, among whom were several persons of large property and high standing in society. John Winthrop, one of the purest characters in England, had been chosen governor. Taken as a whole, it is thought that no single colony could ever be compared with them. One may form some idea of the elevated piety that pervaded the higher classes among the Puritans of that day, from the language of the younger Winthrop: "I shall call that my country," said he to his father, "where I may most glorify God, and enjoy the presence of my dearest friends. Therefore herein I submit myself to God's will and yours, and dedicate myself to God and the company with the whole endeavors both of body and mind. The 'Conclusions,' which you sent down, are unanswerable; and it can not but be a prosperous action which is so well allowed by the judgments of God's prophets, undertaken by so religious and wise worthies in Israel, and indented to God's glory in so special a service."*

Governor Winthrop had a fine estate which he sacrificed. Many others sacrificed what were considered good estates in England in those days. One of the richest of the colonists was Isaac Johnson, "the father of Boston." As proof that he was a man of wealth, it may be mentioned that, by his will, his funeral expenses were limited to £250. His wife, the Lady Arabella, was a daughter of the Earl of Lincoln. . . . They were almost without exception godly people, and when they embarked for America were members of the Church of England, being that in which they had been born and brought up. Though of the party that were opposed to what they considered Romish superstitions and errors, they still cleaved in their conscientious convictions to the National Church; and though they could not in all points conform to it, yet they had not separated from it, but sought the welfare of their souls in its ministrations, whenever they could possibly hope to find it there. They lamented what they regarded as its defects, but not in a spirit of bitter hostility. . . .

The ships that bore Winthrop and his companions across the Atlantic, reached Massachusetts Bay in the following June and July [still 1630]. After having consoled the distresses and relieved the wants of the Salem colonists, the newly-arrived emigrants set about choosing a suitable place for a settlement; a task which occupied the less time, as the bay had been well explored by preceding visitors. The first landing was made at the spot where Charlestown now stands. A party having gone from that place up the Charles River to Watertown, there some of them resolved to settle; others preferred Dorchester; but the greater number resolved to occupy the peninsula upon which Boston now stands, the settlement receiving that name from the fact that part of the colonists had come from Boston in England. For a while they were lodged in cloth tents and wretched huts, and had to endure all kinds of hardship. To complete their trials, disease made its

---

* Winthrop's Journal, i., pp. 359, 360. [Ed.—Baird probably consulted a recent edition of Winthrop's *Journal*, entitled *The History of New England* (Boston: James Savage, 2 vols., 1825) or the more complete edition, 1853.]

attacks, and carried off two hundred of them at least before December. About a hundred lost heart, and went back to England. Many who had been accustomed in their native land to ease and plenty, and to all the refinements and luxuries of cultivated life, were now compelled to struggle with unforeseen wants and difficulties. . . . They were sustained by a profound belief that God was with them, and by bearing in mind the object of their coming to that wilderness.

Amid all this gloom, light began to break in at last. Health returned, and the blanks caused by death were filled up by partial arrivals of new emigrants from England in the course of the two following years. The colony becoming a little settled, measures were taken to introduce a more popular government, by extending the privileges of the charter, which had established a sort of close corporation. By it all fundamental laws were to be enacted by general meetings of the freemen, or members of the company. One of the first steps, accordingly, was to convene a General Court at Boston, and admit above a hundred of the older colonists to the privileges of the corporation; and from that they gradually went on, until, instead of an aristocratic government conducted by a governor, deputy-governor, and assistants, holding office for an indefinite period, these functionaries were elected annually, and the powers of legislation were transferred from general courts of all the freemen joined with the assistants, to a new legislature, or "general court," consisting of two branches, the assistants constituting the upper, and deputies from all the "towns" forming the lower branch. Within five years from the foundation of the colony, a Constitution was drawn up, which was to serve as a sort of Magna Charta, embracing all the fundamental principles of just government; and in fourteen years the colonial government was organized upon the same footing as that on which it rests at the present day.

But with these colonists the claims of religion took precedence of all other concerns of public interest. The New England fathers began with God, sought His blessing, and desired, first of all, to promote His worship. Immediately after landing they appointed a day for solemn fasting and prayer. The worship of God was commenced by them not in temples built with hands, but beneath the wide-spreading forest. The Rev. Mr. [John] Wilson, the Rev. Mr. [George] Philips, and other faithful ministers, had come out with them; and for these, as soon as the affairs of the colony became a little settled, a suitable provision was made.

In the third year of the settlement there came out, among other fresh emigrants, two spiritual teachers, who were afterward to exercise a most extensive and beneficial influence in the colonies. One of these was the eminently pious and zealous [John] Cotton, a man profoundly learned in the Holy Scriptures, as well as in the writings of the Fathers and the Schoolmen; in the pulpit rather persuasive than eloquent, and having a wonderful command over the judgments and hearts of his hearers. The other was [Thomas] Hooker, a man of vast endowments, untiring energy, and singular benevolence; the equal of the Reformers, though of less harsh a spirit than that which marked most of those great men. These and other devoted servants of God were highly appreciated, not only for their works' sake, but also for their great personal excellence.

Before long the colony began to extend, in all directions, from Boston as a centre and capital; and as new settlements were made, additional churches were also planted; for the New England fathers felt that nothing could be really and permanently prosperous without religion. Within five years a considerable population was to be found scattered over Dorchester, Roxbury, Watertown, Cambridge, Charlestown, Lynn, and other settlements. Trade was spreading wide its sails; emigrants were arriving from Europe; brotherly intercourse was opened up with the Plymouth colony, by the visits of Governor Winthrop and the Rev. Mr. Wilson. Friendly treaties were made not only with the neighboring Indian tribes, the Nipmucks and Narragansetts, but also with the more distant Mohigans and the Pequods in Connecticut. . . .

CHAPTER 12

Religious Character of
the Early Colonists
—Founders of New England
—Colonies of Connecticut, Rhode Island,
New Hampshire, and Maine
—General Remarks

Plymouth colony had been planted only three years when it began to have off-shoots, one of which, in 1623, settled at Windsor, on the rich alluvial lands of the Connecticut: led thither, however, more by the advantages of the spot as a station for trading in fur, than by the nature of the soil. . . . Two years later, the Dutch, who, in right of discovery, claimed the whole of the Connecticut territory, sent an expedition from their settlement at Manhattan up the River Connecticut, and attempted to make good their claim by erecting a block-house, called Good Hope, at Hartford. In 1635, the younger Winthrop, the future benefactor of Connecticut, came from England, with a commission from the proprietors to build a fort at the mouth of the river, and this he did soon after. Yet, even before his arrival, settlers from the neighborhood of Boston had established themselves at Hartford, Windsor, and Weathersfield. Late in the fall of that year, a party of sixty persons, men, women, and children, set out for the Connecticut, and suffered much from the inclement weather of the winter that followed. In the following June, another party, amounting to about a hundred in number, including some of the best of the Massachusetts Bay settlers, left Boston for the Valley of the Connecticut.

They were under the superintendence of Hayes, who had been one year governor of Boston, and of Hooker, who, as a preacher, was rivaled in the New World by none but Cotton, and even Cotton he excelled in force of character, kindliness of disposition, and magnanimity. Settling at the spot where Hartford now stands, they founded the colony of Connecticut. They, too, carried the Ark of the Lord with them, and made religion the basis of their institutions. Three years sufficed for the framing of their political government. First, as had been done by the Plymouth colony, they subscribed a solemn compact, and then they drew up a Constitution on the most liberal principles. The magistrates and legislature were to be chosen every year by ballot, the "towns" were to return representatives in proportion to their population, and all members of the "towns," on taking the oath of allegiance to the commonwealth, were to be allowed to vote at elections. Two centuries have since passed away, but Connecticut still rejoices in the same principles of civil polity.

But before this colony had time to complete its organization, the colonists had to defend themselves and all that was dear to them against their neighbors, the Pequods. This was the first war that broke out between the New England settlers and the native tribes, and it must be allowed to have been a just one on the part of the former, if war can ever be just. The Pequods brought it upon themselves by the commission of repeated murders. In less than six weeks, hostilities were brought to a close by the annihilation of the tribe. Two hundred only were left alive, and these were either reduced to servitude by the colonists, or were incorporated among the Mohigans and Narragansetts.

The colony of New Haven was founded in 1638 by a body of Puritans, who, like all the rest, were of the school of Calvin, and whose religious teacher was the Rev. John Davenport. The excellent Theophilus Eaton was their first governor, and continued to be annually elected to that office for twenty years. Their first Sabbath, in the yet cool month of April, was spent under a branching oak, and there their pastor discoursed to them on the Saviour's "temptation in the wilderness." After spending a day in fasting and prayer, they laid the foundation of their civil government, by simply convenanting that "all of them would be ordered by the rules which the Scriptures held forth to them." A title to their lands was purchased from the Indians. The following year, these disciples of "Him who was cradled in a manger" held their first Constituent Assembly in a barn. Having solemnly come to the conclusion that the Scriptures contain a perfect pattern of a commonwealth, according to that they aimed at constructing theirs. Purity of religious doctrine and discipline, freedom of religious worship, and the service and glory of God, were proclaimed as the great ends of the enterprise. God smiled upon it, so that in a few years the colony could show flourishing settlements rising along the Sound, and on the opposite shores of Long Island.

While the colonization of Connecticut was in progress, that of Rhode Island commenced. Roger Williams, a Puritan minister, had arrived in Boston the year immediately following its settlement by Winthrop and his companions; but he soon advanced doctrines on the rights of conscience, and the nature and limits of human government, which were unacceptable to the civil and religious authorities of the colony. For two years he avoided coming into collision with his opponents, by residing at Plymouth; but having been invited to become pastor of a church in Salem, where he had preached for some time after his first coming to America, he was ordered, at last, to return to England; whereupon, instead of complying, he sought refuge among the Narragansett Indians, then occupying a large part of the present State of Rhode Island. Having ever been the steady friend of the Indians, and defender of their rights, he was kindly received by the aged chief, Canonicus, and there, in 1636, he founded the city and plantation of Providence. Two years afterward, the beautiful island called Rhode Island, in Narragansett Bay, was bought from the Indians, by John Clarke, William Coddington, and their friends, when obliged to leave the Massachusetts colony, in consequence of the part which they had taken in the "Antinomian Controversy," as it was called, a discussion of which we shall have occasion to speak further. These two colonies of Providence and Rhode Island, both founded on the principle of absolute religious freedom, naturally presented an asylum to all who disliked the rigid laws and practices of the Massachusetts colony in religious matters; but many, it must be added, fled thither only out of hatred to the stern morality of the other colonies. Hence Rhode Island, to this day, has a more mixed population, as respects religious opinions and practices, than any other part of New England. There is, however, no inconsiderable amount of sincere piety in the State, but the forms in which it manifests itself are numerous.

As early as 1623, small settlements were made, under the grant to Mason, on the banks of the Piscataqua, in New Hampshire; and, in point of date, both Portsmouth and Dover take precedence of Boston. Most of the New Hampshire settlers came direct from England; some from the Plymouth colony. Exeter owed its foundation to the abandonment of Massachusetts by the Reverend Mr. Wheelwright and his immediate friends, on the occasion of the "Antinomian Controversy."

The first permanent settlements made on "the Maine," as the continental part of the country was called, to distinguish it from the islands—and hence the name of the State—date as early, it would appear, as 1626. The settlers were from Plymouth, and no doubt carried with them the religious institutions cherished in that earliest of all the New England colonies.

Within twenty years from the planting of the colony at Plymouth, all the other chief colonies of New England were founded, their governments were organized, and the coast of the Atlantic, from the Kennebec River, in Maine, almost to the Hudson, in New York, was marked by their various settlements. Offshoots from these original stocks gradually appeared, both at intervening points near the ocean, and at such spots in the interior as attracted settlers by superior fertility of soil or other physical advantages. . . . Hope of future comfort sustained them amid present toils. They were cheered by the thought that the extension of their settlements was promoting also the extension of the kingdom of Christ.

But while such, during the early years of their existence, was the temporal prosperity of these colonies, not less great was their spiritual advance. In 1647, New England had forty-three churches united in one communion; in 1650, the number of churches was fifty-eight, that of communicants 7,750, and in 1674, there were more than eighty English churches of Christ, composed of known pious and faithful professors only, dispersed through the wilderness. Of these, twelve or thirteen were in Plymouth colony, forty-seven in Massachusetts and the province of New Hampshire, nineteen in Connecticut, three in Long Island, and one in Martha's Vineyard. Well might one of her pious historians say, "It concerneth New England always to remember that she is a religious plantation, and not a plantation of trade. The profession of purity of doctrine, worship, and discipline, is written upon her forehead."*

The New England colonists may have been "the poorest of the people of God in the whole world," and they settled in a rugged country, the poorest, in fact, in natural resources, of all the United States' territories; nevertheless, their industry and other virtues made them increase in wealth, and transformed their hills and valleys into a delightful land. Their commerce soon showed itself in all seas; their manufactures gradually gained ground, notwithstanding the obstacles created by the jealousy of England, and, with the increase of their population, they overspread a large extent of the space included in their charters.

Many, indeed, affect to sneer at the founders of New England; but the sneers of ignorance and prejudice can not detract from their real merits. Not that we would claim the praise of absolute wisdom for all that was done by the "New England fathers." Some of their penal laws were unreasonably and unjustly severe, some were frivolous, some were even ridiculous. Some of their usages were dictated by false views of propriety. Nor can it be denied that they were intolerant to those who differed from them in religion; that they persecuted Quakers and Baptists, and abhorred Roman Catholics. But all this grew out of the erroneous views which they, in common with almost all the world at that time, entertained on the rights of human conscience, and the duties of civil government, in cases where those rights are concerned. We shall see, likewise, that they committed some most serious mistakes, resulting from the same erroneous views, in the civil establishment of religion adopted in most of the colonies. Notwithstanding all this, they will

---

* Prince, in his Christian History, p. 66. [Ed.—Probably the more accessible editions of this work, originally printed in 1736, must have been Thomas Prince, *A Chronological History of New England in the Form of Annals* (Boston: Cummings, Hilliard & Co., 1826 or 1852).]

be found to have been far in advance of other nations of their day.

With respect to their treatment of the native tribes, they were led into measures which appear harsh and unjust, by the fact that their laws were modeled upon those of the Jews. Such, for example, was their making slaves of those Indians whom they made prisoners in war. There were cases, also, of individual wrong done to the Indians. Yet never, I believe, since the world began, have colonies from civilized nations been planted among barbarous tribes with so little injustice perpetrated upon the whole. The land, in almost all cases where tribes remained to dispose of it, was taken only on indemnification being given, as they fully recognized the right of the natives to the soil. The only exceptions, and these were but few, were the cases in which the hazards of war put them in possession of some Indian territory. Nor were they indifferent to the spiritual interests of those poor people. We shall yet see that for these they did far more than was done by any other colonies on the whole American continent, and I shall explain why they did not do more.

CHAPTER 13

Religious Character of the Early Colonists
—Founders of the Southern States

Widely different in character, I have already remarked, were the early colonists of the Southern from those of the Northern States. If New England may be regarded as colonized by the Anglo-Saxon race, with its simpler manners, its more equal institutions, and its love of liberty, the South may be said to have been colonized by men very Norman in blood, aristocratic in feeling and spirit, and pretending to superior dignity of demeanor and elegance of manners. Nor has time yet effaced this original diversity. On the contrary, it has been increased and confirmed by the continuance of slavery in the South: an institution which has not prevailed much at any time in the North, but has immensely influenced the tone of feeling and the customs of the Southern States.

If the New England colonies are chargeable with having allowed their feelings to become alienated from a throne from which they had often been contemptuously spurned, with equal truth might those of the South be accused of going to the opposite extreme, in their attachment to a line of monarchs alike undeserving of their love, and incapable of appreciating their generous loyalty.

We might carry the contrast still further. If New England was the favorite asylum of the Puritan "Roundhead," the South became, in its turn, the retreat of the "Cavalier," upon the joint subversion of the altar and the throne in his native land. And if the religion of the one was strict, serious, in the regard of its enemies unfriendly to innocent amusements, and even morose, the other was the religion of the court, and of fashionable life, and did not require so uncompromising a resistance "to the lust of the flesh, the lust of the eyes, and the pride of life."

Not that from this parallelism, which is necessarily general, the reader is to infer that the Northern colonies had exclusive claims to be considered as possessing a truly religious character. All that is meant is to give a general idea of the different aspects that religion bore in the one and the other.

Virginia, as we have already stated, was of all the colonies the first in point of date. Among its neighbors in the South it was what Massachusetts was in the North—the mother, in some sense, of the rest, and the dominant colony. Not that the others were planted chiefly from it, but because, from the prominence of its position, the amount of its population, and their intelligence and wealth, it acquired from the first a preponderating influence, which it retains as a State to this day.

The records of Virginia furnish indubitable evidence that it was meant to be a Christian colony. The charter enjoined that the mode of worship should conform to that of the Established Church of England. In 1619, for the first time, Virginia had a Legislature chosen by the people; and by an act of that body, the Episcopal Church was, properly speaking, established. In the following year the number of boroughs erected into parishes was eleven, and the number of pastors five, the population at the time being considerably under three thousand. In 1621–22, it was enacted that the clergy should receive from their parishioners fifteen hundred pounds of tobacco and sixteen barrels of corn each, as their yearly salary, estimated to be worth, in all, £ 200. Every male colonist of the age of sixteen or upward was required to pay ten pounds of tobacco and one bushel of corn.

In proportion as the population began to spread along the large and beautiful streams that flow from the Allegheny Mountains into the Chesapeake Bay, more parishes were legally constituted, so that in 1722 there were fifty-four, some very large, others of moderate extent, in the twenty-nine counties of the colony. Their size depended much on the number of titheable inhabitants within a certain district. Each parish had a convenient church built of stone, brick, or wood, and many of the larger ones had also chapels of ease, so that the places of public worship were no fewer than seventy in all. To each parish church there was attached a parsonage, and likewise, in almost all cases, a glebe of two hundred and fifty acres, and a small stock of cattle. But not more than about half, probably, of these established churches were provided with ministers; in the rest the services were conducted by lay readers, or occasionally by neighboring clergymen. When the war of the Revolution commenced, there were ninety-five parishes, and at least a hundred clergymen of the Established Church.

We shall yet have occasion to speak of the Church Establishment in Virginia, and of its influence upon the interests of religion, as well as of the character of the clergy there during the colonial period. I can not, however, forbear saying, that although the greater number of the ministers seem at that epoch, to have been very poorly qualified for their great work, others were an ornament to their calling. I may mention, as belonging to early times, the names of the Rev. Robert Hunt and the Rev. Alexander Whitaker. The former of these accompanied the first settlers, preached the first English sermon ever heard on the American continent, and by his calm and judicious counsels, his exemplary conduct, and his faithful ministrations, rendered most important services to the infant colony. The latter was justly styled "the apostle of Virginia." . . .

In point of intolerance, the Legislature of Virginia equaled, if it did not exceed, that of Massachusetts. Attendance at parish worship was at one time required under severe penalties; nay, even the sacramental services of the Church were rendered obligatory by law. Dissenters, Quakers, and Roman Catholics were prohibited from settling in the province. People of every name entering the colony, without having been Christians in the countries they came from, were condemned to slavery. Shocking barbarity! the reader will justly exclaim; yet these very laws prove how deep and strong, though turbid and dark, ran the tide of religious feeling among the people. As has been justly remarked, "If they were not wise Christians, they were at least strenuous religionists."

I have said enough to show that, in the colonization of Virginia, religion was far from being considered as a matter of no importance; its influence, on the contrary, was deemed essential to national as well as individual prosperity and happiness.

Maryland, we have seen, though originally a part of Virginia, was planted by Lord Baltimore, as a refuge for persecuted Roman Catholics. When the first of its colonists landed, in 1634, under the guidance of Leonard Calvert, son of that nobleman, on an island in the Potomac, they took possession of the province "for their Saviour," as well as for "their lord the king." They planted their colony on the broad basis of toleration for all Christian sects,* and

---

* It is due to truth to say that much more credit has been given to Lord Baltimore for the "toleration" in matters of religion which characterized his colony in Maryland than has been merited. He was undoubtedly a man of liberal and tolerant views. But from whom did he obtain the charter for his projected colony? From the government of Protestant England. Who can believe that that government would have granted Lord Baltimore a charter that did not guarantee religious liberty, in a good measure, to Protestants? Lord Baltimore could have obtained no other charter from the government of England than that which he did. And when Roman Catholic orators wish to prove to us that their Church is a tolerant Church, let them give us an instance of a Roman Catholic country granting to a Protestant colony such a charter as England, Protestant England, gave to Lord Baltimore and his Roman Catholic colony in Maryland. [Ed.—Whether through pointed exclusion or inadvertent omission, Baird failed to include in his discussion the fact that Puritan forces gained control of the government in Maryland and revoked toleration for all but the most rigorous Calvinists. From 1654 to

in this noble spirit the government was conducted for fifty years. Think what we may of their creed, and very different as was this policy from what Romanism elsewhere might have led us to expect, we can not refuse to Lord Baltimore's colony the praise of having established the first government in modern times, in which entire toleration was granted to all denominations of Christians; this too, at a time when the New England Puritans could hardly bear with one another, much less with "papists;" when the zealots of Virginia held both "papists" and "Dissenters" in nearly equal abhorrence; and when, in fact, toleration was not considered in any part of the Protestant world to be due to Roman Catholics. . . .

North Carolina was first colonized by stragglers from Virginia, settling on the rivers that flow into Albemarle Sound, and among these were a good many Quakers, driven out of Virginia by the intolerance of its laws. This was about the middle of the seventeenth century. Puritans from New England, and emigrants from Barbadoes, followed in succession; but the dissenters from Virginia predominated. Religion for a long while seems to have received but little attention. William Edmonson and George Fox visited their Quaker friends among the pine groves of Albemarle, in 1672, and found a "tender people." A Quarterly Meeting was established, and thenceforward that religious body may be said to have organized a spiritual government in the colony. But it was long before any other made much progress. No Episcopal minister was settled in it until 1703, and no church built until 1705.

The Proprietaries, it is true, who obtained North as well as South Carolina from Charles II., professed to be actuated by a "laudable and pious zeal for the propagation of the Gospel;" but they did nothing to vindicate their claim to such praise. In their "Constitutions" they maintained that religion and the profession of it were indispensable to the well-being of the State and privileges of citizenship; vain words, as long as no measures were taken to promote what they thus lauded. But we shall yet see that, little as true religion owed in North Carolina to the first settlers, or to the

1657 and from 1692 until after the Revolution, Catholics were denied religious freedom in the land where they had welcomed all sects. In 1704 the Mass was outlawed; in 1718 all Roman Catholics were disenfranchised.]

Proprietaries, that State eventually obtained a large population of a truly religious character, partly by the emigration of Christians from France and Scotland, partly by the increase of Puritans from New England.

South Carolina began to be colonized in 1670, by settlers shipped to the province by the Proprietaries, and from that time forward it received a considerable accession of emigrants almost every year. Its climate was represented as being the finest in the world; under its almost tropical sun, flowers were said to blossom every month of the year; orange groves were to supplant those of cedar; silk-worms were to be fed on mulberry-trees introduced from the south of France; and the choicest wines were to be produced. Ships arrived with Dutch settlers from New York, as well as with emigrants from England. . . .

Such was the character of what might be called the substratum of the population in South Carolina. The colonists were of various origin, but many of them had carried thither the love of true religion, and the number of such soon increased.

Georgia, of all the original thirteen colonies, ranks latest in point of date. The good Oglethorpe, one of the finest specimens of a Christian gentleman of the Cavalier school, one who loved his king and his Church, led over a mixed people to settle on the banks of the Savannah. Poor debtors, taken from the prisons of England, formed a strange medley with godly Moravians from Herrnhut, in Germany, and brave Highlanders from Scotland. To Georgia, also, were directed the youthful steps of those two wonderful men, John and Charles Wesley, and the still more eloquent Whitfield, who made the pine forests that stretch from the Savannah to the Altamaha resound with the tones of their fervid piety. . . .

Thus we find that religion was not the predominating motive that led to the colonization of the Southern States, as was the case with New England; and yet that it can not be said to have been altogether wanting. It is remarkable that in every charter granted to the Southern colonies, "the propagation of the Gospel" is mentioned as one of the reasons for undertaking the planting of them. And we shall see that that essential element of a people's prosperity ultimately received a vast accession of strength, from the emigrants whom God was preparing to send from the Old World to those parts of the New.

CHAPTER 14

Religious Character of the Early Colonists

—Founders of New York

. . . The first attempts to establish trading stations, for they could hardly be called settlements, were made by the merchants of Amsterdam. But when the Dutch West India Company was formed, in 1621, it obtained a monopoly of the trade with all parts of the Atlantic coast claimed by Holland in North America. Colonization on the Hudson River does not appear to have been the main object of that Company. The territory of New Netherlands was not even named in the charter, nor did the States General guarantee its possession and protection. Trade with the natives in skins and furs was, in fact, the primary and almost exlusive object.

But in a few years, as the families of the Company's factors increased, what was at first a mere station for traders, gradually bore the appearance of a regular plantation; and New Amsterdam, on Manhattan Island, began to look like some thriving town, with its little fleet of Dutch ships almost continually lying at its wharves. Settlements were also made at the west end of Long Island, on Staten Island, along the North River up to Albany, and even beyond that, as well as at Bergen, at various points on the Hackensack, and on the Raritan, in what was afterward New Jersey.

Harmony at this time subsisted between the Dutch and their Puritan neighbors, notwithstanding the dispute about their respective boundaries. In 1627, we find the Governor of New Netherlands, or New *Belgium,* as the country was sometimes called, paying a visit of courtesy and friendship to the Plymouth colony, where he was received with "the noise of trumpets." A treaty of friendship and commerce was proposed. "Our children after us," said the Pilgrims, "shall never forget the good and courteous entreaty which we found in your country, and shall desire your prosperity forever."

. . . the colony was . . . retarded by the want of a popular form of government, and by the determination of the West India Company not to concede one.

The first founders of New Netherlands were men of a bold and enterprising turn, whose chief motive in leaving Holland was, no doubt, the acquisition of wealth. But educated in the National Dutch Church, they brought with them a strong attachment to its doctrines, worship, and government; and however deeply interested in their secular pursuits, they unquestionably took early measures to have the Gospel preached among them, and to have the religious institutions of their fatherland planted and maintained in their adopted country. A church was organized at New Amsterdam, now New York, not later, probably, than 1619; and there was one at Albany as early, if not earlier. The first minister of the Gospel settled at New York, was the Reverend Everardus Bogardus.

The Dutch language was exclusively used in the Dutch churches until 1764, being exactly a century after the colony had fallen into the hands of the English. As soon as that event took place, the new governor made great efforts to introduce the language of his own country, by opening schools in which it was taught. This, together with the introduction of the English Episcopal Church, and the encouragement it received from Governor Fletcher, in 1693, made the new language come rapidly into use. The younger colonists began to urge that, for a part of the day at least, English should be used in the churches; or that new churches should be built for those who commonly spoke that tongue. At length, after much opposition from some who dreaded lest, together with the language of their fathers, their good old doctrines, liturgy, catechisms, and all should disappear, the Rev. Dr. [Archibald] Laidlie, a distinguished Scotch minister who had been settled in an English

Presbyterian church at Flushing, in Holland, connected with the Reformed Dutch Church, was invited to New York, in order to commence Divine service there in English. Having accepted this call, he was, in 1764, transferred to that city, and in his new charge his labors were long and greatly blessed. From that time the Dutch language gradually disappeared, so that hardly a vestige of it now remains.

The population of New Netherlands, when it fell into the hands of the English, is supposed to have been about ten thousand, or half as many as that of New England at the same date. There has been a slight emigration to it from Holland ever since; too small, however, to be regarded as of any importance. But all the emigrants from Dutch ports to America were not Hollanders. The Reformation had made the Dutch an independent nation, and the long and bitter experience they had had of oppression led them to offer an asylum to the persecuted Protestants of England, Scotland, France, Italy, and Germany. . . .

Several causes retarded the progress of religion among the Dutch colonists in America. One was the unsettled state of the country, caused by actual or dreaded hostilities with the Indians; another lay in the continued and unnecessary dependence of the churches for their pastors on the Classis, or Presbytery, of Amsterdam; a body which, however well disposed, was at too remote a distance to exercise a proper judgment in selecting such ministers as the circumstances of the country and the people required; a third is to be found in the lateness of the introduction of the English tongue into the public services of the churches, which ought to have occurred at least fifty years sooner.

Notwithstanding these hinderances, the blessed Gospel was widely and successfully preached and maintained in the colony, both when under the government of Holland and afterward. Its beneficial influence was seen in the strict and wholesome morals that characterized the community, and in the progress of education among all classes, especially after the adoption of a more popular form of government. . . .

CHAPTER 15

Religious Character of the Early Colonists

—Founders of New Jersey

Hollanders from New Amsterdam were the first European inhabitants of New Jersey, and, during the continuance of the Dutch dominion in America, it formed part of New Netherlands. The first settlement was at Bergen, but the plantation extended afterward to the Hackensack, the Passaic, and the Raritan. It is probable that a few families had settled even on the Delaware, opposite Newcastle, before the cession of the country to the English in 1664.

But the Dutch were not the only colonists of New Jersey. A company of the same race of English Puritans that had colonized New England, left the eastern end of Long Island in 1664, and established themselves at Elizabethtown. They must have been few in number, for four houses only were found there the following year, on the arrival of Philip Carteret, as governor of the province. Woodbridge, Middletown, and Shrewsbury were founded about the same time by settlers from Long Island and Connecticut. Newark was founded in 1667 or 1668, by a colony of about thirty families, chiefly from Brandon in Connecticut.

Colonists from New Haven bought land on both sides of the Delaware, and fifty families were sent to occupy it, but their trading establishments were broken up, and the colony dispersed, in consequence of the Dutch claiming the country. There are extant memorials, however, in the records of Cumberland and Cape May counties, that colonies from New England established themselves in these, not very long after the province changed its masters. The middle parts were gradually occupied by Dutch and New England settlers in their progress westward, and also by a considerable number of Scotch and Irish emigrants—all Protestants, and most of them Presbyterians.

. . . After some years of severe struggles between the colonists and their governors, Lord Berkeley became tired of the strife, and in 1674 sold the moiety of New Jersey to Quakers for £1,000, John Fenwick acting as agent in the transaction for Edward Byllinge and his assigns. Fenwick left England the following year, accompanied by a great many families of that persecuted sect, and formed the settlement of Salem, on the Delaware. Lands in West Jersey were now offered for sale by the Quaker company, and hundreds of colonists soon settled upon them. In 1676 they obtained from Carteret the right, so far as he was concerned, to institute a government of their own in West Jersey, and proceeded, the year following, to lay the ground-work in the "Concessions," as their fundamental deed was called. Its main feature was, that "it put the power in the people." Forthwith great numbers of English Quakers flocked to West Jersey, with the view of permanently settling there. . . .

After about twelve years of embarrassment, commencing with the Revolution of 1688 in England, the Proprietaries of both East and West New Jersey surrendered "their pretended right of government" to the British crown, and in 1702, both provinces, united into one, were placed for a time under the Governor of New York, retaining, however, their own Legislature. The population, notwithstanding the difficulties and irritation caused by political disputes intimately affecting their interests, steadily increased. Taken as a whole, few parts of America have been colonized by a people more decidedly religious in principle, or more intelligent and virtuous; and such, in the main, are their descendants at the present day. Nowhere in the United States have the churches been supplied with a more faithful or an abler ministry. . . . I may add, that no State in the American Union has more decidedly proved the importance of having a good original population, nor has any State done more, in proportion to its population and resources, to sustain the honor and promote the best interests of the American nation.

CHAPTER 16

Religious Character of the Early Colonists
—Founders of Delaware,
at First Called New Sweden

Though of all the States Delaware has the smallest population, and is the least but one in territorial extent, yet its history is far from uninteresting. Fairly included within the limits of Maryland, it never submitted to the rule of Lord Baltimore's colony; subjected for a time to the dominion of the Quaker province of William Penn, from that it emancipated itself in time to be justly ranked among the original Thirteen States, which so nobly achieved their independence.

. . . Emigrants for Delaware Bay, furnished with provisions for themselves, and with merchandise for traffic with the Indians, accompanied also by a religious teacher, left Sweden in 1638, in two ships, the Key of Calmar and the Griffin. Upon their arrival, they bought the lands on the Delaware from its mouth up to the falls where Trenton now stands; and near the mouth of Christiana Creek they built a fort, to which they gave that name, in honor of their youthful queen. Tidings of their safe arrival, and encouraging accounts of the country, were soon carried back to Scandinavia, and naturally inspired many of the peasantry of Sweden and Finland with a wish to exchange their rocky, unproductive soil for the banks of the Delaware. More bands of emigrants soon went thither, and many who would fain have gone were prevented only by the difficulty of finding a passage. The plantations gradually extended along the Delaware, from the site of Wilmington to that of Philadelphia. A fort constructed of huge hemlock logs, on an island a few miles below Philadelphia, defended the Swedish settlements, and became the head-quarters of Printz, their governor. The whole country, as above described, was called New Sweden, and the few families of emigrants from New England that happened to be within its boundaries, either submitted to the Swedish government, or else withdrew and established themselves elsewhere.

Meanwhile the Dutch reasserted their old claims to the country, planted a fort of Newcastle, and ultimately reduced New Sweden under their dominion, by means of an expedition of six hundred men, under the famous Peter Stuyvesant, Governor of New Netherlands. Thus, in 1655, terminated the power of Sweden on the American continent, after it had lasted above seventeen years. . . .

Interesting as this colony is from its early history, it becomes still more so because of its practical worth. The colonists were amiable and peaceable in their deportment; they maintained the best terms with the Indians; they were frugal and industrious; they were attentive to the education of their children, notwithstanding the want of schools and the difficulty of procuring books in their mother tongue; and, above all, they were careful in upholding religious institutions and ordinances. Lutherans, as their kindred in Sweden are to this day, they long preserved their national liturgy and discipline, besides keeping up an affectionate intercourse with the churches in their mother-country; and from these they often received aid in Bibles and other religious books, as well as in money. Having established themselves in the southern suburbs of Philadelphia, previous to the colonization of Pennsylvania by William Penn, they have always had a church there, known to this day as the "Swedes' Church," and which, with two or three more in Delaware and Pennsylvania, now belongs to the Protestant Episcopal communion. . . .

CHAPTER 17

Religious Character of the Early Colonists
—Founders of Pennsylvania

The history of William Penn, the Quaker philosopher and lawgiver, is very generally known. The son of a distinguished English admiral, heir to a fortune considered large in those days, accustomed from his youth to mingle in the highest circles, educated at the University of Oxford, rich in the experience and observation of mankind acquired by much travel, and versed in his country's laws, he seemed fitted for a course very different from that which he considered to be marked out for him in after life. He inherited from his parents a rooted aversion to the despotism of a hierarchy, and having, when a student at Oxford, ventured to attend the preaching of George Fox, he was for this offence expelled from the university. . . .

William Penn's personal interests, in the course of Providence, coincided with his benevolent views, in leading him to think of founding the colony to which he at length so assiduously devoted himself. His father having a large sum due to him from the crown, left this not very hopeful debt as a legacy to his son. But the son proposed to his royal debtor an easy mode of paying it: the king had only to make him a grant of waste land in the New World; and the suggestion was favorably received, for the profuse and profligate Charles II. had been his father's friend. On the 5th of March, 1681, he received a title to a territory which was to extend from the Delaware River five degrees of longitude westward, and from the thirty-ninth to the forty-second degree of north latitude. . . .

Nor was it only for the persecuted "Friends" in England that William Penn founded his colony: it was to be open, also, to members of the same society in America. Incredible as it may appear, they were persecuted in New England by the very men who themselves had been driven thither by persecution. Twelve Quakers were banished from Massachusetts by order of the General Court, in 1656, and four of these, who had returned, were actually executed, in 1669. That same year an act was passed by the Legislature of Virginia, to the effect "that any commander of any shipp, or vessell, bringing into the collonie any person or persons called Quakers, is to be fined £100; and all Quakers apprehended in the collonie are to be imprisoned till they abjure this countrie, or give securitie to depart from it forthwith. If they return a third time, they are to be punished as felons."*

After making all necessary arrangements, Penn left England for his ample domain in America, and arrived there on the 27th of October, 1682. Having landed at Newcastle, he went from that to Chester, and thence, by boat, up the Delaware, to the spot where now stands the city of Philadelphia. His first care was to acquire, by fair purchase, a title from the Indians to so much land, at least, as might be required for his projected colony, and this transaction took place at a famous council, held under a large elm-tree at Shakamaxon, on the northern edge of Philadelphia. There the hearts of the congregated chiefs of the Algonquin race were captivated by the simplicity and sincerity of Penn's manners, and by the language of Christian affection in which he addressed them. "We will live," said they, in reply to his proposals, "in love with William Penn and his children, and with his children's children, as long as the moon and sun endure."

The first emigrants to Pennsylvania were, for the most part, Quakers; but the principle of unlimited toleration, upon which it was established, made it a resort for people of all creeds and of none. Swedes, Dutch, and New Englanders had previously established themselves within its limits and not many years had elapsed when the Quakers, whom Penn had specially contemplated as the future citizens of his colony, were found to be a minority among the inhabitants. This, however, has not marred the harmony and tranquillity of the province. No act of persecution or intolerance

---

* Hening's "Collection of the Laws of Virginia." [Ed.—The modern reader might wish to consult this source; see W. W. Hening (ed.), *The Statutes at Large Being a Collection of All the Laws of Virginia* (1619–1792), 13 vols. (Richmond, Va., 1809–1823).]

has ever disgraced its statute-book. The rights of the Indians were always respected; their friendship was hardly ever interrupted.

It were superfluous in me to pronounce any eulogium on the morality of the Quakers. The foundations of the colony of William Penn were laid in the religion of the Bible, and to the blessed influence of that religion it is unquestionably indebted for much of the remarkable prosperity which it has enjoyed. . . .

Thus have I completed the notice of the religious character of all the original colonies, which, in settling on the Atlantic slope, may be said to have founded the nation, by founding its civil and religious institutions: or rather I should say, I have spoken of the colonies that had territorial limits as such, and were established under charters from the crown of England. I have spoken of the bases—the lowest strata, so to speak—of the colonization of the United States. I have yet to speak of the superadded colonies, which dispersed themselves over the others, without having any territorial limits marked out to them by charters, but which settled here or there, as individuals or groups might prefer. It will be seen that this secondary, but still early colonization, exerted an immense influence upon the religious character of the country, and in many cases, through the wonderful providence of God, supplied what was wanting in the religious condition of the primary or territorial colonization.

[Six chapters on the "Religious Character of the Early Colonists" followed here in the original. Included were emigrants from Wales, Scotland and Ireland, Huguenots from France, Germany, Poland, and the valleys of the Piedmont.]

CHAPTER 18

Summary

Such, as respects the religious character of the colonists, was the early colonization of the United States. . . . Before leaving the subject, let us take a general survey of their character.

1. They were not composed of the rich, the voluptuous, the idle, the effeminate, and the profligate, neither were they, generally speaking, composed of poor, spiritless, dependent, and helpless persons. They rather came from that middle class of society, which is placed in the happy medium between sordid poverty and over-grown wealth. They knew that whatever comfort or enjoyment they could look for in the New World, was only to be attained by the blessing of God upon their industry, frugality and temperance.

2. They were not an ignorant rabble, such as many ancient and some modern States have been obliged to expel from their borders. Taken in the mass, they were well-informed—many of them remarkably so for the age in which they lived—and which in the case of none of them was an age of darkness. Letters had revived; the art of printing had diffused a great amount of valuable knowledge among the middle ranks of society, and was fast carrying it down to the lowest. With few exceptions, they had acquired the elements of a good education. There were few persons in any of the colonies that could not read. They were, moreover, a thinking people, and very unfit to be slaves of despotic power.

3. They were a virtuous people; not a vicious herd, such as used to be sent out by ancient States, and such as chiefly colonized South America and Mexico, men of unbridled passions and slaves to the basest lusts. The morality of the early colonists of the United States was unrivaled in any community of equal extent, and has been lauded by almost all who have written about them, as well as by those who have governed them.

4. They were religious men. They believed and felt that Christianity is no vain fancy—a fact that holds true even as respects those of them with whom religious motives were not the chief inducement for expatriating themselves. The overwhelming majority stood acquitted of the slightest approach to infidelity. Neither were they what are called "philosophers," attempting to propagate certain new theories respecting human society, and suggesting new methods for rendering it perfect. By far the greater number of them were simple Christians, who knew of no way by which men can be good or happy but that pointed out by God in His Word. There was not a single St. Simon or Robert Owen to be found among them. Some of them, indeed, were irreligious men; some

were even openly wicked, and opposed to all that is good. But these, in most of the colonies, formed a very small minority.

5. With few exceptions, the first colonists were Protestants; indeed, Lord Baltimore's was the only Roman Catholic colony, and even in it the Romanists formed but a small minority long before the Revolution of 1775. The great mass had sacrificed much, some their all, for the Protestant faith. They were Protestants in the sense of men who took the Bible for their guide, who believed what it taught, not what human authority put in its place. . . . There they learned to look upon all men as children of the same heavenly Father, as redeemed by the same Saviour, as going to the same bar of judgment, before which all must stand stripped of the factitious distinctions of this world. They saw no reason, therefore, why one man should lord it over another, since all "are of one flesh," and if Christians, brethren in Christ. And they learned from the Bible that obedience is due to rulers, not because they are different in blood or rank from other men, but because government is "an ordinance of God." Obedience to God secured their obedience to civil rulers. As God can not command what is wrong, no ruler can be justified in doing so, nor can he expect obedience if he does. And while they learned from the Bible what were their duties, so they learned there also what were their rights. This led them at once to practise the former, and to demand the latter.

6. The great majority of them had suffered much oppression and persecution, and in that severe but effectual school had learned lessons not to be acquired in any other. It led them to question many things to which otherwise their thoughts might never have been directed, and it gave them irresistible power of argument in favor of the right of the human mind to freedom of thought. Indeed, it is remarkable how large a proportion of the early colonists of the United States were driven from Europe by oppression. Although Virginia and the Carolinas were not expressly established as asylums for the wronged, yet during the Commonwealth in England they afforded a refuge to the "Cavalier" and the "Churchmen," as they did afterward to the Huguenot and German Protestant. Georgia was colonized as an asylum for

the imprisoned and "persecuted Protestants;" Maryland, as the home of persecuted Roman Catholics; and the colony of Gustavus Adolphus was to be a general blessing to the "whole Protestant world," by offering a shelter to all who stood in need of one. Even New York, though founded by Dutch merchants, with an eye to trade alone, opened its arms to the persecuted Bohemian, and to the inhabitant of the Italian Valleys. So that, in fact, all these colonies were originally people more or less, and some of them exclusively, by the victims of oppression and persecution; hence the remark of one of our historians is no less just than eloquent, that "tyranny and injustice peopled America with men nurtured in suffering and adversity. The history of our colonization is the history of the crimes of Europe."*

7. Though incapable as yet of emancipating themselves from all the prejudices and errors of past ages, with respect to the rights of conscience, they were at least in advance of the rest of the world on these points, and founded an empire in which religious liberty is at this day more fully enjoyed than anywhere else—in short, is in every respect perfect.

8. Lastly, of the greater number of the early colonists it may be said, that they expatriated themselves from the Old World, not merely to find liberty of conscience in the forests of the New, but that they might extend the kingdom of Christ, by founding States where the Trust should not be impeded by the hindrances that opposed its progress elsewhere. This was remarkably the case with the Puritans of New England; but a like spirit animated the pious men who settled in other parts of the country. They looked to futurity, and caught glimpses of the glorious progress which the Gospel was to make among their children and children's children. This comforted them in sorrow, and sustained them under trials. They lived by faith, and their hope was not disappointed.

---

* Bancroft's "History of the United States," vol. ii., p. 251.

CHAPTER 19

Relations Between the Church
and the Civil Power
in the Colonies of America
—In New England

. . . If we consider for a moment what was the state of the Christian world when these colonies were planted, in the early part of the seventeenth century, we must see that the mass of the colonists would be very little disposed to have the Church completely separated from the State in their infant settlements, and the former deriving no support from the latter. The Church and the State were at that time intimately united in all the countries of Europe; and the opinion was almost universally entertained that the one could not safely exist without the direct countenance of the other. It is not even certain that England, or any other country, would have granted charters for the founding of permanent colonies, unless upon the condition expressed, or well understood, that religion was received with public sanction and support. Assuredly, James I., at least, was not likely to consent to any thing else.

Be that as it may, the first colonists themselves had no idea of abolishing the connection which they saw everywhere established between the civil powers and the Church of Christ. To begin with New England, nothing can be more certain than that its Puritan colonists, whether we look to their declarations or to their acts, never contemplated the founding of communities in which the Church should have no alliance with the State. Their object—and it was one that was dearer to them than life itself—was to found such civil communities as should be most favorable to the cause of pure religion. They had left England in order to escape from a government which, in their view, hindered the progress of Divine truth, oppressed the conscience, and was inexpressibly injurious to the immortal interests of men's souls. . . .

In the formation, likewise, of their civil institutions in the New World, they determined that, whatever else might be sacrificed, the purity and liberty of their churches should be inviolate. Bearing this in mind, they founded commonwealths in which the churches were not to be subordinate to the State. . . . they had no wish that the Church should engross to itself the powers of the State, and so rule in civil as well as in ecclesiastical matters. But they thought it better that the State should be accommodated to the Church, than the Church to the State. "It is better," said Mr. Cotton, "that the commonwealth be fashioned to the setting forth of God's House, which is His Church, than to accommodate the Church frame to the civil State."*

With this in view, they sought to avail themselves of all the lights furnished by the experience of ancient as well as modern States, and looking especially to the Constitution of England as it then stood, they framed civil governments in which, as they hoped, not only the temporal, but, still more, the spiritual interests of mankind might best be promoted. . . . the Puritan founders of New England thought that "they were free to cast themselves into that mould and form of commonwealth which appeared best for them," in reference to their grand purpose: nor did they doubt that a government thus originating in voluntary compact, would have equal right to the exercise of civil authority with that of any earthly potentate.

But whatever were the details of their policy, and whatever the results of some parts of it, it is most certain that they intended that the Church should in no sense be subject to the State. They held the great and glorious doctrine that CHRIST IS THE ONLY HEAD AND RULER OF THE CHURCH, and that no human legislation has a right to interfere with His. It has been said that they took the

---

* Cotton's "Letter to Lord Say and Seal," in "Hutchinson's History of New England," vol. i., p. 497. [Ed.—Modern readers could consult Thomas Hutchinson, *The History of the Colony and Province of Massachusetts Bay*, 3 vols. (Cambridge, 1936).]

Hebrew commonwealth for their model in civil politics, and this is so far true. But it holds as to their penal code more than with respect to the forms of their civil governments. With the exception of the first few years of the Massachusetts Bay and New Haven colonies, there was no such blending of civil and religious authority as existed in the Jewish Republic. There was much, however, in the Hebrew commonwealth and laws that seemed adapted to the circumstances of men, who had just exchanged what they considered a worse than Egyptian bondage for a Canaan inhabited by the "heathen," whom they were soon to be compelled to "drive out." . . .

It is remarkable that, with the exception of the Plymouth settlers, all the first New England colonists—all who founded Massachusetts Bay, New Hampshire, Maine, Connecticut, New Haven, Providence, and Rhode Island—up to their leaving England, were members of the Established Church. The Plymouth people alone were Independents,* had had their church organized on that principle for years, and were such even before they went to Holland. If any of the other original colonists of New England had been thrust out from the Established Church of the mother country, they had not organized themselves on any other principle; and, however opposed to the spirit of its rulers and to some of its ceremonies and usages, their attachment to the Church itself, as well as to many of those whom they had left within its pale, is manifest from the letter of Governor Winthrop and his associates, just after embarking for America.

But on arriving there they immediately proceeded to the founding of an ecclesiastical economy upon the Independent plan, having for its essential principles, "That, according to the Scriptures, every Church ought to be confined within the limits of a single congregation, and that the government should be democratical; that Churches should be constituted by such as desired to be

---

* They were not, properly speaking, *Separatists*, in the distinctive sense in which that word was used at that epoch, viz., those who not only refused to have any sort of communion with the Established Church, but denounced all who did. The Separatists were exceedingly bitter in their hostility to every thing which bore the name of the Established Church of England. The farewell address of John Robinson to the Pilgrims who left Leyden to plant the colony at Plymouth, breathed a very different spirit.

members, making a confession of their faith in the presence of each other, and signing a covenant; that the whole power of admitting and excluding members, with the deciding of all controversies, was in the brotherhood; that church-officers, for preaching the Word and taking care of the poor, were to be chosen by the free suffrages of the brethren; that in Church censures, there should be an entire separation of the ecclesiastical from the civil sword; that Christ is the Head of the Church; that a liturgy is not necessary; and that all ceremonies not prescribed by the Scriptures are to be rejected."

But how are we to account for a change in their views so sudden and so great? Even when Winthrop left England, in 1630, neither the Presbyterian nor the Independent doctrines, as to Church government, had made that progress in public opinion which they had made when the Long Parliament, and Cromwell and his army, began to play their parts. . . .

This, it appears to me, may be referred to two or three causes. First, it is natural that, on quitting England, where they had suffered so much from Prelacy, they should renounce an ecclesiastical system that conferred upon any men powers so capable of being abused; nor can it be thought surprising that in such circumstances they should go to the opposite extreme, and prefer an ecclesiastical government of the most democratical sort. Another, and much more powerful reason for their rejecting Episcopacy, would be that they might escape the jurisdiction of the bishops, which would otherwise unquestionably have followed them. And, lastly, there can be no doubt that they were much influenced by what they saw and heard of the Plymouth colony. . . .

Let us now see what were the relations between the Church and the State or "Commonwealth," in New England. In every colony there, except [Providence and Rhode Island], the object of one of the first acts of civil legislation was to provide for the support of public worship; and other laws followed from time to time to the same effect, as circumstances required. Without going into unnecessary details, suffice it to say, that parishes or "towns" of a convenient size were ordered to be laid out, and the people were directed by the proper authorities of their respective towns to levy taxes for erecting and keeping in due repair a suitable "meeting-house," for the maintenance of a pastor or minister, and for all other necessary expenses connected with public worship. I am not aware that any exemption from this law was allowed for a long time after the colonies were founded. Such was the fundamental union of Church and State in the colonies that now form the States of Massachusetts, Connecticut, New Hampshire, and Maine.

The next law adopted in the Massachusetts Bay colony dates from 1631, the year after the arrival of Winthrop and his company, and, as we shall hereafter see, it was pregnant at once with evil and with good. It ran thus: "To the end that the body of the commons may be preserved of honest and good men, it is ordered and agreed, that for the time to come, no man shall be admitted to the freedom of this body politic but such as are members of some of the churches within the limits of the same."* In other words, no one was to vote at elections, or could be chosen to any office in the commonwealth, without being a member of one of the churches. This law was long in force in Massachusetts and in Maine, which, until 1820, was a part of that State; but it never prevailed, I believe, in New Hampshire, and was unknown, of course, in Rhode Island. But a like law existed from the first in New Haven, and when that colony was united, in 1662, with Connecticut, where this had not been the case, it became, I believe, part of the legislation of the united colony.

Thus we find two fundamental laws on this subject prevailing in New England—the one universal, with the exception of Rhode Island; the other confined to Massachusetts, Connecticut, and Maine. In restricting the exercise of political power to men who, as members of the Church, were presumed to be loyal to the grand principle of the colony to which they belonged, namely, the maintenance of purity of doctrine and liberty of worship, as the first consideration, and of free political government as necessary to it, the authors of that law doubtless contemplated rather the protection of their colonists from apprehended dangers than the direct promotion of piety.

---

* Bancroft's "History of the United States," vol. i., p. 360.

In conclusion, I ought to state, that in the New England colonies the ministers of the Gospel had no part, as such, in the civil government. They were confined to their proper office and work. Yet no men had more influence, even in affairs of state. As a body of enlightened patriots, whose opinion it was important to obtain, they were consulted by the political authorities in every hour of difficulty; and although cases might be found in which the leading men among them, at least, did not advise their fellow-citizens wisely, it was much otherwise in the great majority of instances. . . .

CHAPTER 20

Relations between the Church
and the Civil Power
in the Colonies
—The Southern and Middle Provinces

Virginia, too, like New England, was first colonized by members of the Church of England; but there was a vast difference between the views of the admirers of the English Prelacy of that time, and those of the Puritans. The Established Church was then composed, in fact, of two great divisions, which in spirit, at least, have more or less existed ever since, and were represented in the colonization of America by the High Churchmen and Cavaliers of the South, on the one hand, and the Puritans of the North on the other. While the latter left England in order to escape from the oppression inflicted on them by the Prelacy, abetted by the Crown, the former had no complaint against either, but carried with them a cordial attachment to both.

In the original charter of James I. to Virginia, it was especially enjoined that religion should be established according to the doctrines and rites of the Church of England; every emigrant was bound to allegiance to the king, and to conformity with the royal creed. Still, it does not appear that any provision was made for the clergy until 1619, that is, twelve years after the commencement of the colony. A Legislative Assembly, elected by the colonists, met that year for the first time, and passed laws for the formation of parishes and the regular maintenance of the clergy; accordingly, the establishment of the Episcopal Church dates formally, if not really, from that year.

Previously to this, however, and during the governorship of Sir Thomas Dale, the London Company sent over to Virginia a set of "laws, divine, moral, and martial," being, apparently, the first-fruits of Sir Thomas Smith's legislation; and from their Draconian character, they give us some idea of the notions entertained in those times of the ways whereby religion might be promoted by the civil power. They were so bad, it is true, as to be little, if at all enforced. . . .

Previously to the dissolution of the company, in 1624, the colonial Legislature passed a number of laws relating to the Church; three of the most important were as follows:

1. That in every plantation where the people were wont to meet for the worship of God, there should be a house or room set apart for that purpose, and not converted to any temporal use whatsoever; and that a place should be impaled and sequestered only for the burial of the dead.

2. That whosoever should absent himself from Divine service any Sunday, without an allowable excuse, should forfeit a pound of tobacco; and that he who absented himself a month should forfeit fifty pounds of tobacco.

3. That there should be a conformity in the Church as near might be, both in substance and circumstance, to the canons of the Church of England; and that all persons should yield a ready obedience to them upon pain of censure.*

---

* It will be seen, from these laws, that the actual legislation of the more liberal "Cavaliers" of the South was not a whit more tolerant than that of the bigoted "Roundheads" of New England. So it ever is; the religion of the world, with all its vaunted liberality, is found to be more intolerant, wherever it has a chance, than serious, earnest, evangelical piety.

Upon the company being dissolved, the colony fell under the immediate government of the crown, which thenceforth appointed the governors, as well as decided, in the last instance, upon all laws passed by the Assembly, the Council, and the governor. And from about the year 1629, the laws requiring conformity to the Established Church were strictly enforced, and infractions of them visited with severe penalties.

In 1662, in obedience to instructions from the crown, the Virginia Legislature enacted several laws for the more effectual support of the Established Church, the promotion of the education of youth generally, and of candidates for the ministry in particular. But it was long before the "college" contemplated by these laws was actually established [College of William and Mary, 1693].

Early in the eighteenth century, if not even sooner, the laws of Virginia, requiring strict conformity to the Established Church, must either have been modified, or have begun to fall into neglect, there being positive evidence that Presbyterian meetings were held for public worship in 1722. From that period until the Revolution, avowed dissenters increased steadily and rapidly, and previously to 1775 there were many Baptist, Presbyterian, Lutheran, and Quaker churches within the colony. Still, the Episcopal Church predominated, and it alone was supported by law.

Maryland, founded by Roman Catholics, had no union of Church and State, no legal provision for any religious sect, and tolerated all until 1692,* when Protestant Episcopacy was established by law, the country divided into parishes, and the clergy, as in Virginia, supported by a tax upon the inhabitants. This was one of the results of the Revolution of 1688 in England, and of the wide-spread abhorrence of popery which prevailed at that time, and long afterward, both in the mother-country and her colonies. Gradually, and not without encountering many obstacles, the

---

* Strictly speaking, it might be said that this statement is not quite exact. For when Cromwell's commissioners came into possession of the colony, in 1654, the legislature, which was wholly subservient to Clayborne, a tool of the Protector, passed a law suppressing public worship among Roman Catholics and Episcopalians. And four years afterward, [Josias] Fendall, acting as governor, at first in the name of the Proprietaries, and afterward by his own usurpation, undertook to persecute the Quakers. But both these exceptions were of short duration.

Episcopal Church advanced in the number of its parishes and clergy until the American Revolution, and though all other sects had ever been tolerated, was the only one supported by the State. . . .

In South Carolina, all sects were at first protected by the Proprietaries. In 1704, however, the friends of the Episcopal Church having, by the arts of Nathaniel Moore, obtained a majority of one in the Representative Assembly of a colony two thirds of whose inhabitants were not Episcopalians, abruptly disfranchised all but themselves, and gave the Church of England a monopoly of political power. But the dissenters having appealed to the House of Lords in England, the acts complained of were annulled by the crown, and, consequently, repealed by the Colonial Assembly, two years afterward. Nevertheless, although the dissenters were tolerated, and admitted to a share in the civil government, the Church of England remained the Established Church of the province until the Revolution.

In the same year, 1704, influenced by zeal or bigotry, the Proprietaries forced a Church Establishment upon the people of North Carolina, though presenting at that time an assemblage of almost all religious denominations—Quakers, Lutherans, Presbyterians, Independents, etc. But, according to the royalists, the majority were "Quakers, Atheists, Deists, and other evil-disposed persons." From that time glebes and a clergy began to be spoken of, and churches were ordered to be erected at the public cost. But . . . the Established Church made slow progress in North Carolina.

As long as New York was under the Dutch government, the churches of that colony supported their pastors by voluntary contributions, and there was no union of Church and State.* But on

---

* It can not be said, I fear, that the early Dutch colonists, or, rather, their colonial governors, were very tolerant. Though there was no union of the Church and State, they were very jealous of allowing any other than the Reformed Dutch Church to exist among them. A little band of Lutherans, who joined the colony almost at its commencement, were not allowed to hold their worship publicly until the country passed into the hands of the English.—*Professor Schmucker's "Retrospect of Lutheranism in the United States,"* p. 6. [Ed.—This was an address to the General Synod at Baltimore, 1841, and can be found in the collection entitled *The American Lutheran Church, Historically, Doctrinally, and Practically Delineated, in Several Discourses* (Springfield, Ohio: D. Harbaugh, 1851).]

its falling into the hands of the English, as the royal governors and other officers sent over to administer public affairs were all admirers of the Established Church of England, they very naturally wished to see it supersede the Dutch Church, while, at the same time, the English tongue supplanted the Dutch as the language of the colony. Governor [Benjamin] Fletcher, accordingly, in 1693, prevailed on the legislature to pass an act for the establishment of certain churches and ministers, reserving the right of presentation to the vestrymen and churchwardens. This act was so construed, two years after, that Episcopal ministers alone received the benefit of it, although this does not appear to have been the expectation or the intention of the legislature. From that period till the Revolution, the Episcopal was the Established Church, although, at the time of its becoming so, it was reckoned that nine tenths of the population belonged to other communions.

East and West New Jersey, united into one province, and placed under the administration of the crown in 1702, had its future government laid down in the commission and instructions to Lord Cornbury. Toleration being allowed by these to all but papists, and special "favor" invoked for the Church of England, that Church was so far established there, seventy-three years before the American Revolution. In Pennsylvania there never was any union of Church and State, nor, so far as I know, any attempt to bring it about. Delaware was separated from Pennsylvania in 1691, and from that time had its own governors, under the immediate control of the crown. But in Delaware, as well as in New Jersey and in Georgia, the colony of the good cavalier, James Oglethorpe, who loved "the King and the Church," there can hardly be said to have been an establishment: as the "favor" shown to the Episcopal Church secured a maintenance for a very small number of ministers only, and that more for the benefit and gratification of the officers connected with the government, and their families, than with the view of reaching the bulk of the people, who preferred other modes of worship.

Were we to select two colonies from each of these divisions as examples of the two favored types of Church government, so diverse, yet about equally favored by legal enactments and a public provision, we should take Massachusetts and Connecticut in the North, and Virginia and Maryland in the South. In these we may compare and contrast the nature and influence of Independency, or the most popular form of Church organization, with Episcopacy; or Puritanism with High-churchism, among the descendants of the Anglo-Saxons and the Normans of the New World.

CHAPTER 21

The Influences of the Union of Church
and State as It Formerly Existed
in America—In New England

. . . Let us first consider what were the advantages resulting from this union.

1. It is not to be denied that it proved beneficial, by securing the ministrations of the Gospel to the colonial settlements, as fast as these were formed. The law provided that the country occupied should be divided into "towns," or parishes, with well-defined boundaries, and that as soon as a certain number of families should be found residing within these boundaries, a meeting should be called by the proper local officers, and steps taken for the establishment of public worship. The expense of building such a church as the majority of the inhabitants, or legal voters, might choose to erect, was, like other taxes, to be levied on the people of the township, according to their properties and polls, and the pastor's stipend was, in like manner, to be fixed by the decision of the majority at a meeting of legal voters, and raised by a general yearly tax.

Thus it will be seen that the township was left to decide what sort of building should be erected, how much should be expended upon it, and the amount of the pastor's stipend. As the pastor was chosen by the people, without any interference on the part of the civil authorities, or any other person, individual or corporate, the evils of patronage were unknown. In the choice of a pastor, however, be it observed, that it was the invariable rule from the first, that he should be called by the "church," that is, by the body of believers or actual members of the church—the communicants —and afterward by the "town," that is, by the legal voters, the vote of a majority of them being requisite to the validity of a call. . . .

It will be admitted that such a law as this, if enforced, must have made the establishment of public worship keep pace with the increase of the population, wherever that became numerous enough, in any given direction, for the building of churches; and also must have secured to ministers of the Gospel a steadier, and possibly, too, an ampler support than otherwise. . . .

2. I have already stated that in Massachusetts, and if not in the Connecticut colony, at least in that of New Haven, political trust and power were confined to members of the churches. It were absurd to suppose that this law was adopted as a means of promoting religion; its authors were too well acquainted with human nature to have any such expectation. Their grand object was to confine the exercise of political power to persons in which they could confide. . . . They had made a long voyage to establish a colony in the wilderness, where they and their children might enjoy liberty of conscience, and worship God in purity. Being all of one mind on the subject of religion, as well as other great points, they thought that they were fully authorized to establish such a colony, and certainly it would be hard to prove that they were not. In these circumstances, what more natural than their endeavoring to prevent persons from coming in among them to defeat their object? Desiring, above all things, that their institutions might continue to be pervaded in all time coming with the spirit in which they had been commenced, they determined, in order to secure this, that none but the members of their churches should enjoy the rights and privileges of citizens, and by this they hoped to guard against both internal and external enemies. . . .

3. While the above law, no doubt, had the effect of keeping out of the government of the colony all influences which in those trying

times might militate against its best interests, it is no less certain that it kept away men of a troublesome character. Many, in fact, who made the experiment, speedily became weary of a colony where their restless spirits found little or no scope for intereference, and accordingly soon left, either for some other colony, or for England.

Such, I consider, were the most important advantages resulting from the union of Church and State in Massachusetts, and some other of the New England colonies; and I am not disposed to deny that these advantages were of no small moment in the circumstances in which the colonists were placed. I have next to point out some of the evils resulting from it.

1. It gave rise to internal difficulties of the gravest nature with such of the colonists as were not disposed to agree to all the measures by which it was carried out, and led to the adoption of the harshest proceedings against those persons. One of the first cases of this kind was that of Roger Williams, in 1633–35, and it shook the colony to its centre. That remarkable man had been educated for the English bar under the patronage of Sir Edward Coke; but influenced by the conviction that he was called to the ministry, he took orders in the Established Church. Expelled from that Church by the bishops, on account of his Puritanical principles, he came to Boston in 1631.

Taught by persecution to examine how far human governments are authorized to legislate for the human mind, and to bind its faculties by their decisions, Williams soon perceived that a course was pursued in America which he could not but condemn as repugnant to the rights of conscience. Regarding all intolerance as sinful, he maintained that "the doctrine of persecution for cause of conscience is most evidently and lamentably contrary to the doctrine of Jesus Christ." . . . In the end, Roger Williams was banished from the colony, and having retired to Narragansett Bay, there he became a Baptist, and founded what is now the State called Rhode Island. Absolute religious liberty was established there from the first.

The next case occurred in 1637, and ended in the expulsion of [John] Wheelwright, Anne Hutchinson, and [William] Aspinwall, who, although they held some very extravagant notions on certain points, would have been harmless persons had the only weapon employed against them been Truth.

. . . Every thing indicated that this union between Church and State was operating in such a manner as rapidly to undermine the rights and principles of both. The Anabaptists were treated in some cases with great harshness, and when, in 1651, the Quakers made an attempt to establish themselves in the colony, they were expelled and prohibited from returning upon pain of death: a penalty actually inflicted on four of them who returned in contravention of this enactment.

These Quakers, it is true, behaved in the most fanatical and outrageous manner. They attacked the magistrates with the grossest insults, and interrupted public worship with their riotous proceedings. Even women among them, forgetting the proprieties and decencies of their sex, and claiming Divine direction for their absurd and abominable caprices, smeared their faces, and ran naked through the streets! It were absurd to compare them with the peaceable and excellent people who bear that name in our day. They gave no evidence whatever of knowing what true religion means. Still, their punishment ought not to have been so extreme, and should have been inflicted for violating the decorum of society, not for their supposed heretical opinions.* Now, measures so disgraceful and injurious to the colony, and so contrary to what one would expect from men of such excellence in other respects, would never have been adopted had it not been for laws unhappily dictated by the colonial union between Church and State.

Forty years later, twenty persons were put to death for witchcraft! Now it is obvious that so absurd a spectacle would never have taken place, had not the union of the Church and the State led the government so often to act on grounds purely religious, and

---

* Penalties involving mutilation, such as boring the tongue with a hot iron, and cutting off the ears, were enacted against the Quakers in 1657, and thus found a place in the statute-book of Massachusetts, but were soon repealed, the colony being ashamed of them. The fact was, as Mr. Bancroft says, vol. i., p. 451, "the creation of a national and uncompromising Church led the Congregationalists of Massachusetts to the indulgence of the passions which disgraced their English persecutors, and Laud was justified by the men whom he wronged." . . .

to take cognizance of subjects which no political government is capable of deciding upon.* . . .

2. Much more disastrous were the consequences flowing from another and still more fundamental law, passed by the Conscript Fathers of Massachusetts and Connecticut—that of making church membership requisite to the enjoyment of the rights and privileges of citizenship. Nor was it long before these consequences appeared. Not only did many persons find admission into the colonies as settlers who were not members of any church, in the sense almost invariably attached to the term in America—that is, communicants, or, as they are sometimes called, "full members"—but, what the worthy founders seem not to have anticipated, some of their own children grew up manifestly "unconverted," and, consequently, did not become communicants; the churches planted by the New England Fathers having maintained at first the strictest discipline, and allowed none to become communicants until they had satisfied the proper church authorities that they were converted persons, and had the religious knowledge without which they could not fitly come to the Lord's Supper. Persons who had not these requisites, as might be expected, thought it very hard to be excluded from the privilege of citizenship, although, as was generally the case, their lives were perfectly regular and moral. They therefore complained, and their complaints were felt to be reasonable, and such as parental love, even in the breast of a Brutus, could not long resist.

In these circumstances, what was the course pursued by the colonial legislators, after taking council of their spiritual guides?

---

* The putting of witches to death in Massachusetts was a legitimate result of the attempt to build up a sort of theocracy, having for its basis the civil institutions of the Jewish commonwealth. But were witches nowhere put to death in those days save in New England? Let the reader search and see.

I ought to add, that the rules of Massachusetts put the Quakers to death, and banished the "Antinomians" and "Anabaptists," not because of their religious tenets, but because of their violations of the civil laws. This is the justification which they pleaded, and it was the best they could make. Miserable excuse! But just so it is: wherever there is such a union of Church and State, heresy and heretical practices are apt to become violations of the civil code, and are punished no longer as errors in religion, but as infractions of the laws of the land. So the defenders of the Inquisition have always spoken and written in justification of that awful and most iniquitous tribunal.

Instead of abolishing the law, they decided that all baptized persons might be regarded as members of the Church, thus directly interfering with matters wholly beyond the sphere of civil legislation, and contravening, likewise, a former decision of the Church: for although there is a sense in which all persons baptized in infancy are in their youth members of the Church, it is only as pupils or wards, and must not be confounded with the membership of persons who have made a profession of their faith after conversion, and at an age that qualifies them for taking such a step. Such, at least, is, I apprehend, the opinion of all churches that maintain a strict discipline. . . .

This law was not so hurtful in its consequences to the State as it was to religion. The churches were filled with baptized persons who "owned the covenant," and with the lapse of time the number of "full members," or communicants, diminished. Many now enjoyed civil privileges in virtue of a less intimate connection with the Church; this was all that they desired, and with this they were too apt to be content. But the evil went far beyond this. To escape from a state of things in which the churches, though filled with baptized people, had comparatively few "communicants," many of the pastors were led into the dangerous, I may say the fatal error, of considering the Lord's Supper to be a means of grace, in the same sense that the preaching of the Word is such, and that all well-disposed persons may be admitted to it as a means of conversion to the unconverted, as well as of edification to "believers," or converted persons.

Not that this was enjoined on the churches as a law of the State. But it was the natural and almost inevitable, though indirect, consequence of the law adjudging all baptized persons who "renewed the covenant" to be considered members of the church, and entitled to the civil privileges attached to that relation. It is easy to see what would follow. The former measure filled the churches with baptized people who owned the covenant; the latter practice filled the churches with unconverted communicants. In the course of a few generations the standard of religious truth and practice fell lower and lower. This decline necessarily bore upon the character of the pastors, for upon the occurrence of a vacancy, the choice, in too many cases, was sure to fall upon a pastor equally low in point of religious character with the parties by whom he was chosen. Such a state of things opened the way effectually for the admission of false doctrine, and the more so, inasmuch as there was no effectual control beyond and above what was to be found in each individual church. . . .

3. As the people were invested by law with an absolute control over the application of the money so raised, no great evil seemed, at first sight, likely to arise from such a mode of supporting the churches: and it may readily be supposed that at the outset, when the colonists formed a homogeneous society, and were all either members of the established churches, or cordial friends and admirers of their system of doctrine and church polity, this assessment for their support would be submitted to without reluctance. But in process of time, when, whether from the accession of fresh emigrants, or from the growing up of the children of the original colonists into manhood, there happened to be found in any particular town a considerable number of inhabitants who either disliked the services of the parish church, or were indifferent to religion altogether, it is clear that such a law would be considered both burdensome and unjust. Men can never be made to feel that they may with equity be required to pay taxes in any shape, to support a church which they dislike, and to which they may have conscientious objections. Hence arose serious difficulties, aggravated afterward when the Legislature was compelled, by the progress of true principles of legislation, to extend the rights of citizenship, and permission to have a worship of their own, to persons of all sects. It seemed unjust that these, while supporting their own churches, should be compelled, in addition, to contribute toward the maintenance of the parish, or "town" churches, which for a long time they were called upon to do.

A law, however, was passed at length, [there were several, but one in 1729 was the most general], not exempting those who did not attend the parish church from all taxation, but allowing them to appropriate their proportion to the support of public worship according to their own wishes. Fair as this seemed, it proved most disastrous in its consequences to the interests of true religion. The haters of Evangelical Christianity could now say, "Well, since we must be taxed in support of religion, we will have what suits us;" and in many places societies, for it would be improper to call them churches, of Universalists* and Unitarians began to be formed, and false preachers found support where, but for this law, no such societies or preachers would ever have existed. It is impossible to describe the mischiefs that have flowed from this unfortunate measure. . . .

4. Only one further measure was required in order to make this law for the support of public worship as fatal as possible to the interests of true religion in Massachusetts. This was a decision of the Supreme Court of that State, pronounced some thirty or thirty-five years ago, [1820, regarding the First Church of Dedham] by which the distinction which had previously existed between the "church" and the "town" or "parish," was destroyed in the view of the law; and the "town," that is, the body of the people who were taxed for the support of the parish church, was allowed to exercise a control in the calling of a pastor and in every thing else. There then ensued great distress in not a few parishes. In every instance in which the majority of the "town" were opposed to evangelical religion, they had it in their power, by stopping his salary, to turn away a faithful pastor, and to choose a Universalist or Unitarian in his place. This actually took place in numerous instances, and the church, or at least the faithful part of it, which was often the majority, was compelled to abandon the edifice in which their fathers had worshipped, with whatever endowments it might have, and to build for themselves a new place of worship, call a pastor, and support him on the voluntary plan. The evil, however, which might have gone to still greater lengths, was arrested in Massachusetts in 1833, by the final dissolution of the union between Church and State, in a way to be hereafter briefly described. . . .

---

* By Universalists I mean those professed Christians in America who, with many shades of difference on the subject, agree in holding that eventually all men will be saved. I shall have to speak of them more at large in another place.

CHAPTER 22

The Influences of the Union

of Church and State

—In the Southern and Middle States

. . . In Virginia, we find that the three main laws connecting the Church and the State were substantially the same as those of Massachusetts at a later date. 1. The country was divided into parishes, the inhabitants of which were required to build, furnish, and uphold churches, or places of worship, and maintain a pastor, by an assessment proportioned to their respective means, these being estimated by the quantity of tobacco that they raised, as that was the chief article of their commerce and of their wealth. 2. The people were required to attend the established churches, which were for a long time the only ones that existed, or that were permitted to exist in the colony. 3. The rights of citizenship were confined to members of the Episcopal Church.

Now, it is beyond dispute that the division of the country into parishes, the erection of churches, and the providing of glebes for the rectors and ministers, was useful both in Virginia and in Maryland. . . .

. . . During a large part of the colonial period . . . the want of ministers greatly diminished the advantages that might have accrued from having parishes marked out and churches built in them. Thus, in 1619, there were eleven parishes and only five ministers; and in 1661, the parishes in Virginia were about fifty, and the ministers only about a fifth part of that number.*

---

* Dr. Hawks's "History of the Episcopal Church in Virginia," p. 64. [Ed.—Modern readers might wish to consult Francis L. Hawks, *Contributions to the Ecclesiastical History of the United States of America, A Narrative of Events connected with the Rise and Progress of the Protestant Episcopal Church in Virginia* (New York: Harper & Brothers, 1836.)]

But granting that the support secured by law to Episcopacy was ample, which in Virginia it was not, let us notice some of the evils attending this union of Church and State, and see whether they did not counterbalance all the admitted good. The first of these, and it was no trifling one, was the antipathy which such compulsory measures created toward the favored Church. Men were displeased, and felt aggrieved at being taxed for the support of a church whose services they did not frequent, but to which they might otherwise have felt no hostility, nay, to which they might by a different course have been won. . . . taxes for the support of a dominant church, representing in some instances but a mere fraction of the population, were extremely offensive to those who were members of other churches or of none, and proved hurtful, in the end, to the Episcopal Church itself. It attached a stigma to it which it took a long time to efface; the more so as, when the Revolution was drawing on, it began to be viewed as the Church favored of the mother-country, with which the colonists were about to enter into a war for what they deemed to be their rights. . . .

2. As respects Virginia, at least, the interests of true religion and of the Episcopal Church were seriously injured by the compulsory attendance upon the services of the churches. . . . In the justness of the following remarks every well-informed man must heartily concur: "To coerce men into the *outward* exercise of religious acts by penal laws is indeed possible; but to make them love either the religion which is thus enforced, or those who enforce it, is beyond the reach of human power. There is an inherent principle of resistance to oppression seated in the very constitution of most men, which disposes them to rebel against the arbitrary exercise of violence seeking to give direction to opinions; and it is not, therefore to be wondered at, that one sanguinary law to compel men to live piously, should beget the necessity for more."*

3. Another evil resulting from the union between Church and State in the Southern colonies, and particularly in Virginia and Maryland, is to be found in the almost incessant disputes that long prevailed between the colonial governors and the parish vestries

---

* Dr. Hawks's "History of the Episcopal Church in Virginia," p. 49.

respecting the right of presentation, which was claimed by both parties. In this contest, the Virginia vestries were, upon the whole, successful; still, as the governor claimed the right of *inducting,* there were often serious collisions.* . . . In Maryland, the governors long insisted on exercising the right of presentation, a right that put it into their power to thrust very unworthy pastors into the Church. But the case was not much better when left to the vestries, these being often composed of men by no means fit to decide upon the qualifications of a pastor. In no case does it appear that the Church itself, that is, the body of the communicants, possessed the privilege of choosing a pastor for themselves.

4. A fourth evil resulting from the union of Church and State in the colonies where the Episcopal Church was established, lay in this, that the ministers required from time to time by the churches behooved to come from England, or, if Americans by birth, to receive ordination from some bishop in England, generally the Bishop of London, to whose superintendence and government the Episcopal Church in America seems to have been intrusted. As there was no bishop in America during the whole colonial period, this disadvantage continued down to the Revolution.

. . . At a distance from England, and beyond the immediate inspection of the only bishop that seemed to have any authority over them, they generally contrived to secure impunity, not only for the neglect of their duties, but even for flagrant crimes. Some cases of the most shocking delinquency and open sin occurred both in Virginia and Maryland, without the possibility, it would seem, of their being reached and punished. All that could be done by persons commissioned by the Bishop of London to act for him, under the name of "commissaries," was done . . . , but the evil was too deep to be effectually extirpated by any thing short of the exercise of full Episcopal authority on the spot. . . .

---

* [Ed.—"Inducting" was the process of designating a particular priest as having permanent charge over a certain parish. An act of 1629 empowered the governor to induct priests who were presented to him, but Anglican laymen were unwilling to destroy their freedom from episcopal control by submitting to that of a temporal magistrate. As vestrymen of local churches, they simply refused to "present" any candidates to the governor for induction, preferring rather to hire priests on a temporary basis. For further clarification, see Winthrop S. Hudson, *Religion in America* (New York: Charles Scribner's Sons, 1965), pp. 13, 33–34.]

5. And, lastly, one of the greatest evils of the Establishment we are speaking of, is to be found in the shameful acts of intolerance and oppression to which it led. Although the Quakers were in no instance put to death in Virginia, yet they were subjected to much persecution and annoyance, and were glad in many cases to escape into North Carolina. The Puritans, too, were much disliked, and severe laws were passed "to prevent the infection from reaching the country."* . . .

In fact, it was not until the lapse of a century after those times that toleration was established in Virginia, through the persevering efforts of the Presbyterians and other non-established denominations, whose friends and partisans had by that time greatly increased, partly in consequence of this very intolerance on the part of the government, but chiefly by immigration, so far as to outnumber the Episcopalians of the province when the war of the Revolution commenced.

As for Maryland, although the Quakers were greatly harassed in that colony for some time, and Roman Catholics were treated with grievous injustice, yet there never was the same intolerance manifested toward those who were called Dissenters, as had been shown in Virginia. The Protestant Episcopal Church was established there by law in 1692, but not in fact until 1702.

But in no colony in which Episcopacy became established by law was there more intolerance displayed than in New York. That establishment was effected in 1693 by Governor Fletcher, who soundly rated the Legislature because [it was] not disposed to comply with all his wishes. But in zeal for Episcopacy he was outdone by one of his successors, Lord Cornbury, a descendant of Lord Clarendon, who would fain have deprived the Dutch of their privileges, and forced them into the Episcopal Church. . . .

In what has been said of the intolerance manifested in several of the colonies in which the Protestant Episcopal Church was established, I would not be understood as charging such intolerance upon that Church. No doubt men of an intolerant spirit were to be found in it, for, alas! true religious liberty, and an enlarged spirit of toleration, were far from being general in those days; but it had

---

* Hening's "Virginia Statutes," 223.

members also of a most catholic spirit, who neither did nor could approve of such acts as the above. The intolerance was rather that of the colonial governments, and to them properly belongs the credit or discredit attached to it.

In conclusion, I can not but think that the union of the Episcopal Church with the State in some colonies, and of the Congregational Church with the civil power in others, was, upon the whole, far more mischievous than beneficial; an opinion in which I feel persuaded that the great body alike of the Episcopal and Congregational ministers with us concur. Had the founders of the Episcopal Church in Virginia and Maryland, excellent men as I believe they were, gone to work in reliance on the blessing of God upon their efforts, and endeavored to raise up a faithful native ministry, trusting to the willingness of the people to provide for their support, I doubt not that they would have succeeded far better in building up the Episcopal Church than they did with all the advantages of the State alliance which they enjoyed. They would doubtless have had to encounter many difficulties, but they would have laid a surer foundation also for ultimate success. Dr. Hawks gives a painfully interesting narrative of the struggles which the established clergy of Virginia and Maryland had to sustain with their parishioners about their salaries: the one party striving to obtain what the law assigned to them; the other, aided even at times by legislative enactments, availing themselves of every stratagem in order to evade the legal claims of the clergy. The time and anxiety, the wearing out of mind and body, which these disputes cost faithful ministers, not to mention the sacrifice of influence, would have been laid out better and more pleasantly in the unembarrassed work of their calling; nor were they likely to have been worse off in respect of this world's blessings than the faithful among them really were. . . .

CHAPTER 23

State of Religion during
the Colonial Era

Before quitting the Colonial Era in the history of the United States, let us take a general view of the state of religion throughout all the colonies during that period of 168 years, from 1607 to the commencement of the war of the Revolution in 1775.

As communities, the Anglo-American colonies, from their earliest days, were pervaded by religious influence, not equally powerful, yet real and salutary in all. This was especially true of New England, whose first settlers openly declared to the world that they left their native land not so much to promote individual religion as to form Christian societies. . . . Religion with them was not only a concern between man and God, but one in which society at large had a deep interest. Hence some fruits of this high and holy principle might be expected in the communities which they founded, and we not unreasonably desire to know how far the result corresponded with such excellent intentions. It were unfair, however, to expect much in this way, considering the circumstances of the colonists, settling in a remote wilderness, amid fierce and cruel savages, and exposed to all the fatigues and sicknesses incident to such a settlement, and to the anxieties and difficulties attending the organization of their governments, collisions with the mother-country, and participation in all that country's wars.

The Colonial Era may, for the sake of convenience, be divided into four periods. The first of these, extending from the earliest settlement of Virginia in 1607 to 1660, was one in which religion greatly flourished, notwithstanding the trials incident to settlements amid the forests, and the troubles attending the establishment of the colonial governments. Peace with the Aborigines suffered few interruptions, the only wars worth mentioning being that with the Pequods in Connecticut, in 1637; that between the Dutch and the Algonquins, in 1643; and those that broke out in Virginia in 1622 and 1644, which were at once the first and the last, and by far the most disastrous of that period. But these wars were soon over, and a few years sufficed to repair whatever loss they occasioned to the colonists.

This was the golden age of the colonial cycle. God poured out His Spirit in many places. Precious seasons were enjoyed by the churches in Boston, in Salem, in Plymouth, in Hartford, and in New Haven. Nor were the labors of faithful men in Virginia without a rich blessing. Days of fasting and prayer were frequently and faithfully observed. The Saviour was entreated to dwell among the people. Religion was felt to be the most important of blessings, both for the individual man and for the State. Revivals were highly prized, and earnestly sought; nor were they sought in vain. The journals of Governor Winthrop, and other good men of that day, present most interesting details in proof of this. America has seen more extensive, but never more unequivocal, works of grace, or more indubitable operations of the Spirit.

The second period is one of sixty years, from 1660 to 1720.

This might be called the brazen age of the colonies. Almost all of them experienced times of trouble. Massachusetts suffered in 1675 from a most disastrous war with "King Philip," the chief of the Pokanokets, and with other tribes which afterward joined in a general endeavor to expel or exterminate the colonists. Violent disputes arose with the government of England respecting the rights of the colony, and to these were added internal dissensions about witchcraft, and other exciting subjects, chiefly of a local nature. In Virginia, in 1675–76, there were a serious Indian war and a "Grand Rebellion," which threatened ruin to the colony. And in the Carolinas a desolating war with the Tuscaroras broke out in 1711–12.

Besides these greater causes of trouble and excitement, there were others which it is not necessary to indicate. The influence of growing prosperity may, however, be mentioned. The colonies had now taken permanent root. They might be shaken, but could not be eradicated or overthrown by the rude blasts of misfortune. Their wealth was increasing; their commerce was already considerable, and attracted many youth to the seas. Every war which England had with France or Spain agitated her colonies also.

These causes concurring with the disastrous consequences of the union of Church and State already described, led to a great decline of vital Christianity, and although partial revivals took place, the all-pervading piety that characterized the first generation suffered a great diminution. The light of holiness grew faint and dim, and morality, in general, degenerated in a like degree. The Fathers had gone to the tomb, and were succeeded, upon the whole, by inferior men. . . .

The third period, comprehending the thirty years from 1720 to 1750, was distinguished by extensive revivals of religion, and this, notwithstanding the agitation produced in the colonies, by the share they had in the war between France and England toward the close of that period, and other unfavorable circumstances besides. The Great Awakening, as it has been called, infused a new life into the churches, more especially in New England, in certain parts of New York, New Jersey, Pennsylvania, and some other colonies, and its effects were visible long afterward in many places. It is true that fanatical teachers did much mischief in several quarters by associating themselves with the work of God, and introducing their own unwarrantable measures, so as to rob it, in the end, of much of the glorious character that distinguished it at first. Yet it can not be denied that it was a great blessing to the churches. Some important, though painful lessons, were learned, in regard to the economy of the Spirit, which have not been wholly forgotten to this day.

This was the period in which [Jonathan] Edwards and [Thomas] Prince, [Theodorus Jacobus] Frelinghuysen, [Jonathan] Dickinson, [Samuel] Finley, and the Tennents [Gilbert and William], labored in the Northern and the Middle States; [Samuel] Davies, and others of kindred spirit, in Virginia; the Wesleys [John and Charles] for a while in Georgia; while [George] Whitfield [sic], like the angel symbolized in the Apocalypse as flying through the heavens, having the everlasting Gospel to preach to the nations, traversed colony after colony in his repeated visits to the New World, and was made an instrument of blessing to multitudes.

The fourth and concluding period of the Colonial Era comprehends the twenty-five years from 1750 to 1775, and was one of great public agitation. In the early part of it, the colonies aided England with all their might in another war with France, ending in the conquest of the Canadas, which were secured to the conquerors by the treaty of Paris in 1763. In the latter part of it, men's minds became universally engrossed with the disputes between the colonies and the mother country, and when all prospect of having these brought to an amicable settlement seemed desperate, preparation began to be made for that dreadful alternative—war. Such a state of things could not fail to have an untoward influence on religion. . . .

Such is the very cursory and imperfect review which the limits of this work permit us to take of the religious vicissitudes of the United States during their colonial days. That period of 168 years was, comparatively speaking, one of decline, and even deadness, in the greater part of Protestant Europe; indeed, the latter part may be regarded as having been so universally. Yet, during the same period, I feel very certain that a minute examination of the history of the American Protestant churches would show, that in no other part of Christendom, in proportion to the population, was there a greater amount of true knowledge of the Gospel, and of practical godliness, among both ministers and their flocks. No doubt there were long intervals of coldness, or, rather, of deadness, as to spiritual things, during which both pastors and people became too much engrossed with the "cares of life." But, blessed be God, He did not abandon us forever. Though He visited our transgressions with a rod, and chastised us for our sins, yet He remembered the covenant which He made with our fathers, and the Word of His promise wherein He had caused them to trust. And though our unworthiness and our unprofitableness had been great, He did not cast us away from His sight, but deigned to hear us when we called upon Him in the dark and gloomy hour, and saved us with a great salvation. And this He did because "His mercey endureth forever."

BOOK III

The National Era

CHAPTER 24

Effects of the Revolution upon Religion
—Changes to Which It Necessarily Gave Rise

. . . The first twenty-five years of the national existence of the States were fraught with evil to the cause of religion. First came the war of the Revolution, which literally engrossed all men's minds. The population of the country at its commencement scarcely, if at all, exceeded three millions; and for a people so few and so scattered, divided into thirteen colonies, quite independent, at the outset, of each other, having no national treasury, no central government or power, nothing, in short, to unite them but one common feeling of patriotism, it was a gigantic undertaking. The war was followed by a long period of prostration. Connection with England having been dissolved, the Colonies had to assume the form of States, their governments had to be re-organized, and a general, or federal government, instituted. The infant nation, now severed from the mother country, had to begin an existence of its own, at the cost of years of anxiety and agitation. Dangers threatened it on every side, and scarcely had the General Government been organized, and the States learned to know their places a little in the federal economy, when the French Revolution burst forth like a volcano, and threatened to sweep the United States into its fiery stream. In the end it led them to declare war against France for their national honor, or, rather, for their national existence.* That war was happily brought to an end by Napoleon, on his becoming First Consul, and thus was the infant country allowed to enjoy a little longer repose, as far as depended on foreign nations.

Unfavorable to the promotion of religion as were the whole twenty-five years from 1775 to 1800, the first eight spent in hostilities with England were pre-eminently so. The effects of war on the churches of all communions were extensively and variously disastrous. To say nothing of the distraction of the mind from the subject of salvation, its more palpable influences were seen and felt everywhere. Young men were called away from the seclusion and protection of the parental roof, and from the vicinity of the oracle of God, to the demoralizing atmosphere of a camp; congregations were sometimes entirely broken up; churches were burned, or converted into barracks or hospitals, by one or other of the belligerent armies, often by both successively; in more than one instance pastors were murdered; the usual ministerial intercourse was interrupted; efforts for the dissemination of the Gospel were, in a great measure, suspended; colleges and other seminaries of learning were closed for want of students and professors; and the public morals in various respects, and in almost all possible ways, deteriorated. Christianity is a religion of peace, and the tempest of war never fails to blast and scatter the leaves of the Tree which was planted for the healing of the nations.

It required some time for the churches to recover from the demoralizing effects of a war which had drawn the whole nation into its circle, and lasted eight long years. But the times immediately following the Revolution were, as I have remarked, far from

---

* [Ed.—Between 1797 and 1800 bellicose notes were exchanged between the United States and her recent ally regarding the seizure of ostensibly neutral merchant shipping. Some naval skirmishes with French privateers occurred, but in point of fact war was never declared. See G. W. Allen, *Our Naval War with France* (Boston: Houghton Mifflin, 1909); S. E. Morison and H. S. Commager, *The Growth of the American Republic* (New York: Oxford University Press, 1962), pp. 358–69.]

being favorable to the resuscitation of true religion, and to the restoration of the churches, even to the condition, unsatisfactory as it was, in which they had stood previously to the contest. Through God's blessing, however, they not only shared in the returning tranquillity of the country, but from that time to this, with some short periods of interruption, they have steadily grown with its growth and strengthened with its strength.

It is not easy to ascertain what was the exact number of ministers and churches in the United States when these became severed from England, but the following estimate can not be very wide of the truth. . . .

The most exact approximation which I make is as follows:

	Ministers	Churches
Episcopalians	250	300
Baptists	350	380
Congregationalists	575	700
Presbyterians	140	300
Lutherans	25	60
German Reformed	25	60
Reformed Dutch	25	60
Associate	13	20
Moravians	12	8
Roman Catholics	26	52
Total	1,441	1,940

If we assume the number of ministers to have been 1,441, and the population 3 millions, in 1775, then we have one minister of the Gospel, on an average, for nearly 2,082 souls, which, I apprehend, is not far from the exact truth.

At that epoch there was no bishop in either the Protestant Episcopal or the Roman Catholic Church. There were nine colleges and two medical schools, but no schools of law or theology.

. . . We have now to see by what means that union of Church and State, which connected the Congregational churches in the North and the Episcopal Church in the Middle and South, with the civil government, was dissolved; what were the results of that dissolution; and what the position in which the churches now stand to the civil power, whether as represented by the General Government or by the individual States.

CHAPTER 25

The Dissolution of the Union of Church
and State Not Effected
by the General Government,
nor Did It Take Place Immediately

More than one erroneous idea prevails, I apprehend, in Europe, with respect to the dissolution of the union of Church and State in the United States. First, many seem to think that it was a natural and inevitable result of the separation of the colonies from the mother country, and of the independent position which they had assumed. But that union connected the established churches of America, not with the mother country, but with the colonial governments; so that, when the colonies became States, the alliance that had subsisted between them and certain churches was not necessarily affected. . . .

Again, many imagine that the union of Church and State in America was dissolved by an act of Congress; that is, by an act of the General Government. But this was not the case. An article of the Constitution, it is true, restrains Congress from establishing any particular religion: but this restriction is not in the original draught of the Constitution; it forms one of certain amendments adopted soon after, and runs as follows: "Congress shall make no laws respecting an establishment of religion, or prohibiting the free exercise thereof." That is to say, the General Government shall not make any law for the support of any particular church, or of all the churches. But neither this, nor any other article in the Constitution of the United States, prohibits individual States from making such laws. The Constitution simply declares what shall be the powers of the General Government, leaving to the State governments such powers as it does not give to the General Government. This, in reference to the subject in hand, is manifest from the fact that "the establishment of religion," as we shall presently see, survived for many years, in some States, their acceptance of the Constitution of the United States.

Lastly, many persons in Europe seem to be under the impression that the union of Church and State was annihilated at the Revolution, or, at all events, ceased upon the organization of the State governments being completed. This, however, was not so in all cases. The connection between the civil power in all the States in which Episcopacy had been established in the colonial period was dissolved, very soon after the Revolution, by acts of their respective Legislatures. But the Congregational Church in New England continued to be united with the State, and to be supported by it, long after the Revolution. Indeed, it was not until 1833 that the last tie that bound the Church to the State in Massachusetts was severed.

CHAPTER 26

Dissolution of the Union of Church

and State in America,

When and How Effected

The first State that dissolved its connection with the Church was Virginia, a circumstance that seems surprising at first sight, inasmuch as its early colonists were all sincere friends of its Established Episcopal Church, and for a long period were joined by few persons of different sentiments. Indeed, for more than a century, dissent was scarcely, if at all, allowed to exist within the commonwealth, even in the most secret manner.

Two causes, however, concurred in producing an alteration of these feelings toward the Established Church. First, many whose attachment to it had been owing to their birth, education, and early prepossessions, became disgusted with the irreligious lives of many of the clergy, and the greediness with which, notwithstanding that most of their time was spent in fox-hunting and other sports, in company with the most dissolute of their parishioners, they were ready to contend for the last pound of tobacco allowed them as their legal salary. Such, indeed, was the character of those clergymen, that any one who makes himself minutely acquainted with their doings, must feel amazed that the Church which they dishonored should have retained its hold upon the respect of the Virginian colonists as long as it did. What attachment to it remained, must be ascribed to its having at all times had some faithful and excellent ministers who mourned over these scandals, and by their personal worth redeemed in some measure the body to which they belonged from the infamy brought upon it by their reprobate fellow-clergymen, or "parsons," as they were oftener called. These exceptions, however, did not prevent multitudes from abandoning the Church of their fathers, around which their earliest and tenderest associations still clustered. . . .

Prior to 1740, there was only one Presbyterian congregation, it is believed, in eastern Virginia, though the Scotch and Irish emigrants from Pennsylvania must have introduced several. . . .* There were also a few Quaker societies, some small German congregations, and a considerable number of Baptist churches, which, though small and scattered, embraced, perhaps, a larger number of persons upon the whole, than all the other dissenting bodies put together. . . .

[In 1747 Samuel Davies was sent by the Presbytery of Newcastle, Delaware; except for a few months' visit to England, he labored in Virginia until 1759.] He succeeded in building up seven churches, and from that time Presbyterianism made very consider-

---

* [Ed.—Baird never mentions explicitly the second cause for an alteration of feelings toward the Established Church in Virginia. But judging from the amount of space given to the activities of dissenting churchmen, Presbyterians and Baptists mostly, during the Revolutionary epoch, one can infer that he considered the influence of dissenting churches as the second cause.]

able progress in eastern Virginia; so that when the war of the Revolution began, the Presbytery of Hanover in that colony was a numerous body, and comprehended some very able and eloquent ministers. The Scotch and Irish Presbyterians were at the same time increasing in the western part of the province. The Baptist congregations increased even more rapidly. Still, it was not always easy to avoid suffering from the interference of the civil authorities. The Act of Toleration, passed in England on the 28th of June, 1687, extended unquestionably to the colonies, yet not a few obstacles continued to be thrown in the way of "dissenters," almost down to the opening scene of the Revolutionary drama.

When the Revolution came at last, the Baptists and Presbyterians were, almost to a man, in its favor; and many of these, but especially of the former, whose preachers had suffered by far the most from the civil authorities in the earlier part of the century, at the instigation, as they believed, whether justly or unjustly, of the clergy of the Established Church, were not a little influenced in the course they then adopted by the hope of seeing the success of the Revolution lead to the overthrow of an establishment which they regarded with feelings of repugnance, and even of hostility. In these circumstances, it was to be expected that before the Revolution had made much progress, an assault would be made on the Established Church; such an assault was made, and not without success.

A very general impression prevails in England, and perhaps elsewhere, that the entire separation of Church and State in America was the work of Mr. Jefferson, the third President of the United States. . . . Now none of Mr. Jefferson's admirers will consider it slanderous to assert that he was a very bitter enemy to Christianity, and we may even assume that he wished to see not only the Episcopal Church separated from the State in Virginia, but the utter overthrow of every thing in the shape of a church throughout the country. Still, it was not Jefferson that induced the State of Virginia to pass the Act of Separation. That must be ascribed to the petitions and other efforts of the Presbyterians and Baptists.

No sooner was war declared, than the Synod of New York and Philadelphia, the highest ecclesiastical body among the Presbyterians of America at that time, addressed to their churches a very judicious and patriotic letter, which, while it displayed a firm spirit of loyalty toward the government of England, evidently and naturally sympathized with the contest then begun—a contest which it was thought could not be abandoned without the sacrifice of their dearest rights. Few persons supposed at that time that the struggle was to end in a separation from the mother country. But when, in the following year, the Congress issued its Declaration of Independence, the whole face of matters was changed, and ministers of the Gospel had to make their election—whether they would recognize and obey the act of the Congress, or still adhere to the sovereignty of England. Then it was that the first body of clergy of any denomination in America that openly recognized that act, and thereby identified themselves with the cause of freedom and independence, was the comparatively numerous and very influential Presbytery of Hanover in Virginia. At its first meeting after the appearance of the Declaration, that body addressed the Virginia House of Assembly in a memorial, recommending the separation of Church and State, and the leaving of the support of the Gospel to the voluntary efforts of its friends. The memorial runs as follows:

"To the Honorable the General Assembly of Virginia. The memorial of the Presbytery of Hanover humbly represents: That your memorialists are governed by the same sentiments which have inspired the United States of America, and are determined that nothing in our power and influence shall be wanting to give success to their common cause. We would also represent that dissenters from the Church of England in this country have ever been desirous to conduct themselves as peaceable members of the civil government, for which reason they have hitherto submitted to various ecclesiastical burdens and restrictions that are inconsistent with equal liberty. But now, when the many and grievous oppressions of our mother country have laid this Continent under the necessity of casting off the yoke of tyranny, and of forming independent governments upon equitable and liberal foundations, we flatter ourselves that we shall be freed from all the incumbrances which a spirit of domination, prejudice, or bigotry has interwoven with most other political systems. . . .

"In this enlightened age, and in a land where all of every denomination are united in the most strenuous efforts to be free, we hope and expect that our representatives will cheerfully concur in removing every species of religious as well as civil bondage. Certain it is, that every argument for civil liberty gains additional strength when applied to liberty in the concerns of religion; and there is no argument in favor of establishing the Christian religion but may be pleaded, with equal propriety, for establishing the tenets of Mohammed by those who believe the Koran; or, if this be not true, it is at least impossible for the magistrate to adjudge the right of preference among the various sects that profess the Christian faith, without erecting a claim to infallibility, which would lead us back to the Church of Rome.

"Neither can it be made to appear that the Gospel needs any such civil aid. We rather conceive that, when our blessed Saviour declares His kingdom is not of this world, He renounces all dependence upon State power, and as His weapons are spiritual, and were only designed to have influence on the judgment and heart of man, we are persuaded that if mankind were left in the quiet possession of their inalienable religious privileges, Christianity, as in the days of the Apostles, would continue to prevail and flourish in the greatest purity by its own native excellence, and under the all-disposing Providence of God.

"Therefore, we ask no ecclesiastical establishments for ourselves; neither can we approve of them when granted to others. This, indeed, would be giving exclusive or separate emoluments or privileges to one set of men, without any special public services, to the common reproach and injury of every other denomination. And, for the reasons recited, we are induced earnestly to entreat that all laws now in force in this commonwealth, which countenance religious domination, may be speedily repealed; that all, of every religious sect, may be protected in the full exercise of their several modes of worship; exempted from all taxes for the support of any Church whatsoever, further than what may be agreeable to their own private choice or voluntary obligation. This being done, all partial and invidious distinctions will be abolished, to the great honor and interest of the State, and every one be left to stand or fall according to his merit, which can never be the case so long as any one denomination is established in preference to others.

"That the great Sovereign of the universe may inspire you with unanimity, wisdom, and resolution, and bring you to a just determination on all the important concerns before you, is the fervent prayer of your memorialists."

Besides this petition from the Presbytery of Hanover, there were others from the Baptists and Quakers. The Baptists had suffered more than any other class of dissenters, and the remembrance of their wrongs, now that their day of power had come, stimulated them to an uninterrupted opposition of seven-and-twenty years to the Established Church. Indeed, they now took the lead in opposing its claims. In 1775 they presented to the General Assembly an address, composed by members who had spontaneously convened, in which they petitioned, "that they might be allowed to worship God in their own way, without interruption; to maintain their own ministers, separate from others; and to be married, buried, etc., without paying the clergy of other denominations."* . . .

The above memorial from the Presbyterians, and petitions from the Baptists, Quakers, and others opposed to the Established Church, were met by counter-memorials from the Episcopalians and Methodists, appealing on behalf of the Establishment to the principles of justice, wisdom, and policy. Public faith, it was said, required that the State should abide by its engagements; and that a system of such old standing, and which involved so many interests on the part of persons who had staked their all upon its continued existence, possessed the nature of a vested right, and ought to be maintained inviolate. . . . And, finally, the memorials prayed that the matter might be referred, in the last resort, to the people at large, as they had the best of reasons for believing that a majority of the citizens would be in favor of continuing the Establishment.

From this it would seem that, in the conviction of these memorialists, a majority of the population of Virginia were Episcopalians; yet it was confidently maintained in other quarters that two

---

* Semple's "History of the Baptists in Virginia," pp. 25–27, 62. [Robert B. Semple, *A History of the Rise and Progress of the Baptists in Virginia* (Richmond, Va.: Published by the author, 1810).]

thirds of the people were at that time Dissenters. I am inclined to think that the greater part professed, or favored Episcopacy, but that a decided majority were opposed to its civil establishment. The memorials led to a long and earnest discussion. The Episcopal Church had for her champions Messrs. [Edmund] Pendleton and R[obert] C. Nicolas, and for her great opponent Mr. Jefferson, who speaks of the contest as the severest in which he was ever engaged.* After discussing the subject for nearly two months, the Assembly repealed all the colonial laws attaching criminality to the profession of any particular religious opinions, requiring attendance at the parish churches, and forbidding attendance elsewhere, with the penalties attached thereto. Dissenters were to be exempted in future from compulsory contributions in support of the Episcopal Church. The clergy, however, were to have their stipends continued until the first day in the ensuing year, and had all arrears secured to them. The churches, chapels, glebes, books, plate, etc., belonging to the Episcopal Church, were to remain in her possession.† This law was passed on the 5th of December, 1776. The question of having a general assessment for the support of religion was at the same time discussed, but the determination of it was put off to a future day.

In the course of 1777 and 1778, petitions and counter-petitions continued to be addressed to the Legislature on the subject of religion. Some of the petitions prayed for the preservation of all that remained of the Establishment; others advocated a general assessment for the support of all denominations; others opposed that suggestion. . . .

[Another petition from the Hanover Presbytery], and probably still more, the strenuous efforts of the Baptists, led, in 1779, to the abandonment of the proposed "general assessment," after a bill to that effect had been ordered to a third reading.

Thus, it was mainly owing to the exertions of the Presbyterians, Baptists, and Quakers, that the union of Church and State in Virginia was dissolved, and the scheme of a general assessment for

---

* Jefferson's Works, vol. i., p. 32.
† Hening's "Statutes of Virginia," p. 34.

the support of all Protestant denominations defeated.* Mr. Jefferson, it is true, when a member of the Assembly in 1776, rendered all the aid in his power, and would have been very well pleased to have had such parties to co-operate with him in some other schemes, if he could. But they, not he, began the movement in this case, and they persevered in their endeavors to render the churches altogether independent of the civil power, and to have all placed precisely on the same footing, as respected the civil government.

Mr. Jefferson's grand achievement, in the line of legislating on the subject of religious rights, was the famous act "for establishing religious freedom," drawn up by him, and adopted by the Legislature of Virginia in 1785.† That act in itself, however, contains nothing to which a friend of full and equal liberty of conscience would perhaps object; but it gave its author great satisfaction, not because it embodied the principles of eternal justice, but because, by putting all religious sects on an equality, it seemed to degrade Christianity, and "to comprehend," to use his own words, "within the mantle of protection the Jew and the Gentile, the Christian and the Mohammedan, the Hindoo and infidel of every denomination." It was this that made the arch-infidel chuckle with satisfaction—not, we repeat, that the great principles embodied in the measure were right.

This early discussion of the propriety of dissolving the union of Church and State in Virginia, after the war of the Revolution had broken out, had some effect, probably, on other States placed in similar circumstances. Such, at least, is the prevailing impression in the absence of authentic documentary proof. After the Declaration of Independence, measures to the same effect were very promptly taken in Maryland. On the 3d of November, 1776, the Legislature of that State put forth a Declaration of Rights similar to that made by Virginia in the early part of the same year, and

---

* A general assessment bill would have done infinite mischief. It never could have been confined to the Evangelical Churches, and would have ended in building up Unitarianism, Universalism, etc., in Virginia, just as a similar measure did in New England.

† [Ed.—Baird includes in a note here the text of the act that passed both houses on January 16, 1786.]

embodying principles directly subversive of the union of Church and State. . . .

In the Maryland "Declaration of Rights," it was set forth "that as it is the duty of every man to worship God in such a manner as he thinks most acceptable to Him, all persons professing the Christian religion are equally entitled to protection in their religious liberty; wherefore no person ought by any law to be molested in his person or estate on account of his religious persuasion or profession, or for his religious practice, unless, under color of religion, any man shall disturb the good order, peace, or safety of the State, or shall infringe the laws of morality, or injure others in their natural, civil, or religious rights." It was further declared that no one ought to be compelled to frequent or maintain the religious worship of any denomination; but, at the same time, it was affirmed that the Legislature might, in its discretion, impose a common and equal tax for the support of the Christian religion in general; in such case, however, every individual paying the tax was held to possess the right of designating the religious denomination to the support of which it was to be applied; or he might resolve this legislative support of Christianity in general into mere almsgiving, and direct his tax to be applied to the maintenance of the poor.*

The union of Church and State was dissolved in like manner, by acts of their respective Legislatures, in New York, South Carolina, and all the other colonies in which the Protestant Episcopal Church was predominant.

It was not until about forty years subsequent to the separation of Church and State in Virginia that the example was followed by Connecticut. It will be recollected that in the latter State the Established Church was the Congregational. In 1816, shortly after the

---

* See Dr. Hawks's "History of the Episcopal Church of Maryland," p. 288. [Ed.—This book by Hawks has the same title as the 1836 volume on Virginia, except for designating Maryland as the subject. Harper is still the publisher, and it appeared in 1839. Baird does not criticize this enactment as a general assessment bill, and one is led to think he found such taxes acceptable as long as they could serve general charity instead of local churches.]

close of the last war between the United States and Great Britain, all parties that differed from it—Episcopalians, Baptists, Methodists, Universalists, etc.—combined to effect its overthrow. These various parties having succeeded in gaining a majority in the Legislature, proceeded to abolish the legal assessment for the parish churches, and by a new law left it optional to the rate-payers to support either the parish church, or any other, as each thought fit. The same system was adopted by New Hampshire and Maine. Vermont, I believe, has at all times had essentially the voluntary scheme; that is, the people of each township have supported such churches within their respective boundaries, and in such a measure, as they have thought proper.

Of all the States in which there had ever been any connection between the Church and the civil power, Massachusetts was the last to come under the operation of the voluntary principle. The fathers of that colony, in the indulgence of their theocratic principles and ideas, had ever prided themselves on the union made by the vine of the Lord's planting and the State. They had with great satisfaction reposed under the shadow of both, and discoursed of the happy fruits of such a union. . . .

Before the Revolution took place, the Episcopalians had been relieved by a special act of the Legislature, from contributing to the support of the parish churches, and their congregations had been erected into incorporated societies, or poll-parishes; that is, parishes comprising only individuals, and not marked by geographical limits. But though the Constitution of 1780, which maintained the old assessment for religious worship, allowed every person to appropriate his taxes to whatever society he pleased, it was still held by the courts of that State, until the year 1811, that a member of a territorial parish (which is a corporation) could not divert the taxes imposed on him for the support of religious worship to the maintenance of a teacher of an unincorporated society. By the statute of 1811, amended in 1823, a duly-attested certificate of membership in any other religious society, whether incorporated or not, sufficed to relieve the holder of it from all taxes for the support of the parish church; but it was still the law and practice of Massachusetts to regard all persons, in any town or parish, who belonged to no religious society whatever, as regular members of the parish or Congregational church, and taxable for the support of its clergy.

I have elsewhere spoken of the accumulated evils which grew out of the connection between the Church and the State in Massachusetts. Those evils became so great that the friends of evangelical religion, in other words, of the orthodox faith of every name, resolved to unite in urging an amendment of the Constitution of the State, by which some better results might be obtained. Their efforts were crowned with success. The amendment having been voted by the Legislature in three successive sessions, 1831–33, became part of the organic law of the State, and the union of Church and State was brought to a close.

CHAPTER 27

Effects of the Dissolution
of the Union of Church and State
in the Several States
in Which It Once Existed

It will be readily believed that the union of Church and State, in any country where it has once existed, can not be dissolved without some attendant inconvenience. If such has been the nature of the connection, that the Church has been wholly dependent on the State for its support, for the keeping of its places of worship in repair, the maintenance of its pastors, and the incidental expenses of public worship, very serious embarrassments must inevitably attend a sudden dissolution of such a union. Such was unquestionably the case in some of the States of America. In others, again, in which the connection had been one of no long duration, had never been very close, and had not been carried out to a great extent, that result was attended with but little evil, and that not very lasting.

Nowhere were the ill consequences of the dis-establishment of the Church felt more seriously than in Virginia, and this may be ascribed to several causes. The worthless character of many of the clergymen sent over from England, had bred in many places, from the very first, great indifference to the Church and its services. The people had become tired of compulsory payments, for the support of a form of worship which they had ceased to love or respect. . . .

In the second place, a large majority, some say rather more than two thirds of the Episcopal clergy in Virginia, were opposed to the Revolution, and most of these returned to England. Nor are they to be blamed without mercy for so doing. . . . But this loyalty to the British crown was not likely to find much forbearance among a people, so many of whom were republican in sentiment, and hostile for the time to the mother country; and the Episcopal Church could not fail to suffer from the sympathy shown by many of its clergy for those who were considered the country's enemies. . . .

In the third place, Virginia was the immediate theatre of no small part of the war, and was repeatedly overrun by the armies of both sides. Now, without attributing too much to wantonness, though much, no doubt, was owing to that, it may readily be supposed that the Episcopal churches, the best in the colony, would be sure to be used as barracks, store-houses, hospitals, etc., thus losing at once their sacred character, and suffering much in their furniture. Partly, indeed, from accident, partly, it is believed, from design, many were destroyed by fire and other causes.

In the fourth place, so engrossed were all men's minds with the war, that the time was very unfavorable for doing good. Many of the ministers who remained in the province found great difficulty in collecting the people together, or obtaining for themselves the means of subsistence. . . .

Bearing these things in mind, it may be supposed that the state of the Episcopal churches* in Virginia was deplorable enough on the return of peace, and that they little needed the aggravation of

---

* Not that the damage done by the war to other denominations was inconsiderable. The Presbyterians probably suffered more in their church edifices, from being far more obnoxious to the resentment of the enemy.

being thrown for their support entirely upon their own members, when these were impoverished by the length of the war, and rendered by it incapable of doing much for the Church, however well disposed to make sacrifices in her cause. . . .

. . . in the gloomy years that followed the Revolution, the Episcopal Church continued prostrate, and felt the loss of her establishment most severely. Then did it seem as if nothing short of her utter ruin would satisfy the resentment of her enemies. She had, indeed, in the day of her power, been exclusive, domineering, and persecuting; her own sins had brought upon her this severe visitation. From her case, as well as from all past experience, persecuting Churches should learn that a Church that oppresses, will one day be herself oppressed, and most likely by those on whose neck she had placed her foot.

But let us turn to a brighter page. . . . Her people learned by degrees to trust in themselves, or, rather, in God, and began to look to their own exertions rather than to a tobacco-tax for the support of their churches and pastors. Faithful ministers multiplied; an excellent bishop [David Griffith] was elected and consecrated; benevolent societies began to spring up; a theological school was planted within her borders, where many youths of talent and piety have been trained under excellent professors to preach the unsearchable riches of Christ. And although the ministers and parishes are not now much more numerous than they were at the commencement of the war of the Revolution, yet their number is considerable, and constantly increasing. There are more than 110 ministers and churches. But, above all, I do not think it possible to find a body of ministers of equal number, in any denomination, who, in point of theological education, prudent zeal, simple and effective eloquence, general usefulness, and the esteem in which they are held by the people, can be regarded as superior to the Episcopal clergy of the present day in Virginia. . . .

In Maryland as well as Virginia, though in a much less degree, the dissolution of the union of Church and State produced serious embarrassments and long-continued difficulty. In none of the colonies had the established clergy received such an ample maintenance as in Maryland. Their stipends were in many cases most liberal and even large for those days, so that to throw them at once on the voluntary support of their parishioners was a hazardous step, and for the time led to many cases of hardship. . . . the Episcopal Church gradually recovered from its depression, and ever since it has made pretty steady progress, and been decidedly prosperous. Dr. [Thomas] Clagget was appointed its first bishop in 1792, its Convention was organized, and canons established, by which proper discipline was secured. The clergy were for a long time less numerous than before the Revolution; not so much, however, for lack of the means of supporting them, as for lack of suitable men. . . . At no period of its establishment by the State was the Episcopal Church of Maryland so prosperous as it has been during some years back. Not that in all cases the clergy are supported as they ought to be, or as they were during the union of Church and State; but in point of talents and sound learning, combined with piety and other ministerial gifts, they are immeasurably superior to their predecessors before the Revolution.

In North and South Carolina, and in New York, though the disestablishment of the Episcopal Church produced, as in other cases, a kind of syncope for a time, from this it ere long recovered, and its prosperity is now incomparably greater than it ever was when it was supported by the State. . . .

But in no part of the United States was the proposal to disestablish the Church received with more serious apprehension than in New England. The language in which the celebrated Dr. [Timothy] Dwight, president of Yale College, and author of a very valuable system of theology, as well as other distinguished men of that State, deprecated the measure, is still extant in pamphlets and in journals, and these have often been quoted in England by the friends of the Church Establishment there in opposition to its opponents. But it ought to be known that not a single survivor at this day, of all who once wrote against the separation of Church and State in Connecticut, has not long since seen that he was mistaken, and has not found that to be a blessing which he once regarded as a calamity. And had not Dr. Dwight died just as the change came into operation, no doubt he, too, would have changed his opinion. Forty years have elapsed since that time, and although I have been much in Connecticut during the last twenty-five years, know many of the clergy, and have conversed much with them on the subject, out of the three or four hundred ministers of that State, I am not aware of there being one Congregational minister who would like to see the union of Church and State restored in it. On no point, I am confident, are the evangelical clergy of the United States, of all Churches, more fully agreed than in holding that a union of Church and State would prove one of the greatest calamities that could be inflicted on us, whatever it may prove in other countries. This is the very language I have heard a thousand times from our best and ablest men when speaking on the subject.

In Massachusetts, which was the last of the States to abolish the union of the Church and the civil power, the change was adopted from a conviction of the evils, on the one side, resulting from the union in that State, and of the advantages, on the other side, that would accrue from its dissolution: a conviction that led all the evangelical denominations to combine for its overthrow. In fine, after nearly a quarter of a century's experience of the change, I apprehend not one person of influence in all their ranks will be found to regret it.

And now, throughout the whole of the United States, Truth stands on its own immovable vantage-ground. So far as the civil power is concerned, there is not the slightest intereference with the rights of conscience or with the religious worship of any one. Religious liberty, fettered by no State enactment, is as perfect as it can be. Nor is any sect or denomination of Christians favored more than another. All depend, under God, for their support on the willing hearts and active hands of their friends, while the civil government, relieved from the ten thousand difficulties and embarrassments which a union of Church and State would involve, has only to mete out justice with even scales to all the citizens, whatever may be their religious opinions and preferences.

CHAPTER 28

Whether the General Government of the United States Has the Power to Promote Religion

It seems to be inferred by some that because [the First Amendment to] the Constitution declares that "Congress shall make no law respecting an establishment of religion, or prohibiting the free exercise thereof," the General Government can do nothing whatever to promote religion. This is certainly a mistake.

A great variety of opinions has been expressed by writers on public and political law on the question, How far any government has a right to interfere in religious matters; but that such a right exists to a certain extent, is admitted by all of them. Nor can it be otherwise so long as religion shall be thought necessary to the well-being of society, and to the stability of government itself. It is essential to the interests of men, even in this world, that they should be neither ignorant of, nor indifferent to, the existence, attributes, and providence of one Almighty God, the Ruler of the universe; and, above all, a people that believe in Christianity can never consent that the government they live under should be indifferent to its promotion, since public as well as private virtue is connected indissolubly with a proper knowledge of its nature and its claims, and as the everlasting happiness of men depends upon its cordial reception.

There is . . . a manifest difference between legislating directly for religion as an end of jurisdiction, and keeping it respectfully in view while legislating for other ends, the legitimacy of which is not questioned; so that if we admit that the States alone could do the former, the General Government might, at least, be competent to the latter, and in this way the harmony of the whole might be preserved.

But this restricted view of the case is not necessary. All that the Constitution does is to restrain Congress from making any law "respecting an establishment of religion, or prohibiting the free exercise of the same." Every thing that has no tendency to bring about an establishment of religion, or to interfere with the free exercise of religion, Congress may do. And we shall see, hereafter, that this is the view of the subject taken by the proper authorities of the country.

CHAPTER 29

Whether the Government of the United States
May Justly Be Called
Infidel or Atheistical

Because no mention of the Supreme Being, or of the Christian religion, is to be found in the Constitution of the United States, some have pronounced it infidel, others atheistical. But that neither opinion is correct, will appear from a moment's consideration of the case.

Most certainly, the Convention which framed the Constitution in 1787, under the presidency of the immortal Washington, was neither infidel nor atheistical in its character. All the leading men in it were believers in Christianity, and Washington, as all the world knows, was a Christian. Several of the more prominent members were well known to be members of churches, and to live in a manner consistent with their profession. Even Franklin, who never avowed his religious sentiments, and can not be said with certainly to have been an infidel, proposed, at a time of great difficulty in the course of their proceedings, that a minister of the Gospel should be invited to open their proceedings with prayer.

Many members of the Convention had been members also of the Continental Congress, which carried on the national government from the commencement of the Revolution until the Constitution went into effect. Now the religious view of that Congress we shall presently see from their acts.

. . . I am of opinion that the Convention, while sensible that it was unwise to make religion a subject of legislation for the General Government, thought that this, or even any mention of the thing at all, was unnecessary. The Constitution was not intended for a people that had no religion, or that needed any legislation on the subject from the proposed General or National Government; it was to be for a people already Christian, and whose existing laws, emanating from the most appropriate, or to say the least, the most convenient sources, gave ample evidence of their being favorable to religion. Their doing nothing positive on the subject seems, accordingly, to speak more loudly than if they had expressed themselves in the most solemn formulas on the existence of the Deity and the truth of Christianity. These were clearly assumed, being, as it were, so well known and fully acknowledged as to need no specification in an instrument of a general nature, and designed for general objects. The Bible does not begin with an argument to prove the existence of God, but assumes the fact, as one the truth of which it needs no attempt to establish.

This view is confirmed by what is to be found in the Constitution itself. From the reference to the Sabbath, in Article I., section vii., it is manifest that the framers of it believed that they were drawing up a Constitution for a Christian people—a people who valued and cherished a day associated, if I may so speak, with so large a part of Christianity. Regarding the subject in connection with the circumstances that belong to it, I do not think that the government of the United States can justly be called either infidel or atheistical, on account of its Federal Constitution. The authors of that Constitution never dreamed that they were to be regarded as treating Christianity with contempt, because they did not formally mention it as the law of the land, which it was already, much less that it should be excluded from the government. If the latter was intended, we shall presently see that their acts, from the very organization of the government, belied any such intention.

Should any one, after all, regret that the Constitution does not contain something more explicit on the subject, I can not but say that I participate in that regret. Sure I am that, had the excellent men who framed the Constitution foreseen the inferences that have been drawn from the omission, they would have recognized, in a proper formula, the existence of God, and the truth and the importance of the Christian religion.

I conclude this chapter in the language of one who has ably treated this question. ". . . admitting that the Constitution framed on that occasion does not in terms proclaim itself a Christian document, what then? Does it proclaim itself unchristian? For if it is merely silent in the matter, law and reason both tell us that its religious character is to be looked for by interpretation among the people who fashioned it; a people, Christian by profession and by genealogy; what is more, by deeds of fundamental legislation that can not deceive."*

[Two chapters, "The Government of the United States Shown to Be Christian by Its Acts," and "The Governments of the Individual States Organized on the Basis of Christianity," followed here in the original.]

---

* "An Inquiry into the Moral and Religious Character of the American Government," pp. 84, 85. [Ed.—This volume, published by Wiley & Putnam (New York, 1838), has often been ascribed to the pen of Senator Theodore Frelinghuysen because it defends a co-operative relation between religion and politics and thus accords with the Senator's views on that score. Some, however, say that Henry Whitings Warner wrote it. See Arthur M. Schlesinger, Jr., *The Age of Jackson* (Boston: Little, Brown & Company, 1945), pp. 351–52; and Anson P. Stokes, *Church and State in the United States* (New York: Harper & Brothers, 1950), vol. I, p. 702.]

CHAPTER 30

The Legislation of the States
Shown to Be in Favor of Christianity

We have said that the organic laws of the State governments have been so far modified as to extend political rights to citizens of all shades of religious opinions; that in every State the rights of conscience are guaranteed to all men; and that in these respects, the whole thirty-one States and seven Territories composing the American Union are as one. But we must not be understood as meaning thereby, that irreligion and licentiousness are also guaranteed by the organic laws, or by any laws whatever. This would be absurd. Rights of conscience are religious rights, that is, rights to entertain and utter religious opinions, and to enjoy public religious worship. Now this expression, even in its widest acceptation, can not include irreligion—opinions contrary to the nature of religion, subversive of the reverence, love, and service due to God, of virtue, morality, and good manners. What rights of conscience can atheism, irreligion, or licentiousness pretend to? It may not be prudent to disturb them in their private haunts and secret retirements. There let them remain and hold their peace. But they have no right, by any law in the United States that I am aware of, to come forward and propagate opinions and proselytize. Such attempts, on the contrary, are everywhere opposed by the laws, and if, at times, these laws are evaded, or their enforcement intentionally intermitted, this does not proceed from any question of their being just, but from a conviction that, in some circumstances, it is the less of two evils not to enforce them. It is sometimes the best way to silence a noisy, brainless lecturer on atheism, to let him alone, and the immoral conduct of some preachers of unrighteousness is the best refutation of their impious doctrines. At times, however, another course must be pursued. Profane swearing, blasphemy, obscenity, the publication of licentious books and pictures, the interruption of public worship, and offences of a like nature, are punishable by the laws of every State in the American Union. Now, whence had these laws their origin, or where do we find their sanction? Take the laws against profane swearing. Where did men learn that that is an offence against which the law should level its denunciations? Surely from the Bible, and from no other source.

I am not aware that there is one State that has no laws for the due observance of the Sabbath. But whence came such regulations? From the light of Nature? From the conclusions of human wisdom? Has philosophy ever discovered that one day in seven should be consecrated to God? I know that experience and a right knowledge of the animal economy show that the law setting apart one day in seven is good, favorable to human happiness, and merciful to the beasts of burden. But the Sabbath is of God; and putting aside some dim traditions and customs among nations near the spot where the Divine command respecting it was first given to Moses, or the people in whose code it afterward held a permanent place, we find it only in the Bible.

But it is not only by the statute law of the United States that such offences are forbidden, they are punishable likewise under the common law, which has force in that country, as well as in England. Of this admirable part of the civil economy, Christianity is not merely an inherent, it is a constituent part. . . .

A person was indicted at New York, in 1811, for aspersing the character of Jesus Christ, and denying the legitimacy of his birth. He was tried, condemned, fined, and imprisoned. On that trial, the late Chancellor [James] Kent, an authority believed to be second to none in the country, expressed himself as follows:

. . . "the Constitution has discarded religious establishments. It does not forbid judicial cognizance of those offences against religion and morality which have no reference to any such establishment, or to any particular form of government, but are punishable because they strike at the root of moral obligation, and weaken the security of the social ties. To construe it as breaking down the common law barriers against licentious, wanton, and impious attacks upon Christianity itself, would be an enormous perversion of its meaning."*

The application of the common law, by the courts of Pennsylvania, to the protection of clergymen living in the discharge of their official duties, confirms all that has been said respecting the light in which Christianity is regarded by the State governments.

Further, every State has laws for the protection of all religious meetings from disturbance, and these are enforced when occasion requires. Indeed, I am not aware of any offence that is more promptly punished by the police than interference with religious worship, whether held in a church, in a private house, or even in the forest.

All the States have laws for the regulation of church property, and of that devoted to religious uses. In some States, every religious body, immediately on being organized, is pronounced *de facto* incorporated; and in none, generally, is there any difficulty in procuring an act of incorporation, either for churches or for benevolent societies.

No State allows the oath of an atheist to be received in a court of justice, and in one only, in so far as I am aware, is that of a disbeliever in a *future* state of rewards and punishments; in other words, if a man believes that there is a God who punishes men for evil actions, and rewards them for their good ones, whether in this world or in that which is to come, his oath will be received in a court of justice. Of course, the man who believes neither in the existence of God, nor in any sort of divine punishment, can not be sworn, nor can his testimony be allowed, in a court in that State.

[One chapter, "The Legislation of the States often bears favorably, Though Incidentally, on the Cause of Religion," followed here in the original.]

---

* Johnson's "Reports," p. 290. [Ed.—William Johnson, *Reports of cases argued and determined in the Supreme Court of judicature, and in the Court for the trial of impeachment and the correction of errors in the state of New York, 1806–1823* (Albany, N.Y.: 1852–53), 20 vols.; see vol. VIII, pp. 290–95, *The People* v. *Ruggles*.]

CHAPTER 31

In What Cases the Action of
the Civil Authority May Be Directed
in Reference to Religion

Besides the incidental bearing which the legislation of the individual States has upon religion, and which sometimes comes not a little to its help, there are cases in which the civil authority intervenes more directly, not in settling points of doctrine, but in determining questions of property; and these are by no means of rare occurrence where there are conflicting claims in individual churches. This, indeed, has happened several times, in reference to property held by large religious denominations. [Cases which Baird enumerates were those involving disputes between Orthodox Quakers and Hicksite separatists, Old School and New School Presbyterians, and the Northern and Southern branches of the Methodist Episcopal Church. None of the decisions was based on doctrinal considerations, though each involved the volatile question of which faction was the true representative of the total group prior to schism.] . . .

CHAPTER 32

Review of the Ground
Gone Over

. . . A review of the ground which we have gone over may be given almost in the very words of an able author, to whom we have been repeatedly indebted.

1. "The first settlers of the United States went to it as Christians, and with strong intent to occupy the country in that character.

2. "The lives they lived there, and the institutions they set up, were signalized by the spirit and doctrine of the religion they professed.

3. "The same doctrine and spirit, descending upon the patriots of the federal era, entered largely into the primary State Constitutions of the Republic, and, if analogy can be trusted, into the constructive meaning of the Federal Charter itself.

4. "Christianity is still the popular religion of the country.

5. "And, finally, notwithstanding some untoward acts of individual rulers, it is to this day, though without establishments, and with equal liberty to men's consciences, the religion of the laws and of the government. If records tell the truth—if annals and documents can outweigh the flippant rhetoric of licentious debate, our public institutions carry still the stamp of their origin: the memory of better times is come down to us in solid remains; the monuments of the fathers are yet standing; and, blessed be God, the national edifice continues visibly to rest upon them."*

---

* "An Inquiry into the Moral and Religious Character of the American Government," pp. 139, 140.

BOOK IV

The Voluntary Principle in America; Its Action and Influence

CHAPTER 33

The Voluntary Principle the Great Alternative
—The Nature and Vastness
of Its Mission

The reader has remarked the progress of Religious Liberty in the United States from the first colonization of the country until the present time, and traced the effects of its successive developments in modifying the relations between the Churches and the State.

He has seen that when that country began to be settled by

European emigrants, in the beginning of the seventeenth century, freedom of conscience and the rights of the immortal mind were but little understood in the Old World. Those even who fled to the New, to enjoy this greatest of all earthly blessings, had but an imperfect apprehension of the subject and its bearings. That which they so highly prized for themselves, and for the attainment of which they had made such sacrifices, they were unwilling to accord to others.

Not that men were not allowed, in every colony, to entertain whatever opinions they chose on the subject of religion, if they did not endeavor to propagate them when contrary to those of the Established Church, where such a church existed. In the colonies where the greatest intolerance prevailed, men were compelled to attend the National Church, but they were not required, in order to be allowed a residence, to make a profession of the established faith. This was the lowest possible amount of religious liberty. Low as it is, however, it is not yet enjoyed by the native inhabitants of the greatest part of Italy, and some other Roman Catholic countries.

But it was not long before a step in advance was made by Virginia and Massachusetts, of all the colonies the most rigid in their views of the requirements of a Church Establishment. Private meetings of dissenters for the enjoyment of their own modes of worship began to be tolerated.

A second step was to grant to such dissenters express permission to hold public meetings for worship, without releasing them, however, from their share of the taxes to support the Established Church.

The third step which religious freedom made, consisted in relieving dissenters from the burden of contributing in any way to the support of the Established Church.

And, finally, the fourth and great step was to abolish altogether the support of any Church by the State, and place all, of every name, on the same footing before the law, leaving each Church to support itself by its own proper exertions.

Such is the state of things at present, and such it will remain. In every State, liberty of conscience and liberty of worship are complete. The government extends protection to all. Any set of men who wish to have a church or place of worship of their own, can have it, if they choose to erect or hire a building at their own charges. Nothing is required but to comply with the terms which the law prescribes in relation to holding property for public uses. The proper civil authorities have nothing to do with the creed of those who open such a place of worship.* They can not offer the smallest obstruction to the opening of a place of worship anywhere, if those who choose to undertake it comply with the simple terms of the law in relation to such property.

Upon what, then, must Religion rely? Only, under God, upon the efforts of its friends, acting from their own free will, influenced by that variety of considerations which is ordinarily comprehended under the title of a desire to do good. This, in America, is the grand and only alternative. To this principle must the country look for all those efforts which must be made for its religious instruction. . . .

Let us look for a moment at the work which, under God's blessing, must be accomplished by this instrumentality.

The population of the United States in 1850 was, by the census, ascertained to be 23,191,876 souls. At present (January, 1856) it surpasses twenty-seven millions. Upon the voluntary principle alone depends the religious instruction of this entire population, embracing the thousands of churches and ministers of the Gospel, colleges, theological seminaries, Sunday-schools, missionary societies, and all the other instrumentalities that are employed to promote the knowledge of the Gospel from one end of the country to the other. Upon the mere unconstrained good-will of the people, especially of those among them who love the Saviour and profess His name, does this vast superstructure rest. Those may tremble for the result who do not know what the human heart is capable of doing when left to its own energies, moved and sustained by the grace and the love of God.

Now we shall see in the sequel to what extent facts show that provision is actually made to meet this vast demand, and even more. For the present, all that I contemplate in giving this statis-

---

* In California, the Chinese have opened temples for their heathenish worship without molestation.

tical view of the subject is, to enable the reader to form some idea of the work to be accomplished on the voluntary principle in America, if religion is to keep pace with the increase of the population.

CHAPTER 34

Foundation of the Voluntary Principle to Be Sought in the Character and Habits of the People of the United States

Some minuteness of detail will be found necessary, in order to give the reader a proper idea of the manifestations of what has been called the Voluntary Principle in the United States, and to trace it throughout all its many ramifications there. But, before entering upon this, I would fain give him a right conception of the character of the people, as being that to which the principle referred to mainly owes its success.

Enough has been said in former parts of this work to show, that whether we look to the earlier or later emigration to America, no small energy of character must have been required in the emigrants before venturing on such a step; and with regard to the first settlers in particular, that nothing but the force of religious principle could have nerved them to encounter the difficulties of all kinds that beset them. But if great energy, self-reliance, and enterprise, be the natural attributes of the original emigrant, as he quits all the endearments of home, and the comforts and luxuries of States far advanced in civilization, for a life in the woods, amid wild beasts, and sometimes wilder men, pestilential marshes, and privations innumerable, the same qualities are very much called forth by colonial life, after the first obstacles have been overcome. It accustoms men to disregard trifling difficulties, to surmount by their own efforts obstacles which, in other states of society, would repel all such attempts, and prompts them to do many things which, in different circumstances, they would expect others to do for them.

Thus have the Americans been trained to exercise the same energy, self-reliance, and enterprise in the cause of religion which they exhibit in other affairs. Thus . . . when a new church is called for, the people first inquire whether they can not build it at their own cost, and ask help from others only after having done all they think practicable among themselves—a course which often leads them to find that they can accomplish by their own efforts what, at first, they hardly dared to hope for.

Besides, there has grown up among the truly American part of the population a feeling that religion is necessary even to the temporal well-being of society, so that many contribute to its promotion, though not themselves members of any of the churches. This sentiment may be found in all parts of the United States, and especially among the descendants of the first Puritan colonists of New England. . . .

These remarks point the reader to the true secret of the success of the voluntary plan in America. The people feel that they can help themselves, and that it is at once a duty and a privilege to do so. Should a church steeple fall to the ground, or the roof be blown away, or any other such accident happen, instead of looking to some government official for the means of needful repair, a few of them put their hands into their pockets, and supply these means themselves, without delay or the risk of vexatious refusals from public functionaries.

[Four chapters, "How Church Edifices Are Built in Cities and Large Towns," "How Churches Are Built in the New Settlements." "How the Salaries of Pastors Are Raised," and "How Ministers of the Gospel Are Brought Forward," followed here in the original.

In those chapters Baird discusses in a generalized way the various methods for building churches in cities and in new settlements. It is also relevant to his treatment of voluntary support for religious affairs to include the different means of selecting ministers and of raising salaries for them. Since Baird considered the ministry a sacred position to which only godly men could hope to obtain, it confirms one's understanding to see him write, (in chapter VI of the original text): "All denominations of evangelical Christians in the United States hold it to be of the highest and most solemn importance, that no man should enter the holy ministry without well-founded scriptural evidence to his own mind and conscience, that he is 'called of the Holy Ghost' to take that office upon him: nor is he admitted to it until he has satisfied the proper authorities of the Church to which he belongs of the manifestation of that 'call,' and of his possessing, in addition to an unblemished character, the talents and acquirements necessary to his being a competent expounder of God's Word.

". . . A regenerated and devoted ministry must be the first of all earthly blessings to a Church, and it is the only instrument that can effectually secure the morals of a community, and the stability of a government. In these sentiments I feel assured all evangelical Christians in the United States will concur. No greater curse could, in their opinion, befall a Church, next to the abandonment of the true Gospel, than to have an unconverted ministry thrust upon it; and, indeed, the latter evil would soon be followed by the former."]

CHAPTER 35

The Voluntary Principle Developed

in Home Missions—American Home

Missionary Society

Thus much has the voluntary principle done for the parts of the country longest-settled and most densely-peopled. Let us now see what it does for new and thinly-peopled regions, where hundreds of new congregations are rising annually, without the means of maintaining the institutions of the Gospel by their own efforts. Such churches are to be found not only in the new settlements of the Far West, but also in the growing villages of the East.

This inability to support the public preaching of the Gospel often arises from the number of sects to be found in new settlements, and even in some districts of the older States. In this respect diversity of sects sometimes causes a serious though temporary evil, not to be compared with the advantages resulting from it in the long run. It is an evil, too, which generally becomes less and less every year in any given place: the little churches, however weak at first, gradually becoming, through the increase of population, strong and independent, and what is now an evil disappearing, or, rather, as I hope to prove, being converted into a blessing.

The most obvious way of aiding such feeble churches is, to form societies for this express object among the older and more flourishing churches. This has been done, and in this the voluntary principle has beautifully developed itself, particularly during the last thirty years. It began with some denominations not long after the Revolution; and early in this century we find missionary societies formed among the Congregational Churches of Massachusetts and Connecticut, for the purpose of sending ministers to "the West," that is, the western part of the State of New York. The "Far West" to them was the northern part of Ohio, which was then beginning to be the resort of emigrants. The faithful men sent by these societies into the wilderness were greatly blessed in their labors, and to them, under God, many of the now flourishing churches of those regions owe their existence. Missionary societies were subsequently formed in the other New England States, for supplying destitute places within their own bounds with the preaching of the Gospel, as well as to help in sending it to the other parts of the country.

Two societies were formed, likewise, about the year 1819, for the same object, among the Presbyterians and Reformed Dutch in the city of New York, and these supported a goodly number of missionaries, chiefly in the new and feeble churches in the State of that name. In 1826 they were united into one body, and now form the American Home Missionary Society.

This society, from its very outset, has advanced with great vigor, and has been directed with singular zeal and energy. At its first meeting in 1827, it reported that in the course of the year just closed it had employed 169 ministers, who had labored in 196 congregations and missionary districts. Its receipts for the same period amounted to $20,031. This auspicious commencement must be ascribed to its having assumed all the engagements of the Domestic Missionary Societies, out of which it sprang. The Society soon drew into affiliation with it all the State Domestic Missionary Societies of New England, some of which, such as those of Massachusetts and Connecticut, had been of long standing [and] were well established.

It would be interesting to trace the history of an institution which has been so much blessed to a vast number of new and poor churches throughout all the States and Territories of the American Confederacy. But we can only present a summary of its operations . . . during the thirty years that it has been distributing blessings with a liberal hand.

. . . The number of ministers of the Gospel in the service of the Society, in twenty-seven different States and Territories, during the year, [as of May, 1855] was 1,032. Of the whole number, 528 were the pastors or stated supplies of single congregations; 328 ministered to two or three congregations each; and 176 extended their labors over still wider fields. Ten missionaries preached to congregations of colored people; and sixty in foreign languages:—nineteen to Welsh, and thirty-four to German congregations, and seven to congregations of Norwegians, Swedes, Swiss, Frenchmen, and Hollanders. The number of congregations and missionary stations supplied, in whole or in part, was 2,124. The aggregate of ministerial labor performed was equal to 815 years. The number of pupils in Sabbath schools was 64,800. There were added to the churches 5,634 persons, viz.: 2,948 on profession, and 2,686 by letter. Forty-eight missionaries made mention in their reports of revivals of religion in their congregations; and 366 missionaries reported 2,434 hopeful conversions. Sixty-six churches were organized by missionaries during the year; and forty, that had been dependent, assumed the support of their own ministry. Sixty-one houses of worship were completed, thirty-eight repaired, and fifty-two others in process of erection. Eighty-nine young men, in connection with the missionary churches, were in preparation for the Gospel ministry. The disbursements of the society were $177,717; the receipts, $180,136.

The plan pursued by this society, and by all the other societies and boards established for the promotion of home missions, is never to support a missionary at its sole charges, if it can be avoided; but to give $100, or $150, or $200, rarely more than $100 or $120 to a young and feeble church, or two congregations near to each other, on condition of their making up the deficiency in the missionary's salary. Thus they are stimulated and encouraged to help themselves, and as soon as they can walk alone, the society leaves them for others which have been just organized, and which need assistance. In this way hundreds of congregations have been built up, and hundreds are at this moment emerging from the weakness of childhood into the vigor of youth and manhood. In no case, however, does the society do any thing toward the erection of church edifices. The people must find these for themselves, or get help from societies which have been formed for that object. The cheapness of materials in the new settlements and in the villages of the interior, renders it easy to erect such houses as will suffice until the flock gathers strength, and can do something more.

The society engages, in some cases, men of talent and experience to travel over a given district, and to ascertain at what points the people attached to one or other of the denominations which it represents might, with proper efforts, be formed into congregations. The labors of such agents are of the utmost importance, and they necessarily receive their whole salaries from the society.

It is a beautiful feature in our institutions for domestic missions, that while encouraging and stimulating new and feeble congregations to do their utmost to secure for themselves the regular enjoyment of Gospel ordinances, they cultivate the kindly feelings of churches more favorably situated in the older parts of the country. Many of the latter support one missionary, and some of them several each, in the new and destitute settlements, through the agency of the American Home Missionary Society. Nay, there are juvenile societies in the Sunday-schools that support each of them one, and some even two or three missionaries, if not more. Individuals are to be found in the Atlantic States who support a missionary each, and thus preach the Gospel, as they say, "by proxy." Still more, there are persons in New York and other cities, who have each paid the entire salary and traveling expenses of an agent laboring in a large district. . . .

CHAPTER 36

Presbyterian Board of Domestic Missions, Under the Direction of the General Assembly

Presbyterianism owes its foundation in the United States chiefly to persons who had been exiled from Scotland on account of their religious principles, and to Presbyterian emigrants from the north of Ireland. . . .

The first presbytery was constituted in 1705, and the first synod (that of Philadelphia) in 1716. After that the work of home missions began to acquire greater consistency. Ministers were sent out on preaching tours among the small Presbyterian flocks, or, rather, scattered groups of Presbyterian families, particularly in the middle and southern provinces. In 1741, the synod was divided into two bodies, one retaining the old name of Synod of Philadelphia, the other calling itself the Synod of New York. . . .

At the first meeting of the synod of New York, in 1745, the circumstances of the people of Virginia were brought before them, and the opinion unanimously expressed that Mr. [William] Robinson* was the proper person to visit that colony. He visited it

---

* This Mr. Robinson was a remarkable man. His manners were plain, his eloquence simple, animated, and attractive. He had but one eye, and was from that circumstance called "one-eyed Robinson." Dr. Archibald Alexander, late professor in the Theological Seminary at Princeton, New Jersey, says that it was no uncommon thing for people to go twenty, thirty, and even forty miles, to hear him preach a single sermon.

accordingly, and on that, as well as on a former visit, was the instrument of doing much good. He was followed by the Rev. Samuel Davies, formerly mentioned.

In 1758, the two synods were merged in the one Synod of New York and Philadelphia, and from that time domestic missions began to receive considerable attention, and collections for that object were ordered to be made in the churches. In 1767, or 1768, the Synod received an overture, or proposal, from the Presbytery of New York, "that there should be an annual collection in every congregation; that every presbytery should appoint a treasurer to receive and transmit the funds thus obtained; that the Synod should appoint a general treasurer, to whom all these presbyterial collections should be sent; and that every year a full account of the receipts and disbursements should be printed and sent down to the churches." This was the germ of the present Board of Missions. . . .

Collections were thenceforward made in the churches. In 1772, it was ordered that a part of these moneys should be appropriated to the purchase and distribution of useful religious books, and to the promotion of the Gospel among the Indians. Two years afterward it was seriously contemplated to send missionaries to Africa; but the war of the Revolution breaking out the following year, the project fell to the ground. Even during the war there was a considerable demand for ministers from destitute congregations, and to meet this many faithful ministers made missionary tours, at no small personal hazard from the dangers of war. Measures were taken in 1788 for forming the General Assembly, which was organized in 1789, and at its very first meeting much attention was paid to the subject of missions.

. . . In 1802, the General Assembly appointed a "standing committee," to attend to the greatly-increased interests in the missionary cause—a measure which led to a further extension of the work. A correspondence was commenced with all the known missionary societies of Europe. The committee gave much of its attention to the colored population, a class among whom the late John Holt Rice, D.D., one of the most able ministers that the Presbyterian Church in the United States has ever possessed, labored as a missionary during seven years.

In 1816, the General Assembly enlarged the powers of the standing committee, and gave it the title of "the Board of Missions, acting under the authority of the General Assembly." Many missionaries went forth under its auspices, to labor among the destitute Presbyterian congregations that were continually forming in the Southern and Western States. Meanwhile, many local societies, under the direction of synods, presbyteries, and other bodies, had sprung up, and were separately prosecuting the same objects to a considerable extent.

The cause of domestic missions in the Presbyterian Church . . . went on with fresh vigor, and the synodical and presbyterial societies becoming either merged in the Assembly's Board, or affiliated with it, the whole assumed a more consolidated form and greater consistency. . . . The Report for [1855] presents a summary of 525 missionaries employed; 305 Sunday-schools, attended by 14,548 scholars, connected with the churches under their care; 3,346 members added to the churches, of whom 1,778 were received upon examination of their faith, and 1,568 upon letters of recommendation from other churches; the receipts were $71,834, and the expenditures $78,944. The average expense of each missionary is about $150. The Board pursues the wise course of simply *helping* congregations that as yet are unable to maintain pastors, by granting them so much on their undertaking to make up the deficiency.

Such is a brief notice of the operations of the Home Missions of the General Assembly of that branch of the Presbyterian Church commonly called the Old School, to distinguish it from another branch called the New School.* . . .

---

* [Ed.—In 1837 the above-mentioned factions split the Presbyterian church in the United States. While those of New School sympathies supported different missionary plans, the Old School did not back the interdenominational endeavor begun in 1826; and after 1837 they were in almost total control of explicitly Presbyterian missions. These statistics, then, do not include all contributions made by American Presbyterians to the missionary enterprise.]

CHAPTER 37

Home Missions of the Episcopal,

Baptist, and Reformed Dutch Churches,

and American and Foreign Christian Union

A Society was formed in the year 1822, in the Protestant Episcopal Church of the United States, for the promotion of Home and Foreign Missions. . . . up to 1835, it had employed fifty-nine laborers in its home missions, occupying stations in various parts of the Union, but chiefly in the West. This society was re-organized in 1835, and . . . is under the direction of a Board of thirty members, appointed by the General Convention of that Church. The bishops, together with such persons as had become patrons of the society previously to the meeting of the Convention in 1829, are members of the Board, and to it is committed the whole subject of missions. But the better to expedite the business intrusted to it, the Home and Foreign departments are directed, respectively, by two committees, each consisting of four clergymen and four laymen, under the presidency of the bishop of the diocese in which the committee resides, and the members of both committees are *ex officio* members of the Board.

It is only since 1835 that the home missions of the society have been prosecuted with much vigor, but every year now bears witness to the increasing interest felt by the Episcopal churches of the United States in the work of building up churches in the new settlements, and other places where no congregation of that communion had before existed.

During the year ending June, 1855, the Board had employed ninety-eight missionaries; and that they did not labor without effecting much good, is apparent even from the imperfect statements of the Report. The income for the home missions was $42,107. From 1822 to 1841, 186 stations were adopted as fields of special, permanent, and, as far as practicable, regular labor. During the same period eighty church edifices had been erected in those stations, and the number of these once aided, but no longer requiring assistance, was forty-four.

From this it will be seen that this society, like those already mentioned, is an instrument by which churches that have long been favored with the Gospel, and that highly prize it, are enabled to assist others, until they, too, have grown up into a vigorous independence of foreign aid. "Freely ye have received; freely give;" this admonition and command should never be forgotten. It is the true basis of the whole Voluntary System.

We shall only add, that the missionaries employed by the Board of the Episcopal Church are chiefly stationed in the Western States and Territories, California, and Oregon.

The American Baptist Home Missionary Society was instituted in 1832, and has been eminently useful in building up churches of that denomination, both in the West and in many of the Atlantic States, where the assistance of such an institution was required; as well as in establishing Sunday-schools and Bible-classes. Its great field of labor, however, like that of all the other Societies and Boards for domestic missions, has been in the Valley of the Mississippi. Within a few years, it has extended its operations to California and Oregon, in which countries it has several missionaries. It has numerous branches and auxiliaries in all parts of the United States. During the year ending in May, 1855, it had 179 agents and missionaries in its own immediate service, while its auxiliaries employed many more, all of whom were ministers of the Gospel, and believed to be faithful and capable laborers. The receipts of the society amounted to $60,043. The Southern Baptist Convention had eighty-eight missionaries.

In addition to what the regular Baptists are doing for home missions, it ought to be stated that the Free-Will Baptists have a Home Missionary Society, which employs some fifteen or twenty laborers.

The General Synod of the Reformed Dutch Church has a Board of Domestic Missions, which is now prosecuting, with zeal and wisdom, the work of gathering together new congregations, and fostering them during their infancy, wherever it can find openings for so doing. For several years past it has been extending its operations, and during the year ending in June, 1855, it had fifty missionaries.

The American and Foreign Christian Union, composed of good men of nearly all the Evangelical churches, had, in 1855, sixty-two missionaries in the home field.

If the truth is to be carried into every hamlet and neighborhood of the United States, it can only be by the energetic efforts of all denominations of evangelical Christians; and it is delightful to trace the proofs that this conviction is wide and deep. All those denominations are actually engaged in the good work, and send forth and support missionaries in some portion or other of the country.

CHAPTER 38

Home Missions of the Methodist

Episcopal Church

It has been said, with truth, that the Methodist Church is in its very structure emphatically a missionary Church; and how inestimable its office in this respect, the religious history of the United States will strikingly prove. . . .

It was a remark, I believe, of the celebrated Dr. Witherspoon, that "he needed no other evidence that the Rev. John Wesley was a great man, than the system of itinerating preaching of which that wonderful man was the author." The observation was a just one. It is a system of vast importance in every point of view; but that from which we are at present to contemplate it is its filling up a void which must else remain empty. . . .

Yet, capable as the system is of being made to send its ramifications into almost every corner of the country, and to carry the glad tidings of salvation into the most remote and secluded settlements, as well as to the more accessible and populous towns and neighborhoods, many places were found, particularly in the South and West, so situated as to be beyond the reach of adequate supply from itinerant laborers: a fact which led to the formation of the Missionary Society of the Methodist Episcopal Church in 1816.

This society, like that of the Protestant Episcopal Church, was formed for the double object of promoting missions at home and abroad. . . .

In the year 1855 the various branches of the Methodist family of churches employed nearly twelve hundred missionaries in the home field.

Perhaps of all the fields cultivated by this society, the two most interesting, and, in some respects, most important, are those presented by the slaves in the extreme Southern States, and by the German emigrants found in great numbers in our chief cities. The missions among the former were commenced in 1828,* and originated in a proposal made by the Hon. Charles C. Pinckney, a distinguished Christian layman of the Episcopal Church in South Carolina, and which has been carried into effect with much success: the slaveholders themselves, in many places, if not in all, being pleased to have the missionaries preach the Gospel to their people.

These brief notices of the home missions of the chief Evangelical Churches in the United States, will give the reader some idea of the mode in which new and feeble congregations are aided by the older and stronger, until able to maintain the institutions of religion themselves. The societies which we have passed under review in these four chapters, supported, in all, in the year 1855, 3,337 ministers of the Gospel, and at an expense of $728,539, in new, and, as yet, feeble churches and flocks. Year after year many

---

* I speak here of missions technically so called, for, in their ordinary labors, the Methodists, from the first, have had much to do with the slaves in the South, as well as with the free negroes of the North. In fact, no other body of Christians, perhaps, has done so much good to the unfortunate children of Africa in the United States as the followers of John Wesley.

of these cease to require assistance, and then others are taken up in their turn. Be it remembered, that the work has been systematically prosecuted for no long course of time. Thirty-five years ago, in fact, the most powerful of these societies did not exist; others were but commencing their operations. It is an enterprise with respect to which the Churches have as yet but partially developed their energies and resources; still, they have accomplished enough to demonstrate how much may be done by the voluntary principle, toward calling into existence churches and congregations in the settlements rapidly forming, whether in the new or the old States.

CHAPTER 39

The Voluntary Principle Developed
—Influence of the Voluntary Principle
on Education—Of Primary Schools

We have seen how the voluntary principle operates in America in relation to the building of churches, and the support of ministers of the Gospel in the new settlements that are forming every year. We now come to consider its influence on education. Hundreds of ministers, it will be perceived, are required, to meet the demands of the rapidly-augmenting population. Where are these to come from? Besides, in a country where the right of suffrage is almost universal, and where so much of the order, peace, and happiness, that are the true objects of all good government, depend on officers chosen in the most direct manner from among themselves, these must be instructed before they can become intelligent, virtuous, and capable citizens. Ignorance is incompatible with the acquisition or preservation of any freedom worth possessing; and, above all, such a republic as that of the United States must depend for its very existence on the wide diffusion of sound knowledge and religious principles among all classes of the people. Let us, therefore, trace the bearings of the voluntary principle upon education, in all its forms, among the various ranks of society in the United States. We shall begin with primary schools.

It may well be imagined that emigrants to the New World, who fled from the Old with the hope of enjoying that religious freedom which they so much desired, would not be indifferent to the education of their children. Especially might we expect to find that the Protestant colonists, who had forsaken all for this boon, would not fail to make early provision for the instruction of their children, in order that they might be able to read that Book which is the "Religion of Protestants." And such we find to have been the fact. Scarcely had the Puritans been settled half-a-dozen years in the colony of Massachusetts, before they began to make provision for public primary schools, to be supported by a tax assessed upon all the inhabitants.* And such provision was actually made, not only in Massachusetts, but in every New England colony. And such provision exists to this day in all the six New England States. Schools are by law maintained in every school district, during the whole or a part of every year.

. . . Wherever we find the descendants of the Puritans in America, we find a people who value education as the first of all earthly blessings; and when a colony from New England plants itself, whether amid the forests of Ohio, or on the prairies of Illinois, or on the plains of California, two things are ever considered indispensable alike to their temporal and to their spiritual and their eternal welfare—a church and a school-house.

---

* The small colony of Plymouth, as soon as it was in some measure settled, set about providing schools for the children, and this was several years before the colony of Massachusetts Bay was planted.

But if the New England Puritans were zealous in the cause of education and learning, the Virginia colonists seem not to have had any such spirit, for one of their governors, Sir William Berkeley, in 1670, in replying to the inquiries addressed to him by the Lords of Plantations, says, "I thank God, *there are no free schools nor printing,* and I hope we shall not have them these hundred years; for learning has brought *disobedience,* and *heresy,* and *sects* into the world, and printing has divulged them, and libels against the best government. God keep us from both!"—*Hening's Laws of Virginia,* Appendix.

Nor was this thirst for education confined to the New England Puritan: it prevailed to no small degree among the Scotch and Irish Presbyterians, the Huguenots, the early German emigrants; among all, in fact, who had fled from Europe for the sake of their religion. . . .

The right of giving instruction is, in the United States, universal. Even where there is an all-pervading system of public schools, any number of families may join together, and employ any teacher for their children whom they may prefer. Nor has that teacher to procure any license or "brevet of instruction" before entering on the duties of his office. His employers are the sole judges of his capacity, and should he prove incapable or inefficient, the remedy is in their own hands. The teachers employed by the State pass an examination before a proper committee. In all the States where there is a legal provision for primary schools, there is a yearly report from each to a committee of the township, from which, again, there is a report to a county committee, and that, in its turn, sends a report to the Secretary or School Commissioner of the State.

In most cases, a pious and judicious teacher, if he will only confine himself to the great doctrines and precepts of the Gospel, in which all who hold the fundamental truths of the Bible are agreed, can easily give as much religious instruction as he chooses. Where the teacher himself is not decidedly religious, much religious instruction can not be expected; nor indeed should any but religious teachers attempt to give more than general moral instruction, and make the scholars read portions of the Scriptures, and of other good books.

The Bible is very generally used as a reading-book in our primary schools, though in some places the Roman Catholics have succeeded in excluding it, and they have been striving to do the same in the city of New York. In so far as relates to public schools, I see no other course but that of leaving the question to the people themselves; the majority deciding, and leaving the minority the alternative of supporting a school of their own. This will generally be done by Protestants rather than give up the Bible.

Primary instruction in the United States owes almost every thing to religion, as the most efficient of all the principles that prompt to its promotion. Not that the Protestants of that country interest themselves in the primary schools for the purpose of proselytizing children to their views, but rather that at these schools the youth of the nation may be qualified for receiving religious instruction effectually elsewhere, and for the due discharge of their future duties as citizens. And, however much they may wish to see religious instruction given at the common schools, they will not for a moment give in to the opinion that all is lost where this can not be accomplished. Primary instruction, even when not accompanied with any religious instruction, is better than none; and in such cases, they that love the Gospel have other resources—in the pulpit, the family altar, the Bible-class, and the Sabbath-school.

[One chapter, "Grammar-schools and Academies," followed here in the original.]

CHAPTER 40

Colleges and Universities

In the census of the United States for 1850, the number of universities and colleges is put down at 239, and that of students at 27,821. This, however, includes not only the Theological, Medical, and Law schools, but several other institutions improperly called colleges. A more accurate list makes the colleges amount to 119, and the students to 11,903. But even this estimate includes several institutions which, though incorporated as colleges, are scarcely so far organized as to be entitled to the name. . . .

It would be absurd to compare the colleges of America with the great universities of Europe. The course of studies is widely different. For while sufficiently comprehensive in almost all the colleges that deserve that name, it is not to be compared, in general, as respects depth and extent of investigation in particular branches, with that of the older universities of Europe. But, upon the whole, if one may be allowed to judge from experience, the education to be had at one of our colleges better capacitates a man for the work that is likely to await him in America, than would that which the universities of Europe could give him.

In almost all instances, the colleges in the United States have been founded by religious men. The common course in establishing them is as follows: A company is organized, a subscription list opened, and certain men of influence in the neighborhood consent to act as trustees. A charter is then asked from the Legislature of the State within which the projected institution is to be placed, and a grant in aid of the funds at the same time solicited. The charter is obtained, and with it a few thousand dollars, perhaps, by way of assistance. What else is required for the purchase of a site, erecting buildings, providing a library, apparatus, etc., etc., must be made up by those interested in the project. Thus have vast sums been raised, particularly during the last twenty years, for founding colleges in all parts of the country, especially in the West. A great portion of these sums have been subscribed by persons in the neighborhood, and more directly interested in the success of the undertakings subscribed for; but in many cases, money to a large amount has been obtained from the churches along the Atlantic coast.

I have said that the State gives some aid to many such enterprises. But, excepting the Universities of Virginia, Alabama, Michigan, and those of Ohio and Miami, both in the State of Ohio, and Jefferson College in Louisiana, I am not aware of any in the country that can be said to have been wholly endowed by the government of any State. . . .

There are not above six or seven colleges or universities in the United States over which the civil or political governments can exercise any direct control. It is well that it should be so. A State Legislature, or Congress itself, would be found very unfit to direct the affairs of a college or university. Wherever, in fact, they have reserved such power to themselves in the charters they have granted, they have sooner or later nearly, if not altogether, ruined the institutions on which they have laid their unhallowed hands. A college or university is no place for party politics. . . .

I have said that almost every college existing in the country may be traced to religious motives; and how true this is, will appear from the fact, that of the 119 colleges now in operation, eight are under the influence of the Protestant Episcopal Church, twenty-four under that of the Methodists, twenty-five under that of the Baptists, forty-five under that of the Presbyterians and Congregationalists; two are Lutheran, twelve are Roman Catholic, one Universalist, two Unitarian. In this calculation, I place each institution under the Church to which its president belongs. This rule is the best that I know, and although it does not hold in every case, the exceptions are few; and, without any exception, it indicates the general faith by which the institution is influenced.*

Thus we see that of these 119 universities and colleges, 104 are under decided evangelical and orthodox influence. Their presidents, and, I may add, many of their professors, are known to be religious men, and sound in the faith; all of the former, with three or four exceptions, are ministers of the Gospel, and many of them men of great eminence in the Church. I need not say how much cause for gratitude to God we have, that so many young men of the first families, and possessing fine talents, should be educated in colleges that are under the influence of evangelical principles. In many of them the Bible is studied by the students every Sabbath, under the guidance of their teachers. In all they receive a great deal of religious instruction, and are daily assembled for prayers. God has often visited some of them with the outpourings of His Spirit. Not that this religious instruction is intended to proselytize from one Protestant and evangelical church to another. In that respect, a Presbyterian father might with all safety commit his son to an Episcopalian, Methodist, or Lutheran college. Here I speak from facts that I myself have known. Several of the most distinguished dignitaries of the Episcopal Church were educated at Princeton College, New Jersey: a Presbyterian institution, and

---

* The reader will remember that the statements given above refer to the year 1850. At present, the number of colleges and universities in the United States is not far from 135. The Roman Catholics claim to have twenty-four, many of which are little better than academies or grammar-schools.

founded by Presbyterians. Some of them received their first religious convictions there, and yet, I believe, they can testify that no office-bearer of that college ever attempted to bring them over to the Presbyterian Church. Any advice given, on the contrary, would have been that they should join the church of their parentage and birth. . . .*

CHAPTER 41

Sunday-Schools—American Sunday-School Union

and Other Sunday-School Societies

One of the most efficient, as well as the simplest instruments of doing good, is the Sunday-school; an institution, the history of which is too well known to require any detail in this work. . . .

The first attempt to introduce Sabbath-schools into the United States was made by the Methodists in 1790, but from some cause or other it failed. A society was soon after formed at Philadelphia, with the late Bishop [William] White at its head, and a few schools were established for the benefit of the poor, taught by persons who received a certain compensation for their trouble. Early in the present century, schools began to be established in various places under voluntary and gratuitous teaching, and gradually becoming better known and appreciated, the number was found very considerable in 1816. Associations for promoting them more extensively began then to be formed in Philadelphia, New York, and other cities, and the publication of spelling and hymn books, scriptural catechisms, etc., for the children was com-

---

* The Rev. Dr. [Charles] M'Ilvaine, the distinguished Bishop of Ohio, and the no less excellent Assistant Bishop of Virginia, the Rev. Dr. [John] Johns, were both educated and converted at Princeton College. The late Bishop [John Henry] Hobart, of New York, was educated in that institution, and was for some time a tutor there.

menced. Some persons also did much to advance this good work by their individual efforts.

Measures were taken in 1823 for the forming of a national society which should extend the benefit of Sunday-schools to all parts of the country; and, accordingly, the American Sunday-school Union was instituted: an association composed of excellent men of all evangelical denominations, but in which no particular denomination is represented as such. It has now been diffusing its blessings for more than thirty-one years. The board of managers is composed of intelligent and zealous laymen of the various evangelical denominations, the greater part residing in Philadelphia and its vicinity, as that is the centre of the society's operations.

Its grand object is twofold: to promote the establishment of Sunday-schools where required, and to prepare and publish suitable books, some to be employed as manuals in the schools, and others for libraries, intended to furnish the children with suitable reading at home. . . .

. . . the society has rendered great service to the cause of religion, and, I may add, to that of literature also. Exclusive of the Scriptures, spelling-books, primers, catechisms, maps, cards for infant-schools, etc., it has published 813 volumes of books for libraries, a complete set of which, well bound, costs $145. It has published, likewise, selections from these as libraries for families and common schools. Among its publications may be mentioned its admirable manuals or aids for studying the Bible: namely, a Geography of the Bible, Natural History of the Bible, Dictionary of the Bible, Antiquities of the Bible, Scriptural Biographies, Maps of the Holy Land, and Books of Questions, in several volumes, on almost all parts of the Bible, for the use of children and teachers. While all these publications are thoroughly Protestant in their character, they contain nothing repugnant to the doctrines of any of the evangelical denominations, so that there is nothing to forbid their being used in the Sunday-schools of any of the Protestant churches. This is a great advantage, and enables the society to establish hundreds of schools in places where various religious bodies intermingle, and where none of them is strong enough to support a school by itself. The society publishes also a very valuable journal, which appears once in a fortnight. It is replete with interesting and instructive matter, and adapted alike to scholars, teachers, and parents. It also publishes small monthly magazines and gazettes for children.

But besides this great society, which stands ready to promote the cause any where, and on the most catholic principles, there are other Sunday-school societies, not less efficient in their respective spheres. . . . This is not unnatural, for each school is mainly attended by the children of parents attached to churches of the same denomination with that of the society that supports the school. Not that all the publications of a denominational Sunday-school society are of what may be termed a sectarian character. This is by no means the case, and, besides, these more limited societies buy from the American Sunday-school Union whatever books upon its list they may think proper to add to their own.

It is impossible to calculate the extent to which the Sunday-school libraries, composed as they are of most interesting books on almost all subjects of a moral and religious character, are fostering a taste for reading among the rising youth, and the adult population, also, of the country. The scholars receive from them one or two volumes each, according to the size, every Sabbath, to read in the course of the week, and return on the Sabbath following, and these volumes thus pass into the hands of older brothers and sisters, parents, and other members of the household. The proceeds of the sales of books by the American Sunday-school Union amounted last year (1855) to $184,227. If we add to this the value of those sold by the denominational Sunday-school societies, we shall find it rise to at least $350,000. And if we further add the cost of Sunday-school books purchased from the booksellers, we shall have a total far exceeding the last amount, as the value of books bought in one year for the use of Sunday-schools, and mainly for the libraries attached to them.

Sunday-schools are held in various places: sometimes in churches, or in the lecture-rooms attached to many of our large churches, or in rooms fitted up expressly for the purpose in the basement story of many of them; sometimes in the school-houses, which are very numerous; and, especially in the new settlements, in private houses. In summer they sometimes meet in barns; and I once superintended a Sunday-school which met for many months in a large kitchen attached to a farm-house in the State of New Jersey.

The hours of meeting are very various. In the cities and large towns they commonly meet twice in the day; at eight or nine o'clock in the morning, according to the season, and two o'clock in the afternoon, for about an hour and a half each time. In the villages and country churches they usually meet for two hours, once a day, immediately before, or immediately after, the public services. . . .

A word or two may not be amiss on the manner of conducting our Sunday-schools. Each is under a superintendent—a gentleman where there are scholars of both sexes, but usually a lady where there are only girls. The scholars are divided into classes, according to their age and capacity. . . . The service begins with prayer by the superintendent or some other person. Each class—composed usually of six or eight persons—has its teacher, to whom the scholars repeat the lesson in the Scriptures for the day. When that is done the teacher takes the book of Bible Questions (a copy of which each scholar should have), and asks the questions in it relating to the passage which the class, in common with the others, have learned. The answers to these questions the pupils must find out through their own efforts, or with help from their parents, during the week. The teacher asks, also, such other questions as he may think useful, and calculated to lead to a more perfect understanding of the subject. An hour, perhaps, is spent in this exercise. After that the scholars return the books which they had received from the librarian on the preceding Sabbath, and obtain others. Then the superintendent, or pastor, if he be present, addresses a few words to the whole school on the passage which they have learned, and endeavors to impress upon their minds the importance of the truths which it teaches. A hymn is sung, and a prayer offered up, and the school closes.

If there be any children that can not read, they are arranged in classes by themselves, and taught that important acquirement. In many of the schools there is a considerable number of such; and sometimes persons beyond the years of childhood, who have had no opportunities of learning to read before, make the attainment in the course of a few months at a Sunday-school.

In all the free States, and in such of the slaveholding ones as permit the slaves to be publicly taught, there are Sunday-schools for the colored people.* In these schools thousands and tens of thousands of them have learned to read the sacred Scriptures, and have made much progress in Divine knowledge.

. . . A Sabbath-school is so simple an enterprise that it may be begun wherever two or three persons are found disposed to undertake it. . . . Why, then, should not Sabbath-schools be established in every city, town, hamlet, and neighborhood, where there are only two or three persons with hearts to love the kingdom of God, and hands to promote it? Were such a spirit to prevail in all lands professedly Christian, how soon would they show a very different aspect from the present?

. . . It is probable that there are . . . 2,500,000 pupils in the Sunday-schools in the United States at present. Who can estimate the amount of good resulting from two millions of minds being brought into contact every Sabbath with the Word of Him who hath said that it "shall not return unto Him void?" Thousands and tens of thousands, both teachers and scholars, are known to have become enlightened and saved, by means of the lessons given and received at Sunday-schools. But a whole volume would not suffice to unfold all the benefits conferred by this blessed institution, to which may be emphatically applied the words of the celebrated Adam Smith, in speaking of popular education in general, that it is "the cheap defence of nations."

[Two chapters, "Bible-Classes" and "Maternal Societies," followed here in the original.]

---

* There are Sunday-schools held by some pious slaveholders in Georgia, South Carolina, and perhaps some other States, in which portions of Scripture are often repeated to the assembled slaves, and remarked upon until they have committed much of them to memory. Prayer and singing are added to these exercises. Such schools no laws can well hinder, any more than they can the preaching of the Gospel to the slaves. These schools have only been commenced within a few years, and are spreading in several places.

CHAPTER 42

Education Societies

One of the most interesting developments of the voluntary principle in promoting religion in the United States, is seen in the Education Societies: institutions of comparatively recent date, and having for their object the granting of assistance to pious youths of promising talents, but small means, in preparing for the ministry.

In all denominations of evangelical Christians in the United States, there are to be found among those classes of society whose means are too limited to give their sons a college education, young men of talent, to whom God has been pleased to impart the knowledge of His grace, and in whose hearts he implants a strong desire to preach the Gospel. Now, before the Education Societies appeared upon the field, such youths used to find it very difficult, and sometimes even impossible, to obtain such an education as was required by the rules of the church in whose ministry they wished to place themselves. . . . Others, more fortunate, might be so far assisted by a church or some wealthy and benevolent patron or friend. But the greater number, in despair of success, were likely to renounce all expectation of being able to preach the Gospel, and to resign themselves to the necessity of spending their lives in the ordinary pursuits of business, not in making known the "unsearchable riches" of Christ to their fellow-men.

To meet the demands of the churches for a vastly-augmented number of ministers of the Gospel, and to help those young men who desire to respond to this demand, the American Education Society was formed [Boston, 1816] on the broad basis of rendering its aid to all pious young men, of suitable talents, who appear to be called to preach Christ, and who belong to any of the evangelical denominations. The only conditions imposed upon the recipients of its bounty are an engagement, 1. To go through a full course of collegiate and theological education in some approved college or seminary; and 2. To refund the sums advanced to aid them, should the providence of God, in after life, give them the means of doing so.

Such are, in few words, its principles. A rigid supervision is maintained over those who accept its patronage. And setting out in its admirable career with a few young men, it has gone on, under the favor of God, diffusing its blessings far and wide. It has rendered aid to young men belonging to eight different Evangelical Churches. At one period, some twenty years ago, the number of persons whom it was aiding exceeded 1,100! During the year ending May 1st, 1855, the number aided was 610. These were pursuing their education at institutions in different parts of the country; some in academies and grammar-schools, some in colleges, and the rest in theological schools. And the whole number of those who had been aided, up to that time, was 3,482. The receipts for that year were $33,789, and the expenditures $29,290. The amount refunded that year by beneficiaries who had completed their course of education was $2,157. . . .

Of late years, however, the number of young men assisted by this society has greatly diminished: partly owing to the very difficult times through which the country has passed; partly because of higher requirements in the department of preliminary studies; and partly from the fact that most of the evangelical communions have now education societies of their own. . . .

These statements will give the reader some idea of our Education Societies. Though of recent origin, they are exercising an immense influence in training up a more thoroughly-educated ministry. In the absence of precise information, the young men now receiving assistance from them may be moderately estimated at 2,000 in all, and of these at least 350 finish their studies, and enter on the work of preaching the Gospel.

CHAPTER 43

Theological Seminaries

. . . Formerly the young men who sought to enter the ministry among the denominations which require, in those who occupy their pulpits, a collegiate and theological education, were compelled to study theology, more or less immediately under some individual pastor, and it was common for six or eight of them to place themselves under this, or that other, distinguished divine. They often resided in the house of their spiritual teacher; sometimes they boarded in families near his house; they availed themselves of his library, and were directed by him in their studies.

But this was obviously a very imperfect method. Few pastors could afford time to do their pupils justice; fewer still possessed such a range of learning as to fit them for conducting others to the acquisitions, in various branches of knowledge, required in order to a competent preparation for the ministry.

. . . these institutions have wonderfully increased. Most of them, like those at Andover and Princeton, are quite distinct from any college or university; some, under the title of *Theological Departments,* are connected with literary institutions, but have their own professors, and, in reality, are very distinct. The following table, presenting a summary of the whole, will probably be found interesting.

The reader will remark that the number of students in the theological seminaries contained in the following table is that for the year 1855. The whole number of students in these seminaries may fairly be put down at 1,300 at least.

Denominations	Name and Locality of the Institution	State in Which It Is Situated	Year When Founded, When Known	Number of Professors	Number of Students, When Known
Congregationalists	1. Andover	Massachusetts	1808	5	101
	2. Bangor	Maine	1820	3	37
	3. Gilmanton	New Hampshire	1835	3	23
	4. Theological Department of Yale College	Connecticut	1822	3	24
	5. Theological Institute of Connecticut, at East Windsor	Connecticut	1833	3	17
	6. Theological Department of the Oberlin Institute	Ohio		3	23
Old School Presbyterians	1. Theological Seminary at Princeton	New Jersey	1812	4	153
	2. Western Theological Seminary at Allegheny city, near Pittsburgh	Pennsylvania	1828	3	48
	3. Union Theological Seminary	Virginia	1821	3	20
	4. Southern Theological Seminary at Columbia	South Carolina	1832	4	40
	5. Indiana Theological Seminary at New Albany	Indiana	1829	3	15
	6. Danville Theological Seminary at Danville	Kentucky	1852	2	45
New School Presbyterians	1. Union Theological Seminary, in New York City	New York	1836	4	106
	2. Theological Seminary at Auburn	New York	1821	4	8
	3. Theological Department of Western Reserve College	Ohio		3	14
	4. Lane Seminary at Cincinnati	Ohio	1832	3	105
	5. Southwestern Theological Seminary at Maryville	Tennessee		2	25
Episcopalians	1. General Theological Seminary of the Protestant Episcopal Church, New York	New York	1817	5	75
	2. Theological Seminary, Fairfax county	Virginia	1828	4	43
	3. Theological Seminary of the Diocese of Ohio, at Gambier	Ohio		4	10
	1. Thomaston Theological Institute	Maine	1837	2	23
	2. Theological Institution at Newton	Massachusetts	1825	4	35
	3. Hamilton Literary and Theological Institute, at Hamilton	New York	1820	2	20
	4. Virginia Baptist Seminary at Richmond	Virginia	1832	3	67

Denominations	Name and Locality of the Institution	State in Which It Is Situated	Year When Founded, When Known	Number of Professors	Number of Students, When Known
Baptists	5. Furman Theological Seminary at High Hills	South Carolina	1826	2	30
	6. Literary and Theological Seminary at Eaton	Georgia	1834	2	10
	7. Theological Department in Granville College	Ohio	1832	2	8
	8. Howard Theological Institution at Marion	Alabama	1850	1	13
	9. Rochester Theological Seminary at Rochester	New York	1840	2	30
	10. Western Baptist Theological Institution at Covington	Kentucky		4	20
Ref. Dutch	1. Theological Seminary, New Brunswick	New Jersey		3	36
Lutherans	1. Hartwick Seminary	New York		2	5
	2. Theological Seminary at Gettysburg	Pennsylvania	1826	3	20
	3. Theological Seminary at Lexington	South Carolina	1835	2	10
	4. Theological Seminary at Columbus	Ohio		1	10
Ger. Ref.	Theological Seminary at Mercersburg	Pennsylvania	1825	2	20
Assoc. Ch.	Theological Seminary, Xenia	Ohio	1855	2	40
Assoc. Ref. Ch.	1. Theological Seminary at Newburg	New York	1836	1	11
	2. Theological Seminary at Allegheny city	Pennsylvania	1828	2	45
Method.	3. Methodist Biblical Institute at Concord	New Hampshire	1847	3	40

151

The above enumeration comprises the orthodox evangelical denominations of Protestants only. The Unitarians have a theological department at Harvard University, which had two professors and fourteen students in 1855; and a theological school at Meadville, Pennsylvania, which had last year four professors and twenty-five or thirty students.

The Roman Catholic theological seminaries, according to the Catholic Almanac, stood as follows in 1855:

Location		Students	Location		Students
At Baltimore,	Md.	27	At Carondelet, Mo.		28
" Frederick,	"	16	Near Florissant,	"	21
Near Emmitsburg,	"	24	At Barrens, Perry Co., O.		32
At Cumberland,	"	28	" St. Paul, Minnesota		4
" Philadelphia,	Pa.	19	" Buffalo, N.Y.		8
" Villa Nova,	"	—	" Springhill, Ala.		5
" Latrobe,	"	31	" Fordham, N.Y.		40
Near Cincinnati,	Ohio	14	" Milwaukee, Wis.		12
" Somerset,	"	17	" Dubuque, Iowa		10
" Springfield,	Ky.	10	" Sinsinawa Mound, Wis.		1
" Bardstown,	"	5	" San Francisco, Cal.		10
At Cleveland,	Ohio	14	" Benicia,	"	4
" Thompson,	"	7	" Santa Ynes,	"	12
Near Vincennes,	Ind.	15	" Santa Barbara,	"	3
At Notre-Dame,	"	10	" Chicago, Ill.		—
" Wheeling,	Va.	7	Near Pittsburg, Pa.		7
" Lafourche,	La.	12			

In all, 33 institutions and 453 students.

I shall conclude by stating that the entire number of theological schools and faculties belonging to the orthodox Protestant Churches is forty-five, with about 120 professors, and nearly, if not quite, 1,350 students at the present time. The greater number of these institutions are in their infancy. Where they are connected with colleges, the theological professor generally gives lectures in the literary department also, on moral philosophy, metaphysics, logic, etc. Many of the professors in the new and smaller seminaries are pastors of churches in the neighborhood, and all that are not, preach much in vacant churches, or on extraordinary occasions, such as before benevolent or literary societies and bodies, ecclesiastical assemblies, etc. Many of them, too, are expected to employ their leisure moments in giving instruction through the press. Though the number of professors seems large when compared with that of the students, few men have more to do, or, in point of fact, achieve more for the cause of Christ. There are to be found among them many of the first ministers of the Churches to which they respectively belong. If not quite equal in point of science to some of the great professors in the Old World, they are all, God be praised, believed to be converted, and are devoted, faithful men. Their grand object is to train up a pious, as well as a learned ministry. I am not aware that there is one of them that does not open every meeting of his class with earnest prayer, is which he is joined by his pupils—a striking contrast to what one sees, alas! at too many of the theological lectures in the universities of Europe.

CHAPTER 44

Efforts to Diffuse
the Sacred Scriptures

Much has been done in the United States to place the Sacred Scriptures in the hands of all who can read them, and in this endeavor there is a delightful co-operation of good men of every name. Even statesmen, though they may not be decidedly religious, or, by outward profession, members of any church, lend their aid in this enterprise; and it is not uncommon to hear men of the first rank in the political circles, some occupying high places in the council of the nation, advocate at Bible Society anniversaries the claims of the Word of God. The impression prevails among our statesmen that the Bible is emphatically the foundation of our hopes as a people. Nothing but the Bible can make men the willing subjects of law; they must first acquiesce with submission in the government of God before they can yield a willing obedience to the requirements of human governments, however just these may be. It is the religion of the Bible only that can render the population of any country honest, industrious, peaceable, quiet, contented, happy.

It is forty years since the American Bible Society was instituted [1816], and it now has branches in all parts of the country. It has sent out, in all, 10,653,647 copies of the Bible, or of the New Testament, from its depository.* Last year alone 749,896 copies went forth to bless the nation. In the years 1829 and 1830, great and systematic efforts were made to place a Bible in every family that was without one throughout the whole land. Much was accomplished, yet so rapid is the increase of the population, that these efforts must be repeated from year to year; and the work can only be done by dividing the country into small districts, and engaging active and zealous persons to visit every house from time to time, ascertain what families are destitute of the Scriptures, and supply them by selling or giving away copies, according to circumstances. Great efforts are also made at New York, and other seaports, to supply foreign emigrants as they arrive on our shores.

It is a remarkable fact, that what has been done by Bible societies seems not to have interfered with the business of the booksellers; for these sell more copies of the Holy Scriptures than they did before the Bible societies existed. The more the Bible is known, the more it is appreciated; in many a family the entrance of a single copy begets a desire to possess several; besides which, the Bible Society's distributions greatly augment the demand for Biblical commentaries and expositions, and thus augment the trade of the booksellers, who publish and put into circulation immense editions of such works. There is a great demand for the Scriptures, also, both in week-day and Sabbath-schools, and great numbers of these are furnished by the book-trade.

In the year 1837, a Bible society was formed among the members of the Baptist churches, entitled the "American and Foreign Bible Society." It was formed with special reference to the circulation of translations in the course of being made by that body

---

* More than eleven and a half million copies of the sacred Scriptures, in whole or in part, had been issued by the Bible Societies in the United States at the commencement of May, 1855. The receipts of these societies in the year 1854 exceeded half a million of dollars.

of Christians. Some, at least, of these translations the American Bible Society thought it could not, consistently with its constitution, aid in publishing, because the original words *baptize* and *baptism* have been translated into words equivalent to *immerse* and *immersion*. However much it may be regretted that these words, about the meaning of which there has been so much philological disputation, are not permitted to remain untranslated, so that all denominations might be put upon the same footing, and be enabled to continue *united* in the work of Bible circulation, the issue will, it is likely, prove that in this, as in many similar cases, God is about to make an apparent obstacle mightily subserve the advancement of His kingdom. The new society has taken up the work of foreign publication with great zeal, and doubtless it will serve to develop the energies of the large and powerful body of Christians who sustain it, to an extent to which they never would have gone but for its formation. . . .

CHAPTER 45

Associations for the Circulation and Publication
of Religious Tracts and Books

No branch of religious enterprise has been more vigorously prosecuted in the United States than that of preparing, publishing, and circulating moral and religious writings in various forms. The wide diffusion of education, at least among the white part of the population, makes it obvious that powerful advantage may be taken of the instrumentality of the press in promoting the truth.

Associations of various kinds are engaged in this good work. We have seen that the Sunday-school societies are doing much for supplying the youth of the country with moral and religious reading; we have now to speak of other societies which aim at benefiting adults, not, however, to the exclusion of the young.

First among these associations may be ranked the American

Tract Society, which, like most others of a general and national character, has its seat in the city of New York. It was instituted in 1825, and hence has been thirty years in existence. It is founded on the broad principle of uniting in its support Christians of all evangelical denominations of Protestants, so far as they may be disposed to co-operate in its objects; its Committee of Publication is composed of ministers of the Gospel of the different orthodox communions; and its publications themselves convey those great truths and doctrines in which all of these communions can agree.

The operations of no society in America seem to have been prosecuted with greater vigor or more wisdom. Its Report for 1855 states that, since its commencement, it has sent forth 1,948 different publications, of which about 150 form volumes of various sizes by themselves, and the remainder are, with few exceptions, what are called tracts, each consisting of four pages and upward.

The society is zealously prosecuting two grand measures, into which I shall enter the more fully, inasmuch as they are of the utmost importance to the religious well-being of the country, and also more or less practicable in other lands. The first of these is the publication of volumes of approved excellence, such as Bunyan's Pilgrim's Progress, and Doddridge's Rise and Progress of Religion in the Soul, and their distribution throughout the country. It proposes to place not only one volume at least, as was resolved some years ago, but even a whole set of its Evangelical Family Library, of fifteen volumes, or its Religious Library, of twenty-five volumes, in as many households as are willing to buy them; and in seeking to accomplish this end, it employs able men, ministers of the Gospel and laymen, as agents. These visit towns and cities, preach in the churches, raise funds to supply the poor with books, organize committees who are to visit all the families in the respective districts, and engage all who are able to buy one book or more, and supply such as are too poor to purchase. Another set of agents consists of plain, but sensible, pious, and zealous *colporteurs,* or hawkers, generally laymen, who are sent into the "Far West" to carry books and tracts to the frontier people, engaged in felling the forests on their ever-onward course toward the setting sun, as well as into the mountainous districts, and the thinly-settled belt of sandy country which stretches along the ocean in the Middle and Southern States. The number of these colporteurs was last year 659*

Who can calculate the amount of good which such a work must, with God's blessing, accomplish?

I ought to add, that not only is care taken that both books and tracts shall be printed with good type, and on excellent paper, but that the books are substantially bound, and the tracts covered, for the most part, with handsome paper coverings. In these respects they form a marked contrast with the publications of some societies of the same kind on the Continent of Europe. It is rightly thought to be a false economy which, for the sake of saving a few hundred dollars, would fail to render attractive in appearance, as well as readable and durable, publications which are intended to be the means of interesting, instructing, and saving men, of whom multitudes are wholly indifferent to religion, and might be repelled from reading them were they to appear in a mean and shabby dress.

The other measure referred to is the systematic periodical distribution of tracts in cities, towns, villages, and even rural districts, though this work can not be done directly by the society, so much as the numerous auxiliaries which it endeavors heartily to engage in carrying it through. The object is to place a tract, at least once in the month, in every family willing to receive one, and, where practicable, to accompany it with religious conversation, especially where ignorance of the Gospel or family affliction renders it peculiarly called for. . . .

Such is the procedure in many places throughout the United States. In the city of New York it has been in operation for nearly twenty years, and with abundance of blessed results. . . .

---

* Of these 659 colporteurs 126 labored among Germans and emigrants, and 104 were students from Colleges and Theological Seminaries. They visited 639,193 families, with 281,097 of whom they conversed on personal religion, or prayed. Of the families visited, 83,126 habitually neglected evangelical preaching, 64,686 families were Roman Catholics, 51,302 families were destitute of all religious books but the Bible, and 36,259 households destitute of the Bible; and they held or addressed 12,763 religious meetings. Six colporteur conventions were held.

I shall conclude by giving the summary of what was accomplished in New York during one year, as presented at the regular annual public meeting, held in one of the churches of that city:

1,050 average number of visitors (or distributors).
732,155 tracts distributed, containing 3,425,781 pages.
  936 Bibles and 558 Testaments received from the New York Bible Society, and supplied to the destitute.
4,496 volumes lent from the ward libraries.
2,200 children gathered into Sabbath-schools.
  315 children gathered into public schools.
  131 persons gathered into Bible-classes.
  904 persons induced to attend church.
  705 temperance pledges obtained.
1,433 district prayer-meetings held.
   43 backsliders reclaimed.
  396 persons hopefully converted.
  342 converts united with evangelical churches.

Such is the tabular view presented by a single year's labor in the field of tract distribution in one city.

Besides the American Tract Society, which may be regarded as a vast reservoir of common truth—of doctrines about which all Evangelical Protestants are agreed—there are other societies that publish religious tracts and books; and among these I may mention, as distinguished for the energy of their management and the extent of their operations, the "Book Concerns" of the two great branches of the Methodist Episcopal Church. . . . And who can calculate the good that may result from reading the biographical and didactic volumes thus put into circulation? Who can tell what triumphs over sin, what penitential tears, what hopes made to spring up in despairing hearts, what holy resolutions, owe their existence, under God, to these books? . . .

. . . The amount of evangelical tracts and books every year put into circulation by all these "societies," "boards," and "committees," together, can not be exactly ascertained. Their value in money, I mean for what they are sold, can hardly be less than $600,000. They all help to swell the great stream of Truth, as it rolls its health-giving waters through the land. May God grant that these efforts may go on continually increasing from year to year, until every family shall be blessed with a well-stored library of sound religious books.

CHAPTER 46

The Religious Literature

of the United States

While it would be very foreign to the object of this work to enter upon any discussion as to the value and extent of the general literature of the United States, it is not out of place to say something respecting that part of it which falls under the head of Religion.

And first, let me advert, without reference to its origin, to the entire mass of the literature of a religious kind now circulating through the country. In this sense, our religious literature is by far the most extensive in the world, with the single exception of that of Great Britain. We have a population of 27,000,000, if not 27,500,000; and, even including the African race among us, and regarding the country as a whole, we have a larger proportion of readers than can be found in most other nations. Indeed, I am not aware of any whole kingdom or nation that has more. Deducting the colored population, we have 23,000,000 people who, whatever may have been their origin, are Anglo-American in character, and to a great extent speak and read the English language. Not only so, but of these a very large proportion are religious in their character and habits, as we shall show in another place; and, among the rest, there is a widely prevalent respect for Christianity, and a disposition to make themselves acquainted with it.

To meet the demand created by so large a body of religious and serious readers, we have a vast number of publications in every department of Christian theology, and these are derived from various sources. Some have been translated from German and French; some from the Latin of more or less ancient times; some from the Greek; while many of our learned men, and particularly of our divines, read some or all these languages, and would think their libraries very deficient in the literature with which they ought to be familiar, did they not contain a good stock of such books imported from Europe. . . .

Some American reprints of English religious books, particularly of works of a practical character, have had an immense circulation. The commentaries of Scott, Henry, Doddridge, Adam Clarke, and Gill, have been extensively sold, and some booksellers owe a large part of their fortunes to the success of the American editions. . . . In English systematic theology no names are more known or esteemed than the late Andrew Fuller and Thomas Watson. And although it can not be said that every good religious work that appears in Great Britain is republished in the United States, a large proportion of the best certainly are, especially such as are of a catholic nature, and many of them, I am assured, have a wider circulation in the United States than in England itself.

The United States have sometimes been reproached by foreigners as a country without any literature of native growth. M. de Tocqueville, arguing from general principles, and, as he supposes, philosophically, seems to think that, from the nature of things, the country, because a republic, never can have much literature of its own. He forgets that even the purest democratical government that the world has ever seen, that of Athens, produced in its day more distinguished poets, orators, historians, philosophers, as well as painters and sculptors, than any other city or country of the same population in the world. He full well knows, however, that the government of the United States is not an unmixed democracy, and that in every thing that bears upon the higher branches of learning, our institutions are as much above the control of a democracy as those of any other country. . . .

But our literature, it is said, is not known beyond the country itself; and this is to some extent true. But that few, comparatively, even of the distinguished authors of any country, are known beyond its limits, might easily be shown in the case of France, Germany, Holland, Denmark, and Italy. . . .

The United States have unquestionably produced a considerable number of authors in every branch of literature, who, to say the least, are respectable in point of eminence.* Their being unknown to those who make use of the fact as a reproach to the country, may possibly be owing to something else than the want of real merit on their part; and if, upon the whole, they present what appears to foreigners nothing beyond a respectable mediocrity, this may be readily accounted for by other causes than a hopeless peculiarity alleged to exist in the people or their government.

The country is comparatively new. Much has yet to be done in felling the forest and clearing it for the habitations of civilized man. But a small part of our territory bears evidence of having been long settled. Our people have passed through exciting scenes that gave but little leisure for writing. Few families possess much wealth. The greater number of our institutions of learning are of recent origin. None of them have such ancient foundations as exist in many European universities; our colleges have no fellowships; the time of our professors is much occupied in giving instruction;

---

* It would not be difficult to make out a tolerably long list of authors who have lived in recent times, and many of whom are living yet, that must be pronounced, by those who know anything of them, to be such as would be an honor to any country; and many of them are not unknown in Europe. Among writers on law, in its various branches, we have had Kent, Story, Webster, Wheaton; in medicine, Mott, Warren, Beck, Ray, Jackson, and many others; in theology and Biblical science, Stuart, Miller, Woods, the Alexanders, Hodge, Wayland, Robinson, Conant, Barnes, Stowe, Beecher, Schmucker, Hawks, the Abbots, etc.; in belles-lettres and history, Irving, Prescott, Bancroft, Walsh, Cooper, Paulding; in science, Silliman, Hitchcock, Henry, Davies; and in political economy, Carey, Vethake, Biddle, Raymond. These are but a few, selected chiefly with reference to their being known to some extent, at any rate, in Europe. We have also had Marshall, Livingston, Madison, Jefferson, Jay; Rush, Dorsey, Wistar, Dewees, Godman; the Edwardses, Davies, Dwight, Smith, Mason, Emmons, Channing, Griffin, Rice; Wirt, Noah Webster, Ramsey; Franklin, Ewing, and Hamilton. In the fine arts we have had a West, an Alston, and have now a Crawford, a Powers, a Brown; while in the useful arts, as they are called, we have not been without men of some renown, as the names of Fulton, Whitney, and others attest.

Nor are American books unknown in Great Britain, the only country in Europe in which they could be extensively read. In the London Catalogues we find the names of American works on theology, in fiction, of juvenile literature, of travels, on education, on biography, on history, on poetry, on metaphysics, on philosophy, on science, and on law. Besides these, a good many books published in America are imported every year into Great Britain.

our pastors, lawyers, and physicians find but little leisure, amid their professional labors, for the cultivation of literature. We have no sinecures—no pensions—for learned men. There is too much public life and excitement to allow the rich to find pleasure in Sybaritic enjoyments; and they have other sources of happiness than the extensive possession of paintings and statues, though even for these the taste is gaining ground.

But to return to our proper subject, the religious literature of the United States: the number of our authors in this department is by no means small. Many valuable works, the production of native minds, issue year after year from the press, a very large proportion of which are of a practical kind, and exert unquestionably a most salutary influence. They meet with an extensive sale, for the taste for such reading is widely diffused, fostered as it is by the establishment of Sunday-schools and the libraries attached to them.

To the religious literature of books must be added that of periodical works—newspapers, magazines, reviews—and nowhere else, perhaps, is this literature so extensive or so efficient. More than 150 evangelical religious newspapers are published once a week. The Methodists alone publish twenty-four, including one in the German tongue, and nearly all under the direction of their Conferences. The Episcopalians have twelve; the Baptists twenty-eight; the Presbyterians of all classes, including the Congregationalists, Dutch Reformed, Lutherans, etc., about forty more. This estimate includes evangelical Protestant papers only. In all, they can not have fewer than five hundred thousand subscribers. They comprise a vast amount of religious intelligence, as well as valuable selections from pamphlets and books; and though it may be the case that religious newspapers sometimes prevent more substantial reading, yet it must be confessed, I think, that they are doing great good, and are perused by many who would otherwise read little or nothing of a religious character. Besides these newspapers, there is a large number of religious monthly and semi-monthly magazines, and several quarterly reviews, in which valuable essays on subjects of importance may be found from time to time.

[One chapter, "Efforts to Promote the Religious and Temporal Interests of Seamen," followed here in the original.]

CHAPTER 47

Of the Influence of the Voluntary Principle

in Reforming Existing Evils

—Temperance Societies

We have contemplated the Voluntary Principle as the main support of Religion and its institutions in the United States. We have now to consider its powers of correcting, or rather overcoming, some of the evils that prevail in society. And, first, let us see how it has contended with Intemperance, one of the greatest evils that have ever afflicted the human race.

It is not easy to depict in a few words the ravages of drunkenness in the United States. The early wars of the Colonial Age, the long war of the Revolution, and, finally, that of 1812–15 with England, all contributed to promote this tremendous evil. The very abundance of God's gifts became, by their perversion, a means of augmenting it. The country being fertile, nearly throughout its whole extent, and producing immense quantities of wheat, rye, and corn, the last two of which were devoted to the manufacture of whiskey, there seemed no feasible check, or conceivable limit to the ever-growing evil, especially as the government had no such pressure on its finances as might justify the imposing of a tax that would prevent or diminish the manufacture of ardent spirits. Moreover, the idea had become almost universally prevalent that the use of such stimulants, at least in moderate quantities, was not only beneficial, but almost indispensable for health, as well as for enabling men to bear up under toil and fatigue.

In the year 1812, a considerable effort was made to arouse the attention of Christians to the growing evils of intemperance, and a day of fasting and of prayer was observed by some religious bodies. In the following year, the Massachusetts Society for the

Suppression of Intemperance was formed, and its labors were manifestly useful. Still, "the plague was not stayed." The subject, however, was not allowed to drop. It was seen that the Society had not gone far enough, and that it would not do to admit of the use of ardent spirits, even in moderation. The evil of wide-spread drunkenness could never be exterminated by such half-way measures.

It was accordingly proposed, in 1826, to proceed upon the principle of entire abstinence from the use of ardent or distilled spirits, as a beverage, and the same year saw the formation of the American Temperance Society at Boston. The press was soon set in motion to make its objects known, and competent agents were employed in advocating its principles. Great was the success that followed. In the course of a few years, societies were to be found in all parts of the country, and were joined, not by thousands only, but by hundreds of thousands. People of all classes and ages entered zealously into so noble an undertaking. Ministers of the Gospel, lawyers, judges, legislators, and physicians, took a prominent part in urging it forward.

But we need not enter upon the details of this progress. The cause continues advancing to this day. To reach the poor, as well as remove temptation from the rich, the rules of the Temperance Societies have, within the last six or seven years, excluded "all intoxicating drinks." Upon this principle, wines of all descriptions have been generally abandoned, both because of their being mostly impure with us—being, for the most part, imported, and all more or less intoxicating—and because they are not found necessary to persons in health, but, on the contrary, injurious; besides which, it was of consequence that an example of self-denial should be given by those who could afford to buy wine, for the sake of the poor, who could not.

But, in the progress of the Temperance reformation, little was done to reclaim men who had already become drunkards. And yet at the lowest estimate, there were 300,000 such in the United States; many even reckoned them at 500,000 at the commencement of the Temperance movement. No hope seemed to be entertained with respect to these. To prevent such as had not yet become confirmed drunkards from acquiring that fatal habit, was the utmost that any one dared to expect. A few drunkards, indeed, were here and there reclaimed: but the mass remained unaffected by all the cogent arguments and affecting appeals that were resounding through the country.

At length God, in His wonderful providence, revealed the way by which these miserable persons might be reached. And how simple! A few hard drinkers in the city of Baltimore, who were in the habit of congregating at a low tavern for the purpose of revelry, and had been drunkards for years, met one night as usual. All happened to be sober. Apparently by accident, the conversation fell upon the miseries of their life. One after another recounted his wretched history. All were deeply touched with the pictures of their own degradation thus held up. Some one proposed that they should stop in their career of folly and wickedness, and form themselves into a Temperance association. . . . The fire was kindled, and soon it spread. In a few weeks four hundred such persons joined the society. In a few months two thousand drunkards in the city of Baltimore were reclaimed. Then the movement came to light. The newspapers spread the wonderful news. The whole country was astonished. Christians lifted up their hearts in thankfulness to God, and took courage. Benevolent men rallied around these reformed persons, and encouraged them to perseverance.

The society of reclaimed drunkards in Baltimore was invited to send delegates to other cities; and soon the "apostles of Temperance," as these men were called, went forth to every city in the land. Great was their success. . . .

To go further into detail would not consist with the nature of this work. A large proportion of the population of the United States are now under the happy influence of the principle of total abstinence from all intoxicating drinks. In 1826, when the reform commenced, it was estimated that at least sixty million gallons of whiskey were manufactured and consumed annually in the United States, without including the imported brandies, rum, etc. This estimate was unquestionably a very low one. In 1850, that is, twenty-four years afterward, the census stated that the number of gallons of "whiskey," "high wines," and "rum," distilled during that year, was 47,864,724, showing a falling off of more than twelve million gallons: and yet, within the same period, the population had more than doubled. And all this reformation had been brought about solely through the operation of voluntary associations, without the slightest direct aid from the government, with the exception of its abolishing the daily ration of whiskey formerly given to the officers and men in the army. Could any thing in the world show more conclusively the resources which right principles possess in themselves for overcoming, under God's blessing, the evils that are in the world, and even those that derive most power from the depraved appetites of man?

[Two chapters, "The American Prison Discipline Society," and "Sundry Other Associations," followed here in the original.]

CHAPTER 48

Influence of the Voluntary Principle
on the Beneficent Institutions
of the Country

Nor is the Voluntary Principle less operative in the formation and support of beneficent institutions than of associations for attacking and vanquishing existing evils. But these present a field too wide to be fully gone over in this work; besides, they do not properly come within its scope. I shall therefore glance only at a few points, showing how the Voluntary Principle acts in this direction for the furtherance of the Gospel.

In efforts to relieve the temporal wants and sufferings of mankind, as well as in all other good undertakings, Christians, and those, too, with few exceptions, evangelical in their faith, almost invariably take the lead. Whenever there is a call for the vigorous exercise of benevolence, proceeding from whatever cause, Christians immediately go to work, and endeavor to meet the exigency by their own exertions, if possible. But should the nature and extent of the relief required properly demand co-operation on the part of municipal and State authorities, they will bring the case before these authorities, and invoke their aid. It follows naturally that, when this is given, it should be applied through the hands of those who were the first to move in the matter; and this wisely, too, since who can be supposed so fit to administer the charities of the civil government as those who have first had the heart to make sacrifices for the same object? Such alone are likely to have the experience which in such affairs is necessary.

All this I might illustrate by adducing many instances. In this chapter, however, I shall notice but a few, and take these collectively.

There is not a city or large town, and hardly a village, in the whole country, which has not its voluntary associations of good men and women for the relief of poverty, especially where its sufferings are aggravated by disease. These efforts, in countless instances, may not be extensive, only because there is no extensive call for their being made. Created by circumstances, when these disappear, the associations also cease to exist. But where the sufferings to be relieved are perpetually recurring, as well as too extensive to be alleviated by individual effort, these benevolent associations become permanent. . . . Accordingly, the stranger who visits the United States will find hospitals for the sick, alms-houses for the poor, and dispensaries for furnishing the indigent with medicines gratuitously, in all the large cities where they are required. There is a legal provision for the poor in all the States, not such, however, as to do away with the necessity of individual or associated effort to meet extraordinary cases of want, especially when it comes on suddenly, and in the train of disease. The rapid and wide-spread attacks of epidemics may demand, and will assuredly find benevolent individuals ready to associate themselves for meeting such exigencies, before the measures provided by law can be brought to bear upon them.

Of all the beneficent institutions of our large cities, there are none more interesting than those intended for the benefit of *children*. Orphan asylums, well established and properly conducted, are to be found in every city of any considerable size throughout the Union. Nor are these asylums provided for white children only; they are also for the colored. Indeed, it can not be said with truth that the poor and the sick of the African race, in our cities and large towns, are less cared for than those of the white race. . . .

In some of our cities we have admirable institutions, called *houses of refuge,* for neglected children, and for such as are encouraged by their parents to live a vagabond life, or are disposed to lead such a life. In these establishments, now nine in number, they not only receive the elements of a good English education, but are instructed also in the mechanical arts; and with these religious instruction is faithfully and successfully combined. All of these institutions were commenced, and are carried on by the voluntary efforts of Christians, though they have been greatly assisted by appropriations in their favor, in the shape of endowments or annuities from some of the State governments.

Nor are the aged poor neglected. Asylums for widows are to be met with in all our large towns, where they are, in fact, most needed; and old and infirm men are also to be provided for.

At the same time, that "charity which seeketh not her own," but the good of all others, no matter what may have been their character or what their crimes, has not forgotten those unfortunate females who have been the victims of the faithlessness of men. Magdalen asylums have been founded in all our chief cities, especially on the sea-board, and have been the means of doing much good. . . .

[Three chapters on "Influence of the Voluntary Principle on the Beneficent Institutions of the Country" followed here in the original.

Baird gives in these chapters more information about other "beneficent institutions," including asylums for the insane, the deaf and dumb, the blind, and for the mentally retarded. While such discussions preserve some specifics on the early history of these philanthropic organizations, I omit them and follow the author's judgment that they are tangential to voluntary religious endeavors because they "do not properly come within its scope."]

CHAPTER 49

Concluding Remarks on the

Development of the Voluntary Principle

We here close our notice of the development of the Voluntary Principle in the United States. . . . If it is thought that I have dealt too much in details, I can only say that these seemed necessary for obvious reasons. There being no longer a union of Church and State in any part of the country, so that religion must depend, under God, for its temporal support wholly upon the voluntary principle: it seemed of much consequence to show how vigorously, and how extensively, that principle has brought the influence of the Gospel to bear in every direction upon the objects within its legitimate sphere. In doing this, I have aimed at answering a multitude of questions proposed to me during a residence and travels in Europe.

The reader who has had the patience to follow me thus far, must have been struck with the vast versatility, if I may so speak, of this principle. Not an exigency occurs in which its application is called for, but forthwith those who have the heart, the hand, and the purse to meet the case, combine their efforts. Thus the principle seems to extend itself in every direction with an all-powerful influence. Adapting itself to every variety of circumstances, it acts wherever the Gospel is to be preached, wherever vice is to be attacked, wherever suffering humanity is to be relieved.

Nor is this principle less beneficial to those whom it enlists in the various enterprises of Christian philanthropy, than to those who are its express objects. The very activity, energy, and self-reliance it calls forth, are great blessings to the individual who exercises these qualities, as well as to those for whose sake they are put forth, and to the community at large. Men are so constituted as to derive happiness from the cultivation of an independent, energetic, and benevolent spirit, in being co-workers with God in promoting His glory, and the true welfare of their fellow-man.

We now take leave of this part of our subject, to enter upon that for which all that has hitherto been said must be considered preparatory—I mean the direct work of bringing men to the knowledge and possession of salvation.

BOOK V

The Church and
the Pulpit
in America

CHAPTER 50

*Importance of This Part
of the Subject*

It is instructive to mark the influence of Christian institutions upon society—the repose of the Sabbath—the civilizing effect of assemblies of the people in churches—the great amount of knowledge communicated in the numerous discourses of a well-instructed ministry. Apart from higher considerations, the benefits indirectly conferred upon a community by an evangelical ministry are well worth all that it costs. It softens and refines manners; promotes health, by promoting attention to cleanliness and a regard to decency of apparel; it diffuses information, and rouses minds that might otherwise remain ignorant, inert, and stupid. But what is this compared with the preparation of the immortal spirit for its everlasting destiny? This world, after all, is but the place of our education for a better; of how much moment, then, that the period of our pupilage should be rightly spent!

The Church, with her institutions, is of Divine ordination. She was appointed by her great Author to be the depository of the economy of salvation, so far as human co-operation is concerned; designed to combine all the human agencies which God, in infinite wisdom, has resolved to employ in the accomplishment of that salvation. How important, then, that the Church should meet the design of her Divine Founder, not only as regards her proper character, but also in the development and right employment of the influences she was constituted to put forth for the salvation of the world!

As the Church on earth is but preparatory to the Church in heaven, she was obviously intended to bear some resemblance to the celestial state. As the depository to which God has committed the custody of His revealed truth, and as His chosen instrument for its diffusion among mankind, she ought obviously to be kept, so far as an institution placed in the hands of creatures imperfect at the best could be, pure from every thing which would impede the discharge of her high functions.

But we must not misapprehend the office of the Church. She has received no power of original legislation. She is nothing but an agent. Christ is the Lawgiver and the Head of the Church. He has given her the revelation of His will, and has clearly defined her sphere of action. Nor can she justly expect His blessing if she goes beyond the boundaries of her duty.

But a holy life on the part of her members; by a conversation such as becometh saints; by well-directed efforts to make known the Gospel everywhere to dying men, whether by the faithful proclamation of it on the part of the ministry whom God has appointed, or by more familiar instruction in the Sunday-school and the Bible-class, or around the family altar, or by the distribution of the Scriptures and other religious books; united with constant, fervent, and believing prayer that the Holy Spirit may render all these means successful: the Church is required to exert her influence in saving the world. It is thus that she becomes "the light of the world"; it is thus that she proves herself "the salt of the earth." But, in order to fulfill this high mission, she ought to be as nearly as possible what the Saviour of men intended her to be—a company of saints redeemed by His blood, renewed by His Spirit, devoted to His service—ever bearing the cross, that she may wear the crown, and preparing for that day when she shall be presented to her Lord, "not having spot or wrinkle, or any such thing," but "holy and without blemish"—for she is "His Body."

CHAPTER 51

The Evangelical Churches
in the United States
Maintain Discipline

Discipline is a matter of inexpressible importance to the prosperity of a Church; and I rejoice to say that such is the light in which it is viewed by Christians of all the evangelical denominations in the United States, almost without exception.

I do not suppose that there is a single evangelical church in the country that does not keep a record of its members; I mean of those whom it has received according to some regular form or other *as members,* and who, as such, are entitled to come to the Lord's Supper. As this whole subject is not only important, but by some readers may not be easily comprehended, I may venture upon some detail.

1. There is no evangelical church in the United States, that is, no organized body of believers worshipping in one place, that does not hold a creed comprehending at least the following points: the existence of one God, in three Persons, Father, Son, and Holy Ghost, of the same substance, and equal in all the attributes of their nature; the depravity, guilt, condemnation, and misery of all mankind; an all-sufficient and only atonement by the Son of God,

who assumed human nature, and thus became both God and man in one person, and by His obedience, suffering, death, and intercession, has procured salvation for men; regeneration by the Holy Ghost, by which repentance and faith are made to spring up in the soul; the final judgment of all men; and a state of everlasting misery for the wicked, and of blessedness for the righteous. On these doctrines, in their substantial and real meaning, there is no difference among the evangelical churches in the United States.

2. Neither is there any evangelical church in America that does not hold the necessity of a moral life—a life against which no charge inconsistent with a Christian profession can be brought—in order to proper membership of a church of Jesus Christ; or that would not promptly exclude an immoral person, sufficiently proved to be such. No doubt there are immoral persons among the members of churches. They are persons whose guilt can not always be established by such proof as the laws of Christ require; but their number, it is believed, is comparatively small.

3. There are few, if any, evangelical churches in which the profession of a mere general or "historical belief," as it is called, in the great doctrines above states, accompanied even by an outwardly moral life, would be considered sufficient to render a man fit to be admitted to the Lord's Supper. Nineteen twentieths of all the evangelical churches in this country believe that there is such a thing as being "born again," "born of the Spirit." And very few, indeed, admit the doctrine that a man who is not "converted," that is, "renewed by the Spirit," may come without sin to that holy ordinance.

There may be difference of opinion among truly evangelical Christians respecting the amount of evidence of conversion necessary in the case. But I may unhesitatingly affirm that, with few exceptions, all expect some evidence in every candidate for admission to the Church and participation in its most precious privileges; and such evidence, too, as induces the belief that, as the Scriptures express it, he has "passed from death unto life." The belief is almost universal that the sacrament of the Lord's Supper was appointed for the converted or regenerated, and should, as far as possible, be administered only to such. The number of those who hold a different opinion is small. Accordingly, it would be found upon inquiry that all the pastors of our evangelical churches are very careful to explain with what dispositions of the heart and will, as well as with what views of the understanding, one should come to the Lord's Supper, and that these are truly such as no unregenerate person can possess. This holy sacrament is rarely dispensed in our churches without being preceded by a discourse on the nature of the preparation required in order to a right "communicating," or receiving of this ordinance; and all irreligious persons—in fact, all persons, be their lives outwardly what they may—who have not the testimony of their consciences that they possess, so far as they honestly perceive the state of their hearts, the qualifications described, are solemnly warned of the sin, and consequent danger to their souls, incurred by unworthily partaking of that holy Supper.

It is, indeed, too true that, with all this care, unworthy persons do come to the Lord's Table. Many, no doubt, gain admission to the churches who, after all, are not converted. . . . Our pastors and other church officers, whose duty it is to govern the churches, do not profess to be infallible. They can not know the heart. They can only judge according to the evidence presented to them. They lean, very naturally, to the side of charity; and with every desire to do their duty, there are many, doubtless, in every church, admitted by them without being truly converted. . . .

. . . But were there no discipline in our churches, and were all the world permitted to come to the Lord's Supper, the state of things would be in every respect infinitely worse. We make at least the effort to separate the Church from the World, and to render it manifest that there is a difference, and not a small one, between those who belong to the former, and those who seek their happiness in the latter, and have their desires bounded by it.

[Three chapters, "The Way in Which Membership in Our Churches Is Obtained," "The Relations of Unconverted Men to the Church," and "The Administration of Discipline," followed here in the original.]

CHAPTER 52

Character of

American Preaching

Adequately to describe American preaching, one should be intimately acquainted with the Churches of the country throughout its vast extent: but this knowledge it falls to the lot of few to possess. Foreign writers on the subject have been either travelers, whose books betray a very limited acquaintance with the Churches and their ministers; or untraveled authors, whose judgment has been formed upon such specimens as they could find in printed discourses, or hear from the lips of preachers from the United States during visits to Europe. In either case, however impartial the judges, the *data* for forming a sound opinion upon the subject have been manifestly insufficient. . . .

Preaching in the United States varies exceedingly both in *manner* and in *substance;* but most in manner. The clergy in the Presbyterian, Congregational, Episcopal, Reformed Dutch, Lutheran, German Reformed, Moravian, Reformed Presbyterian, Associate, and Associate Reformed Churches, have, with few exceptions, passed through a regular course of education in Latin, Greek, the Natural and Moral Sciences, and Theology, such a course as is now pursued at our colleges and theological seminaries. Many, especially the younger men, have some knowledge of Hebrew. As for the Baptist ministers, it is not easy to say how many have gone through a similar course—certainly not half, perhaps not a fourth. A still smaller proportion of the Methodist preachers have had that advantage, though, upon the whole, they are probably as well informed as the Baptist ministers are. Ministerial education among the Cumberland Presbyterians is much in the same state as among the Methodists.

The clergy of certain denominations, who have not passed through a collegiate course, are often spoken of, but very unjustly, as "uneducated," "unlearned," "illiterate," and so forth. Very many of such, however, have, by great application, made most respectable attainments. Some have acquired a considerable knowledge of the Latin and Greek classics, and a far greater number have, by the diligent perusal of valuable works in English, stored their minds with a large amount of sound learning, which they use with much effect in preaching. . . .

Nearly all the Episcopal and Congregational clergy write their sermons, and read more or less closely when delivering them. So do many of the Presbyterian and Reformed Dutch, and some, also, of the Baptist ministers. A large proportion of the Presbyterian and Baptist clergy, and nearly all the ministers of the Methodist, Cumberland Presbyterian, and some other evangelical denominations, neither write their sermons in full, nor read any considerable part of them. Few, however, of any Church, commit their sermons to memory; the great majority of such as do not read out their discourses, carefully study the subjects of them, and generally note down the principal heads to be used in the pulpit.

The delivery of the ministers who read is not, in general, very animated; still, it is in most instances sufficiently attractive to interest hearers endued with any capacity for distinguishing between sound and sense. Good reading, though in all countries much more rare than attractive and effective speaking, will generally be preferred by hearers of high intellectual acquirements.

Ministers of all denominations who do not read their discourses, possess a much more animated delivery, and generally display more of what may be called "oratory" in their manner, than their brethren who read. But their sermons can hardly have the same order, clearness, and freedom from repetition. Still, they need not be deficient in instructiveness, and they have greatly the advantage in point of fervor, and in those direct and powerful appeals which owe their effect almost as much to look, tone, and manner, as to the truths which the speaker expresses. Not that such appeals can be of much avail if no truth be conveyed by them, but truth may become much more effective when pressed upon the attention in an attractive and impressive manner.

. . . Our Methodist ministers have a certain course of reading prescribed to them for the four probationary years preceding their being ordained elders or presbyters. During that time they have their circuit labors to perform; what they learn is put to instant use, and incorporated, as it were, with their very being. . . . the grand advantage possessed by the Methodist itinerant preacher, and one which, if he has any talent at all, he can not fail to profit by, is, that he may repeat in many or all of the eight, ten, or more places in his circuit, the discourse with which he sets out, prepared during intervals of repose. This frequent repetition of the same sermon is an inestimable means of improvement. Each repetition admits of some modification, as the discourse is not written out; and enables the preacher to remedy what seemed faulty, and to supply what seemed deficient in the preceding effort. No men, accordingly, with us become readier or more effective speakers. Their diction may not always be as pure as that of men who have spent several years in the schools; yet it is surprising with what propriety vast numbers express themselves, while in forcible and effective delivery they far surpass multitudes of preachers who have passed through the colleges.

. . . [Baptist preachers] have not the advantages of the itineracy, and many of them are too much occupied with their secular pursuits to spare much time for study. Still, among them, also, there will be found a great deal of energetic eloquence—rather homely at times, yet often highly effective—and flowing from a mind more intent upon its conceptions than upon the language in which they are to be clothed, and more desirous of producing a lasting effect on the understanding and hearts of the hearers than of exciting admiration for the graces of a fine style and elegant delivery.

Some of the tourists who visit the United States affect to despise our "uneducated" and "ignorant" ministers, and think what they call the "ranting" of such men a fit subject of diversion for themselves and their readers. Such authors know little of the real worth and valuable labors of these humble, and, in comparison with such as have studied at colleges and universities, unlettered men. Their plain preaching, in fact, is often far more likely to benefit their ordinary audiences than would that of a learned doctor of divinity issuing from some great university. Their language, though not always refined, is intelligible to those whom it addresses. Their illustrations may not be classical, but they will probably be drawn either from the Bible or from scenes amid which their hearers move, and the events with which they are familiar. . . . I have often heard most solemn and edifying discourses from such men. I have met with them in all parts of the United States; and though some, doubtless, bring discredit upon the ministry by their ignorance, their eccentricities, or their incapacity, yet, taken as a whole, they are a great blessing to the country. . . . To the labors of such men tens of thousands of neighborhoods in the United States are indebted for their general good order, tranquillity, and happiness, as well as for the humble but sincere piety that reigns in many a heart, and around many a fireside. To them the country owes much of its conservative character, for no men have inculcated more effectively those doctrines which promote obedience to law, respect for magistracy, and the maintenance of civil government. . . .

But the subject of preaching ought to be viewed in its highest and most important aspect—that of the salvation of souls.

The first characteristic of American preaching is, I should say, *simplicity*. . . . The grand aim of our preachers, taken as a body, is rather to present the true meaning of a text than to produce what is called *effect*. Again, preaching in the United States is simple in point of language, the plain and familiar being preferred to the ornate and rhetorical. Such of our preachers as wish to be perfectly intelligible, prefer words of Saxon to those of Latin origin, as being better understood by the people. Vigor, too, is preferred to beauty, and perspicuity to embellishment. Not that we have no preachers whose composition is ornate, and even elegant, but I speak of the mass. Lastly, our preaching is simple in respect to delivery. . . . There may be animation, and in some cases even vehemence, accompanied with a loud and powerful utterance, but the manner remains simple—the hearer's attention is not ordinarily diverted from what is said to him that says it. Truth, accordingly, has, so to speak, a better chance of making its way to the hearts of the audience, than when announced with all the fascinations of a splendid address and captivating manner. . . .

The second grand characteristic of American preaching lies in its being *serious* and *earnest*. Thanks be to God, the preachers of our evangelical Churches seem, in general, to be truly converted men, and preach as if they felt the infinite importance of what they say. "We believe, and therefore speak," seems to be the main-spring of all their endeavors, and to give the tone to all their preaching. They feel it to be a serious office to speak to dying men of their immortal souls, and help them to prepare for death, judgment, and eternity. . . .

A third characteristic of American preaching is its dwelling much upon *immediate reconciliation with God,* by sincere re-pentance toward Him, and faith toward the Lord Jesus Christ. . . . No excuse, no delay on the part of the unconverted sinner can be accepted; the solemn call to repent, and seek *now* the salvation of his never-dying soul is sounded in his ear, and no peace is given until he has not only heard but obeyed it.

A fourth characteristic of American preaching is its *highly doctrinal nature*. This is particularly the case with the discourses of such of our ministers as have passed through a regular course of classical and theological studies; and of these the preachers who write and read their discourses indulge rather more, perhaps, than those who speak from premeditation merely. . . . Many of our pastors expound certain portions of the Bible in order; but this, the most difficult, and yet, when happily done, the most profitable of all methods of presenting truth, is not, I am sorry to say, so common as it ought to be. . . .

As a fifth characteristic of our method of homiletics, I may state that it is *systematic* or *consecutive*. What I mean is, that the best preaching in our evangelical churches maintains a proper connec-tion among the discourses successively delivered from the same pulpit, instead of presenting in each a separate or isolated state-ment of truth. . . . They strive, by all possible means, to present it in all its aspects and bearings, and do not quit one point until they have well established it. They cause every succeeding state-ment and argument to bear upon and strengthen that which preceded, and in this way make it manifest that they are steadily tending to a great final result . . . as the blacksmith can expect to shape the heated iron only by directing his hammer to the same point and its immediate vicinity in many successive blows, so the minister does not hope for success in opening the eyes of blind sinners, or rightly guiding those who are scarcely more than half awake, but by oft-repeated and faithful presentation of the same truths in all their bearings. This characteristic can hardly be called a prevailing one, for, alas! with a good deal of systematic preaching, we have still too much, even among our settled clergy, of that sort which, with more emphasis than elegance, has been called *scattering*.

A sixth characteristic of American preaching is the extent to which it may be called *philosophical*. By philosophical I mean, founded on a knowledge of the faculties and powers of the human mind, and of the principles which govern its operations. . . . True philosophy, in its proper place, is a valuable auxiliary or handmaid, rather than an enemy to theology; but when she ceases to be a servant and assumes the mastery, undertaking that for which she is incompetent, she fails in doing the good she might otherwise have done, and becomes purely mischievous.*

---

* "I think," says M. de Tocqueville, "that in no country in the civilized world is less attention paid to philosophy than in the United States. The Americans have no philosophical school of their own; and they care but little for all the schools into which Europe is divided, the very names of which are scarcely known to them. Nevertheless, it is easy to perceive that almost all the inhabitants of the United States conduct their understanding in the same manner, and govern it by the same rules; that is to say, that without ever having taken the trouble to define the rules of a philosophical method, they are in possession of one, common to the whole people." [*Democracy in America,* trans. Reeves, pt. II, chap. i, p. 1.] I have read with unmingled astonishment these opinions, which are faithfully transferred from the author's original. Certainly one rarely finds such an acknowledgment of a widely-existing effect, for which the proper and only possible cause is denied. The fact is, that in few countries in the civilized world is philosophy, in the sense in which this word is used on the Continent, viz., metaphysical or psychological science, more pursued, at least to all practicable and valuable ends, than in the United States. There is scarcely a college—at least a Protestant one, and there are over one hundred such—in which it is not studied with no little care by the students in the last year of the course. In addition to reading such authors as Locke, Reid, Dugald Stuart, Brown, etc., the professor of that department gives lectures or explanations of the textbook employed. Thus do the thousands of young collegians make considerable proficiency in this science, especially in its more

A seventh feature of the American pulpit is *directness*. This distinguishes our preaching so generally that it were hard to say which of the evangelical denominations has most of it. Everywhere we shall find it the preacher's object, first of all, to be perfectly understood, and then to preach to the heart and conscience, as well as to the understanding. In doing this great plainness of speech is used, and care taken to avoid every thing by which the barbed dart may be arrested before it reaches the heart at which it is aimed.

An eighth characteristic of American preaching is its *faithfulness*. I know not how often I have been asked in Europe whether our ministers are not intimidated by the rich and influential in their congregations who may dislike the truth. The question has not a little surprised me, for I had never dreamed that the courage of evangelical ministers in preaching the Gospel could be doubted. The dependence of our ministers upon their flocks for their salaries seems not to affect in the least their faithfulness in preaching "repentance toward God," and "faith toward our Lord Jesus Christ.". . .

The ninth characteristic of American preaching is, that it is eminently *practical*. Not only are the unconverted urged to "acquaint themselves with God, and be at peace, that thereby good may come to them," and believers exhorted to "grow in grace, and in the knowledge of the Lord Jesus Christ," but the latter are also urged, from the moment of their conversion, to commence living

---

popular and practical aspects. And thus do our public men, our professional men, all, in a word, who have passed through college (and they are the men, with few exceptions, that most influence the public mind), become acquainted with the principles that guide the operations of the human mind. There is not a country in the world, not even excepting Scotland itself, where metaphysics have so much influence upon preaching as in New England; indeed, they have sometimes had too much influence. We have not in the United States great professors who occupy themselves with nothing but philosophy, and who have rivaled Kant, Hegel, and Schelling, in the nature of their speculations; nor is it likely that we ever shall have such. The nature of our Anglo-Saxon mind hardly admits of the thing. Besides, we have too much public life, and too much to engross our attention to allow us to prosecute extensively *unpractical* speculations. Nevertheless, we have a few men, such as Mr. Ralph W. Emerson, of Boston, who equal Mr. Carlyle himself in admiration of the German transcendentalists, and have, probably, come quite as near to understanding them.

for God, and for the salvation of men. The doctrine has of late years been more and more preached, that every Christian, whatever his sphere in life, is under obligation to live for the salvation of others; and that by his conversation, by his holy example, as well as by personal sacrifices, he should do all that he can to promote this salvation far and near. Blessed be God, this style of preaching is not without effect. It is, under God's blessing, the cause of the annually increasing efforts made by Christians of this land, for the building up of Christ's kingdom, both at home and abroad.

A tenth characteristic of American preaching, and the last that we shall name, is, that it *speaks much of the work of the Spirit.* I know of no one idea that has been so *dominant* in the American Churches for the last hundred years as that of the importance of the office and work of the Holy Spirit. The need in which the world lies of the operations of this holy Agent, the indispensableness of His co-operation with the preaching of the Gospel, and the use of all other means to effect the salvation of men, together with the gracious promise of this great ascension gift of the crucified and exalted Saviour, are themes on which the ministry of the evangelical Churches in America often dwells, and not in vain.

CHAPTER 53

Revivals of Religion

Extraordinary seasons of religious interest, denominated Revivals of Religion, have existed in the American Churches from a very early period of their history. The cause of this peculiarity in the dispensation of Divine grace may be traced, in part, to the peculiar character and circumstances of the first settlers of the country. . . .

. . . the attachment of the first settlers of New England to the ordinance of public worship, and especially the reliance they placed on "the preaching of the word" as the chief instrument, under God, for the conversion of their children and dependants, were among the most striking traits in their character. . . . This feeling modified all their habits and institutions as a people. It made them settle in villages around their places of worship, and not, like their Southern neighbors, upon scattered plantations; it led them to support two religious teachers for each of their infant churches; it founded colleges for the preparation of a ministry adequate to these high duties; it established week-day lectures, on which those who lived in the outer settlements, at the distance of six or eight miles, felt it a privilege and a duty regularly to attend; it pervaded, in short, all the arrangements of society, and gave a prominence to *preaching,* a disposition to multiply religious meetings, and a reliance upon this mode of urging truth upon the conscience, greater, perhaps, than has ever existed among any other people.

Another trait in the character of the first settlers of New England, in common with their brethren at home, was a strong faith and expectation of *special* answers to prayer. . . . They did not expect merely the blessing of God *in general* on the requests they made, but direct and specific answers, according to their need, in every pressing emergency. This strong faith in the efficacy of prayer the first settlers of New England carried with them when they fled into the wilderness. It was their support and consolation under all the trials of famine, pestilence, and savage warfare. They felt that special and extraordinary answers were often vouchsafed them when they cried to God. . . .

To see the connection of these two traits of character with the spirit of revivals, we have only to consider the influence they would naturally exert at one of the most interesting crises which can ever happen to a minister and his church—I mean the commencement of increased thoughtfulness among the unconverted part of the congregation. Such seasons exist, at times, in every place where the Gospel is faithfully preached. Some alarming providence, some general calamity which weakens for a time the fascination of worldly things, some impressive sermon, some instances of sudden conversion, may strike upon the consciences of considerable numbers at once, and awaken that latent sense of guilt and danger, which it is impossible for the most thoughtless wholly to suppress. At such a period, how has many a pastor felt, . . . that, by the blessing of God, this interest in religion might extend throughout the whole congregation; might rise to deep anxiety and pungent conviction; that the Holy Spirit might be present to renew the hearts of many; and that more might be done for the salvation of his people in a few weeks or months, than, under ordinary circumstances, in as many years! And what would this be, if his desires were realized, but a *revival of religion,* an outpouring of the Holy Spirit, as a result of the prayers and efforts of the people of God! Now I need not say how entirely the early settlers of New England were prepared, by the traits of character described above, to enter at once on this very course of action. Prayer and preaching were the living principle of their institutions; special prayer upon special emergencies, with the most plain and pungent, enforcing those peculiar doctrines of grace which humble man and exalt God, and which have in every age been made "powerful to the pulling down of strongholds." . . . In these circumstances, how natural was it to multiply the means of grace upon any appearance of increased seriousness; to press with redoubled zeal and frequency to the throne of God in prayer; to urge their children and dependants, with all the fervor of Christian affection, to seize the golden opportunity, and make their "calling and election sure," to remove, as far as possible, every obstacle of business or amusement out of the way; and to concentrate the entire interest of their little communities on the one object of the soul's salvation! How natural that these labors and prayers should be blessed of God; that the Truth preached under these circumstances should be made, like "the fire and the hammer, to break in pieces the flinty rock;" that extraodinary effusions of the Holy Spirit should be granted; that there should be an "awakening," as it was then called, or, in modern language, a REVIVAL OF RELIGION!

The revival of 1735 commenced at Northampton, Massachusetts, under the preaching of Jonathan Edwards. The town, at an earlier period, had enjoyed five awakenings, . . . but at this time religion had suffered a very great decline, not only in Northampton, but in New England at large. A pernicious practice had been gradually introduced of admitting persons to full communion in the Church on the ground of a blameless external deportment, without strict inquiry into their religious experience, or decisive evidence of renewing grace. The disastrous consequences were soon felt. The tone of spiritual feeling was lowered in the churches by the admission of many who had a "name to live, but were dead." Prayer and effort for the salvation of the impenitent had greatly decreased; and, as a natural consequence, there had been for more than thirty years a very marked suspension of Divine influence throughout New England.

The preaching of Mr. Edwards which gave rise to this revival, like all preaching which prepares the way for extensive reformations, was doctrinal in its character. He dwelt with great force of argument and closeness of application on the leading doctrines of grace—which had begun to lose their power in the prevailing declension—justification by faith alone, the necessity of the Spirit's influences, and kindred topics.

Under such preaching, in connection with a sudden and alarming providence, in the beginning of 1735, a solemn, and very soon an overwhelming interest in religious truth, pervaded the whole town. For the space of six months, the revival went on with a power and extent never before known. Hardly a family could be found in the place in which there were not one or more under conviction of sin, or rejoicing in hope. So entire was the absorption in the interests of the soul, that a report went abroad that the people of Northampton had abandoned all worldly employments, and given themselves wholly up to the pursuit of eternal life; and though this was an exaggeration, it is true that Mr. Edwards found it necessary to remind some of his flock that their secular duties were not to be neglected. . . . More than three hundred were added to the Church as the fruits of this revival, making the whole number of communicants about 620, being nearly the entire adult population of the town, which consisted of two hundred families. I will only add, that Mr. Edward's well-known principles on the subject led him to guard his people, throughout the revival, with the most watchful care, against hasty and delusive hopes of having experienced renewing grace. He conversed with each individual separately, not only while under conviction of sin, but in repeated instances after the supposed change of heart took place; pointing out the evidences and nature of true piety; warning them against self-deception, and leading them to the strictest examination into their spiritual state. Such has been the course pursued in the New England churches generally, down to the present day; and the consequence has been, that neither in that revival, nor in most of our well-conducted revivals, has there been reason to suppose that more persons were self-deceived than in the ordinary accessions to the Church at times of no prevailing religious concern.

In 1740, revivals commenced anew at Northampton, Boston, and many other places, very nearly at the same time, and spread within eighteen months throughout all the English colonies. For some time, this appears to have been, to an unusual degree, a silent, powerful, and glorious work of the Spirit of God. An eye-witness states, under date of May, 1741, that from Philadelphia to the remotest settlements beyond Boston, a distance of nearly five hundred miles, there was in *most* places more or less concern for the soul. "Whole colleges are under conviction, and many savingly converted. Our minister (Mr. Pemberton, of New York), being sent for to Yale College on account of the many distressed persons there, in his going and coming preached twice a day on the road, and even children followed him to his lodgings, weeping and anxiously concerned about the salvation of their souls." At a later period, however, some were unhappily betrayed into intemperate zeal, which called forth opposition, and produced great excitement and contention. Mr. Edwards came forward with his usual ability to defend the work, and, at the same time, repress undue excesses. One hundred and sixty of the most respectable ministers of New England, New York, and New Jersey, joined in a public attestation to its genuineness and purity in most places, while they united with Mr. Edwards in condemning the improprieties which had occurred in too many instances. But a spirit of jealousy and strife was engendered, which is always fatal to the progress of a revival. It therefore terminated in the year 1743. Notwithstanding these unfortunate admixtures of human imperfection, the work, as a whole, was most evidently shown by its results to have been of God. Those who had the best means of judging, estimated the number of true converts, as proved by their subsequent lives, at 30,000 in New England alone, at a time when the whole population was but 300,000; besides many thousands more among the Presbyterians of New York, New Jersey, Pennsylvania, and the more southern settlements.

The fifty years that followed were years of war and civil commotion; first in a conflict of nearly twenty years between the English and French for ascendency in North America, and afterward in a struggle of the colonies for independence, and the formation of a Federal Government. During this long period the country was kept in a state of perpetual agitation, under the influence of passions hostile to the progress of spiritual religion in any form, and peculiarly hostile to the prevalance of any extended work of grace. Revivals, however, did not wholly cease, as might reasonably have been expected. On the contrary, I have been struck with surprise, in looking over the accounts of that widespread work of grace which soon after commenced, to see in how many instances they point back to some preceding season of spiritual refreshing during those fifty years of war and civil strife.

The period just referred to, of increased influence from on high, commenced at the close of the last century, and has often been styled the *era of modern revivals*. Owing to its importance in this character, I shall dwell upon it somewhat more fully, and shall then turn to other topics which demand our attention. It was preceded by a spirit of fervent prayer and deep solicitude among Christians, on account of the growing tendency in our country to infidel principles. For this a preparation had been made by the crimes and vices of a long-protracted war; and the breaking out of the French Revolution had given to the enemies of religion the most confident expectations of a speedy triumph. The minds of multitudes had become unsettled. Wild and vague expectations were everywhere entertained, especially among the young, of a new order of things about to commence, in which Christianity would be laid aside as an obsolete system. The people of God, under these circumstances, were driven to the throne of grace with redoubled fervor of supplication, that while the enemy came in like a flood, the Spirit of the Lord would lift up a standard against him.

Another subject of solicitude was the religious wants of our new settlements, which began at this time to spread abroad in the wilderness, to an unparalleled extent. There was every reason to fear that, if left to themselves, in the rapidity of their progress, they would leave behind them the institutions of the Gospel. This gave rise to a missionary spirit in the older States, which has been the salvation of that growing part of our country. . . .

The spirit thus awakened of more fervent prayer to God, and more active zeal in his service, was followed by the Divine blessing. A number of churches in the interior of Connecticut and Massachusetts were favored, in 1797, with an outpouring of the Holy Spirit, which gradually spread into many of the neighboring towns. The utmost care was taken to guard, from the first, against any recurrence of that spirit of intemperate zeal which had brought reproach, to some extent, on the revival of 1740. These efforts, most happily, were attended with complete success. Rarely, if ever, has there been a series of revivals in our country more calm, more pure, more lasting and salutary in their effects. As one means of extending the work, ministers who had enjoyed the presence of God among their own people, were selected by some ecclesiastical body, and sent forth, generally two together, on preaching tours among the neighboring churches. . . . Under these and similar influences, the work of God spread into more than one hundred towns in Massachusetts and Connecticut, and into a still greater number of places in the new settlements of Vermont, New Hampshire, Maine, and New York, which had but recently formed a wide-spread field of missionary labor.

. . . In Kentucky, lying in the centre of these new States of the West, a revival commenced in the year 1801, which spread over the whole State, and within the two following years extended to the North and South, throughout a tract of country six hundred miles in length. Owing to the rude state of society in those new settlements, there occurred in these revivals some irregularities, which threw a suspicion upon them for a time in the view of Christians in the Eastern States. Some, undoubtedly, of the vast multitudes who were then awakened were wrought upon merely by the excitement of the occasion.

But as to the character of the work in general, we have the

following testimony from one of the most enlightened Presbyterian clergymen of Virginia, who visited the scene of those revivals, for the sake of forming for himself a deliberate judgment on the subject. "Upon the whole, I think the revival in Kentucky among the most extraordinary that have ever visited the Church of Christ; and, all things considered, it was peculiarly adapted to the circumstances of the country into which it came. Infidelity was triumphant, and religion on the point of expiring. Something extraordinary seemed necessary to arrest the attention of a giddy people, who were ready to conclude that Christianity was a fable, and futurity a delusion. This revival has done it. It has confounded infidelity, and brought numbers beyond calculation under serious impressions."*

From the period we have now reached it is unnecessary, and, indeed, impossible, to trace distinctly the progress of our revivals. They have become, if I may so speak, a constituent part of the religious system of our country. Not a year has passed without numerous instances of their occurrence, though at some periods they have been more powerful and prevalent than at others. They have the entire confidence of the great body of evangelical Christians throughout our country. There exists, indeed, a diversity of opinion as to the proper means of promoting them, some regarding one set of measures, and some another, as best adapted to this end. But, while these differences exist as to what constitutes a well-conducted revival, all, or nearly all, agree that such a revival is an inestimable blessing: so that he who should oppose himself to revivals, *as such,* would be regarded by most of our evangelical Christians as, *ipso facto,* an enemy to spiritual religion itself.

In the foregoing sketch of the rise and progress of our revivals, I have confined myself chiefly to the Congregational and Presbyterian Churches (which are substantially one), and have described these works of grace, particularly as they exist in New England. I have done so because, having their origin in those Churches, it was proper to trace them forward in the line where they commenced;

---

* [Ed.—The author of this passage was George A. Baxter; the quote, which was part of a letter to Archibald Alexander, can be found easiest in Leonard W. Bacon, *A History of American Christianity* (New York: The Christian Literature Co., 1897), p. 237.]

and because I was best acquainted with their history, and the character they assumed, in the communion to which I belong. It is of such revivals that I shall continue to speak, and, without disparagement to others, I may be permitted to express my preference for that mode of conducting revivals which has generally prevailed in the Congregational churches of New England. These churches have had a longer experience on this subject than any others; they have enjoyed more revivals in proportion to their numbers; and, what I deem of the highest importance is, that they have uniformly kept them under the guidance and control of a learned ministry, whose habits and principles led them to repress all undue excitement, to check every thing extravagant, coarse, or disorderly, and to guard the supposed subjects of the work, by the severest tests, against self-deception. . . .

. . . the ordinary strain of preaching in the Congregational churches of New England, where revivals have prevailed with great frequency, is, to an uncommon degree, *doctrinal* in its character. A preparation is thus made to give the Gospel its full effect whenever a season of religious interest arrives. The mind is preoccupied with clear and discriminating views of Divine truth. The argument, upon every point, has been gone over again and again in its full extent. Those humbling doctrines, especially, which men so love to misrepresent and abuse, are dwelt upon much, explained fully, and argued out at large; and great pains are taken so to state them as to show their perfect consistency with the dictates of right reason and the consciousness of every honest mind. In seasons of revival, the most effective preaching is of the same general character, though, of course, more fervent and urgent. It does not consist, to any great extent, in exhortation, in any appeals, however forcible or just, to mere excited sensibility or feeling. Its object still is to pour *truth* upon the sinner's mind; to make him see, under his new circumstances of awakened interest, the *evidence* of those doctrines which he has admitted, perhaps, in speculation, all his life, and yet never once truly believe; to anticipate all his objections; to strip him of every plea and pretence for delay; to fill and occupy his whole soul with *reasons* for immediate right action, and thus shut him up to "the obedience of the truth." Such preaching, though it be plain, and even homely, if it flows from a full heart and large experience, is ordinarily much blessed of God in seasons of revival.

The leading doctrine at such seasons is that of "the new birth"—of the sinner's entire dependence, for a change of heart, on the direct interposition of God. And yet, for this very reason, the other doctrine implied above, of *duty,* of *obligation* to immediate right action, is urged with redoubled force. Without feeling this, the sinner can not feel his guilt, for there *is* no consciousness of guilt without consciousness of having violated duty; and where guilt is not felt, the influences of the Spirit are not given to renew the heart. And here, at this precise point, is the great difficulty in dealing with the impenitent. They do not believe that God requires them, in their present state, to become instantly holy. . . . These views prevailed in New England previous to the revival of 1735, and were one cause of the great decline in religion which preceded that event. Mr. Edwards was therefore called upon, when that work commenced, to take his ground on this subject, and the principles which guided him in that revival have been the great controlling principles in all our revivals ever since. They are thus stated by his biographer: "To urge repentance on every sinner as his *immediate duty;* to insist that God is under no obligation to any unrenewed man; and that a man can challenge nothing, either in absolute justice or by free *promise,* on account of any thing he does before he repents and believes." . . .

But it may be said, granting (as, indeed, we must on *some* ground) the duty of the unconverted to turn instantly to God, still they will never succeed in doing it without an influence from on high. Why, then, press them so urgently to the act? Why multiply motives, as if you expected to produce the change by the force of moral suasion? Is it not true, after all, that both you and they must "wait God's time?" It would be enough to answer that God himself has set us the example: "Make you a new heart and a new spirit, *for why will ye die?"* Christ and His apostles urged to repentance by argument and persuasion, just as they did to any of the ordinary acts of life. The whole Bible is filled with warnings, expostulations, and entreaties, pressing a lost race, with every motive that two worlds can offer, to immediate right action. Nor is it difficult to see at least some of the reasons. First: Let the sinner really put himself to the act of giving his heart to God, and he will learn, as he can never learn in any other way, the depth of his depravity, the utter and hopeless destitution of all spiritual sensibility within him. Nothing can so effectually crush his pride and self-reliance. This *practical* demonstration of his entire helplessness, in himself considered, may be just the thing that was necessary to bring him to that point where it would be proper for God to grant him the renewing influences of His grace. Secondly: The Spirit, in sanctifying, operates "through the truth;" and the presence of that truth upon the mind as an instrumental cause is, therefore, just as necessary to the result (at least in the case of adults) as the renewing influence itself.

While it was the uniform doctrine of the Apostle Paul, that the redeemed are "begotten of God," he thought it no arrogance to say, "I have begotten you through the Gospel." Without affirming that the influences of the Spirit are granted in exact proportion to the wisdom and power with which truth is urged upon the conscience, we may safely say that such, to a very great and prevailing extent, is the fact. It is, at least, all that man can do; and if the doctrine of the sinner's dependence leads us to do this with one particle of diminished force, if we do not ply him with truth and motive just as earnestly as if we expected to convert him by our own efforts alone, it is a serious question whether our orthodoxy has not lost its true balance. Is there not reason to fear that very excellent men sometimes err on this subject from the best of motives, the desire to exalt the grace of God? . . . No honor is done to the Holy Spirit by exalting His influences in conversion, at the expense of the Truth which He has Himself revealed. It is the glory of that blessed Agent, that in turning the soul to God, He does it in strict accordance with the laws of our moral constitution. . . . Thirdly: The result produced by renewing grace is *right action*. "God," says Edwards, "produces all, and we *act* all. For that is what He produces, viz., *our own acts*."—(*Efficacious Grace,* sec. 64.) Is it not, therefore, most reasonable to suppose that this grace (if bestowed at all) will be granted to those who are putting themselves to the act of giving their hearts to God, "who strive to enter in at the strait gate;" and not to those who remain in the attitude of mere passive recipients? Account for it as we will, there is no fact which our revivals have taught us more fully than this, *the great success which attends the urging of sinners to turn immediately to God, as though we expected them to do it at once and upon the spot.* . . .

This, then, is the point to which all my observations are directed —the union of these two doctrines of *activity* and *dependence,* which are so commonly felt to be subversive of each other; the bringing of both to bear with undiminished force on the minds of the impenitent. Establish one of these doctrines to the exclusion or weakening of the other, and just to the same extent is the Gospel robbed of its power. Inculcate dependence without pressing to the act of instantly giving up the heart to Christ, and the sinner sits down quietly to "wait God's time." Urge him to duty on the ground of his possessing all the requisite power, while (with the Pelagians) you do away his dependence, and his reluctant heart will lead him to take his *own* time, and that is *never.* Address him on the Arminian scheme of *gracious aid,* which is always ready at his call (except in cases of extreme contumacy), and how strongly is he tempted to put off to a more "convenient season" what he feels may at any time be done! But place him under the pressure of both these doctrines—the necessity of action on his part in coming to God, the weighty obligations which urge him to it, the crushing sense of guilt every moment he delays, the momentous interests which seem to be crowded into the decision of the passing hour, the encouragement to "strive as in an agony" afforded by the gift of the Spirit's influences to others around him (an encouragement peculiarly great in seasons of revival, and giving them so much of their power), the feeling that God may justly withhold those influences, and that every moment of delay increases the danger of this fearful doom—and have we not here, most perfectly combined, all the elements of that system of grace which is emphatically the power of God unto salvation?

As far as human instrumentality is concerned, the conversion of sinners depends on two things—the clear and vivid presentation of Divine truth to their minds, and importunate prayer, on the part of Christians, for the influences of the Holy Spirit to give that truth effect. I am, therefore, to show what there is in these seasons of concentrated religious interest, that is peculiarly adapted both to animate the prayers and efforts of the people of God, and to give the Gospel readier access to the hearts of the impenitent, and superior efficacy in bringing them to "the obedience of the truth." In doing so, I shall point to certain original principles of our mental constitution, which have confessedly very great power in moving the minds of men, and shall endeavor to show that revivals appeal to these principles or springs of human action, with a force and effect altogether greater than can ever be realized under any other circumstances. I shall thus give what may not improperly be termed *a theory of revivals,* and shall show that they are not seasons of mere excitement and fanaticism, but might reasonably be expected, from their consistency with the laws of human action, to produce those great and lasting reformations with which they have actually blessed the American Churches. In pursuing the subject, I hope I shall not be suspected of losing sight for one moment of the fact, that the Holy Spirit is the author of all the good produced in this case, both in the hearts of Christians and impenitent sinners. But it is the glory of that blessed Agent, that, in dispensing His sanctifying influences, He does not set aside or destroy the established laws of human agency; and it is not, therefore, detracting from these influences, but rather doing them honor, to point out their perfect consistency with the great principles of mental constitution.

1. The first of these principles to which I shall now advert, and relating particularly to Christianity, is strongly-awakened *desire.*

The scenes presented in a revival are eminently adapted to create those strong spiritual desires which express themselves in fervent prayer, and are indispensable to all successful Christian effort. . . . What more natural, under the impulse of the fervent desires thus awakened, than to "put away all their idols," to bow before God in deep self-abasement for their past backslidings, to mourn over the multitudes around them who are in danger of perishing in their sins. . . . How is all reserve laid aside—all the ordinary backwardness of Christians to speak and act openly on the side of the Redeemer abandoned, and every feeling absorbed amid these triumphs of Divine grace, in the one great question, "Lord, what wilt Thou have me to do" for the advancement of Thy cause? Faint and feeble, indeed, when compared with these, are the spiritual desires which are found to prevail in any ordinary state of the church.

2. The second of these principles, now to be mentioned, is *expectation*.

If I were asked why revivals are so frequent in America, and so rare in Europe, my first answer would be, that Christians on one side of the Atlantic expect them, and on the other they do not expect them. These seasons of "refreshing from on high" are a part of the blessing that rested on our fathers; and the events of the last forty years, especially, have taught us, that if we seek their continuance in the spirit of those with whom they commenced, we shall never seek in vain. . . .

3. A third principle, intimately connected with this subject, is *sympathy*. God, in establishing public worship, has decided that the social and sympathetic feelings of our nature ought to be enlisted in the cause of religion. . . . As the strong images I have used, so perfectly descriptive of the state of things in a revival, are borrowed from the language employed by our Saviour himself, with evident approbation, in describing similar scenes in his own day, it is certain there is nothing inconsistent with perfect soundness of mind, or the presence of the sanctifying Spirit, in a season of simultaneous and highly-awakened interest on the subject of the soul's salvation. That such seasons are liable to be abused, and have, in some instances, actually degenerated, under the guidance of weak and rash men, into scenes of disorder or mere animal excitement, is no more an argument against them, than a similar abuse of any of the great powers of nature, or principles of our mental constitution, is an argument against their legitimate and well-directed use. . . . Our Congregational clergy, when revivals commenced on a broad scale at the close of the last century, [united] from the first to discountenance this practice; to repress mere animal excitement of every kind; to make their religious meetings, especially in the evening, short (not generally exceeding an hour or an hour and a half), in order to prevent exhaustion and

nervous agitation; and to impress upon their people that the presence of the Holy Spirit ought to be recognized in silence and awe, not with noise and confusion. So complete was their success that, although I have been much conversant with revivals for more than thirty years, I have never, but in one instance, and that a very slight one and for a moment, witnessed any audible expression of emotion in a religious assembly. All our experience has shown that it is wholly unnecessary, and from what we see in some sects where it prevails to some extent, we are constrained to feel that it is injurious, not only as creating prejudices against revivals, but as leading many to mistake nervous excitement for the influence of the Holy Spirit.

4. A fourth of these principles is the *spirit of inquiry* awakened among the thoughtless and prejudiced by the striking scenes of a revival.

When crowds are seen flocking to the house of God, many persons are drawn thither by the impulse of mere curiosity, and when thus brought under the power of Divine truth, are often taught of the Spirit. . . . Others still, who were wholly skeptical as to the existence of any inward principle of spiritual life, when they witness the amazing change produced in the character of many around them, are compelled to exclaim, "This is indeed the finger of God." . . .

5. As a fifth of these principles, I may mention the influence of *that prolonged and exclusive attention to Divine truth* which prevails in a revival.

The power of fixed and continuous attention in deepening the impressions of any subject is one of the most familiar principles of mental science. . . .

But the impenitent, to a great extent, are very imperfectly qualified for such a task. Their minds are so wandering, so unused to dwell on spiritual objects, so estranged from the throne of grace, so entirely in the dark as to the nature of those feelings with which they must come to God, that most of the time they give to contemplation is wasted in chaotic thought; and they are often led to relinquish the attempt in despair. It is not, therefore, sufficient, when their attention is awakened, to send them to their Bibles and their closets. In addition to this, they need, at every step, the assistance of an experienced mind to *hold them to the subject,* to remove obstacles out of the way, and throw light on the path before them. Here, then, is the great principle of revivals. At certain seasons which seem peculiarly to promise a Divine blessing, an extraordinary effort is made (such as can not from its nature last many months) to bring the impenitent completely under the power of Divine truth. Religious meetings are made so frequent, as not, on the one hand, to weary and distract the mind, nor, on the other, to leave the impression made at one meeting to be effaced or much weakened before the next arrives; but to keep the impenitent constantly, as it were, in an atmosphere of Divine truth, brightening continually around them, and bringing their minds more and more perfectly under "the power of the world to come." . . .

6. Another principle involved in revivals is, *the removal of many causes which prevent the access of Divine truth to the mind under ordinary circumstances.*

I can barely glance at a few of these. In a season of general religious interest, much of that *reserve* is laid aside which ordinarily prevails in respect to close conversation on personal religion, and which forms so effectual a guard for backsliding Christians and impenitent sinners, against the intrusion of this unwelcome subject. . . .

The *sense of shame,* the *reluctance to be singular*—one of the strongest impediments (especially with the young) to entering on a religious course—loses, at such times, almost all its power. In an extensive revival, the singularity lies on the other side.

Those *changes* in business or family arrangements, which must often be made as the result of becoming religious, are regarded at such seasons with diminished dread and repugnance. . . .

The ordinary *amusements* of life, which interest the feelings and divert the attention, are at such periods wholly laid aside among those who are friendly to revivals.

The concerns of *business* are made to yield on such occasions to the higher interests of eternity. The people of God will find or *make* time for the numerous seasons of prayer and preaching which demand their presence; and will so arrange that their children and dependents shall enjoy every facility that is requisite to the effectual pursuit of eternal life.

Such, without dwelling further on the subject, are some of the ways in which the impediments to the progress of the Gospel are removed out of the way, by extraordinary seasons of attention to religion.

7. The next principle which I shall mention is, the tendency of revivals to bring men to a *decision,* and to make them decide *right* on the subject of religion.

"Hell," says a quaint old writer, "is paved with good intentions"—intentions never carried into effect, because the time for their execution never quite arrived. On these dreams of the future a revival breaks in with startling power, and calls men to instant decision: "Choose ye this day whom ye will serve." . . . The well-known shortness of such a season, to them, perhaps, the end of their day of grace—the uncommon clearness and pungency with which the truth is preached—the solicitude of Christian friends—the importunity of young converts who have just "tasted that the Lord is gracious"—the impulse of the mass of mind around them, moving in one direction, with all the multiplied influences that concentrate in a revival, unite to impress the truth with irresistible force, *"Now* is the accepted time, *now* is the day of salvation." In the mean time, one step prepares the way for another; a decision on one point braces up the mind for further and more important decisions in the onward progress. . . .

8. Another principle involved in revivals is the tendency of that *lively joy which prevails among Christians and especially young converts,* to render religion attractive to the unconverted.

At ordinary seasons, a life of piety too often appears to the impenitent and especially to the young, under a forbidding aspect. Christians find but little in the state of things around them to call forth their affections, before the unconverted, in lively expressions of spiritual joy. If they do not decline in the warmth of their feelings (as they too often do), they are apt at least to retire within themselves, and to seek their chief enjoyment in secret communion with God. But in times of revival every thing is changed. Their hearts naturally flow forth in warm expressions of thankfulness and joy, as they witness again the triumphs of Divine grace. They renew the fervors of their first love. In their intercourse with the unconverted, they naturally assume an unwonted tenderness of manner, as they seek to bring them by their faithful admonitions to the cross of Christ. The effect is often most striking. The impenitent look at religion under a new aspect, as they see the kindness and solicitude of so many around them for their spiritual good. . . .

But the effect on the impenitent is still more striking, when they witness the joy that is manifested in the countenance and conversation of the new converts to religion. Every natural man bears in his bosom a testimony that he is in the wrong. He has, too, a sense of *want,* an insatiable desire of some good which he has never yet obtained; and when he sees multitudes around him who have found that good, where he knows it can alone exist, in the favor of God, how strong is the appeal to one of the deepest principles of our nature, especially in the case of those who are already somewhat convinced of sin, and of the unsatisfying nature of all worldly enjoyment! . . .

9. The last of these principles to which I shall advert is, *the solemnity and awe inspired by a sense of the peculiar presence of God, the sanctifying Spirit.*

The feelings of the supernatural is one of the strongest and most subduing emotions of the human heart. . . . "How dreadful is this place: it is none other than the house of God and the gate of heaven." Such is the feeling with which those who believe in the reality of Divine influence move amid the scenes which are hallowed by the especial presence of the sanctifying Spirit. In the children of God, as they are employed in bearing forward the triumphs of His grace, it awakens that mingled awe and delight which we may imagine filled the breasts of those who bore before the armies of Israel the ark of the covenant. . . . To the enemies of God it comes with a solemnity of appeal second only to that of the bed of death and the scenes of approaching judgment, as they see around them the striking manifestations of His presence who "will have mercy on whom He will have mercy, and whom He will He hardeneth." . . .

Thus have I given a brief sketch of the rise and progress of our revivals; of the mode of presenting Divine truth which has been found most effectual at such periods; and of those principles in our mental constitution which are appealed to with peculiar power by these seasons of concentrated religious interest. As the limits assigned me have already been exceeded, I must here leave the subject, commending the very imperfect exhibition which has now been made to the candor and prayers of the Christian reader.

[One chapter, "Supplementary Remarks on Revivals of Religion," followed here in the original.]

CHAPTER 54

Alleged Abuses in

Revivals of Religion

. . . No man, certainly, who is at all acquainted with human nature, should be surprised to hear that the greatest blessings bestowed on mankind are liable to be abused, and even the purest and noblest qualities to be counterfeited. When, then, is there any matter for astonishment should we find that abuses mingle with religious revivals, through man's imprudence and the malignity of the great adversary, or even should we discover some revivals which deserve to be called spurious?

. . . There are, I admit, persons among us who oppose religious revivals, and it would be sad evidence against them if there were not. There are the openly wicked, the profane, Sabbath-breakers, enemies of pure religion in every form, and avowed or secret infidels. These form the first category, and it is not a very small one. They may be found in our cities and large towns, and sometimes in our villages, and are the very persons whom strangers are most likely to meet about our hotels and taverns. Next, there are Roman Catholics, Unitarians, Universalists, and others whose Christianity is greatly marred with errors and heresies. These, too, almost without exception, hate revivals, nor can we wonder that they should. A third class consists of those members of our evangelical churches who conform too much to the opinions and practices of the world; are so much afraid of what they call enthusiasm and fanaticism as to do nothing, or nothing worthy of mention, for the promotion of the Gospel; and would never be known to be Christians, either by the world or by their fellow-Christians, were they not occasionally seen to take their places at the communion-table. Some such there are in all our evangelical churches, and in one or two of those whose discipline is more lax than it should be, they constitute a considerable party.

Now it is natural that European travelers in the United States, when not decidedly religious themselves, should chiefly associate with one or all of these three classes; and that, taking up their notions from them, they should have their note-books and journals filled with all sorts of misrepresentations with respect to our religious revivals. Hence many, who have never visited America, owe all their ideas on that subject to writers whose own information was partial and incorrect, and who, as their very books show, know nothing of true religion, and would never have touched upon the subject, but that they wished to give piquancy to their pages by working up for the wonder and amusement of their readers every false and exaggerated statement, and foolish anecdote, which had been poured into their ears.

But serious and worthy people in Europe, and particularly in Great Britain, have been prejudiced against revivals in another way. There have been excellent men among us, who, apprehending much danger to the cause of revivals from certain measures taken to promote them by zealous, but injudicious persons, and perceiving the mischievous results of such measures, have faithfully exposed them, and warned the churches to be upon their guard. . . . But, as was natural, the strong language in which they were prompted to indulge by the actual view of some evils, and the apprehension of worse, have impressed foreigners with very exaggerated ideas of those evils. This result was perhaps unavoidable, yet it is much to be deplored; for injury has thus been done to the cause abroad by men who would be the last to intend it.

It is an infelicity to which all endeavors for good are subject in this evil world, that they are liable to be marred by proffered aid from men who, notwithstanding the fairest of professions, prove, at length, to have been more actuated by their own miserable

ambition than by a true zeal for God's glory and man's salvation.
. . . Some good men, as we still consider the greater number of
them to have been, not content with the more quiet and prudent
character which had hitherto marked the revivals, attempted to
precipitate matters by measures which many worthy and experienced persons, both ministers and laymen, deemed unwise and
mischievous. The passions, instead of the judgment and the conscience, were too much appealed to; too much stress was laid on
the sinner's natural ability, and not enough on the needed influence
of the Holy Spirit; too superficial a view of the nature and evidences of conversion was presented; in a word, the Gospel was not
held forth in such a way as to lead to that self-abasement which
becomes a sinner saved wholly by grace.

One of the measures reprehended was the practice of earnestly
pressing those who were somewhat awakened to a sense of their
sin and danger, to come, at the close of the sermon, to seats
immediately before the pulpit, called "anxious seats." These were
seats provided for such as were anxious to be saved, in order that
they might be specially prayed for, and receive some special counsels. . . . It proved a poor substitute for the simpler and quieter
method of meeting such as chose to remain after the public
services, in order to receive the advice that their case might
require; or for the good old practice of holding special meetings at
the pastor's house, or in the church vestry or lecture-room, for
such as were "inquiring the way to Zion."

Another measure, hardly deserving to be called new, for it has
long existed in substance in the Presbyterian churches of the
interior, and at one time, I understand, in Scotland also—that of
having public services during three or four days on sacramental
occasions—was found hurtful, when carried to the extent encouraged by some, in the shape of what are called "protracted meetings." . . . But when prolonged, as they were in some places—I
know not how long, sometimes, I believe, for a month or forty
days—the practice was regarded as an abuse, and as such it was
resisted. . . .

But what was thought worst of all was the proposal, for it
hardly went further, of an order of "revival preachers," who
should go through the churches, spending a few weeks here and

there, for the sole object of promoting revivals. This was justly opposed as subversive of the regular ministry, for it is easy to see that such men, going about with a few well-prepared discourses on exciting topics, and recommended, perhaps, by a popular delivery, would throw the pastors in the background, give the people "itching ears," and in a few weeks do more harm than good. . . . Nothing could be more dangerous to the peace of the churches than that every man, who may fancy himself a "revivalist," or "revival preacher," should be allowed to go wherever people desire to have him, with or without the consent of their pastors. Accordingly, the institution of any such order was opposed, and the preachers who had been thus employed were urged each to settle at some one spot, which they did; and thus the churches hear little more of "revival preachers," or "revival makers," as some deserved to be called.

I have said more on this subject than I intended, but not more, perhaps, than was required. Yet, should any of my readers have been led to suppose that the abuses I have described affected our churches generally, he is mistaken. They began to manifest themselves about the year 1828, and lasted some ten years, without, however, having ever prevailed widely; and in some extensive districts they have been altogether unknown. Of the thrice ten thousand churches of all denominations among us, in which "the truth as it is in Jesus" is preached, only a few hundreds are believed to have been affected by them, and even these have now become pretty well rid both of the abuses and of their consequences. During some of the subsequent years our churches were more extensively blessed with revivals than at any time before, and all well-informed persons, whom I have consulted, agree that those blessed seasons were more free from whatever could offend a judicious Christian. For these things we are glad; they demonstrably prove that, though our sins be great, the God of our fathers has not forsaken us.

Before closing the subject of the abuses attending religious revivals, I may say something, although there be no special connection between them, about camp-meetings, respecting which I have had many questions put to me in some parts of Europe. . . .

Camp-meetings, as they are called, originated in sheer necessity among the Presbyterians of Kentucky, in the year 1801, during that great religious revival, which, after commencing in the western part of North Carolina, penetrated into Tennessee, and spread over all the parts of the West then settled. It so happened that, on one occasion, in the early part of that revival, so many people had come from a distance to the administration of the Lord's Supper at a particular church, that accommodation could nowhere be found in the neighborhood for all, during the successive days and nights which they wished to spend at the place. This induced as many as could to procure tents, and form something like a military encampment, where, as provisions were easily to be had, they might stay till the meetings closed. Such was the origin of camp-meetings. They were afterward held at various points during that extraordinary season of religious solicitude. The country was still very thinly settled, and as a proof of the deep and wide-spread feeling that prevailed on the subject of religion, many persons attended from distances of thirty, forty, and fifty miles; nay, on one occasion, some came from a distance of even one hundred miles. It is not surprising that the meetings should have lasted for several days, since many who attended them had few opportunities of frequenting public worship and of hearing the Gospel in the wilderness where they lived.

These meetings were held, when the weather permitted, in the midst of the noble forest. Seats were made of logs and planks, the under rubbish being cleared away; a pulpit was erected facing the rows of seats; and there, in the forenoon, afternoon, and evening, the ministers of the Gospel made known the "words of eternal life." Public prayer was also held at the same spot early in the morning, and at the close of the services at night. . . . A horn or trumpet announced the hour for the commencement of the public services.

. . . They were confined for years to the frontier settlements, as they ought, perhaps, always to have been, for there they were in some measure necessary. I have attended them in such circumstances, have been struck with the order that prevailed at them, and have seen them become the means of doing unquestionable good. They served to bring together, to the profit of immortal souls, a population scattered far and wide, and remaining some-times for years remote from any regular place of worship.

In the remote settlements of the Far West, the utility of camp-meetings seems to be admitted by all who know any thing about them; but in densely-settled neighborhoods, and especially near cities and large towns, whether in the West or in the East, they are apt to give rise to disorder. The idle rabble are sure to flock to them, especially on the Sabbath, and there they drink and create disturbance, not so much at the camp itself, for the police would prevent them, but at taverns and temporary booths for the sale of beer and ardent spirits in the neighborhood.

Such is the account I have to give of camp-meetings. Wicked men have sometimes taken advantage of them for their own bad purposes, and such abuses have been trumpeted through the world with the view of bringing discredit on the religion of the country. Without having ever been a great admirer of such meetings, I must say after attending several, and carefully observing the whole proceedings, that I am satisfied that the mischiefs alleged to arise from them have been greatly exaggerated, while there has been a failure to acknowledge the good that they have done.

CHAPTER 55

Concluding Remarks on the Church and the Pulpit in America

A stranger upon visiting extensively our evangelical churches of all denominations would be struck, I am sure, with the order that prevails in their public assemblies; and this applies equally to the smaller prayer-meetings to be found in every parish and congrega-tion that possesses any vitality. Foreigners who have never visited the United States, seem impressed with the idea that there is a great deal of disorder and lawlessness in that country, and they infer that there must be no less insubordination in the religious commonwealth than they ascribe to the civil. But both opinions are totally unfounded. It does not follow, because of a few disgraceful disturbances, arising from the opposition made in some places to abolitionists, and the resentment of an exasperated populace against gangs of gamblers in others, that the whole country is a scene of continual commotion. In no part of the world have there been so few dreadful riots, attended with loss of life, as in the United States, during these last sixty years. There are bad men among us, and there are crimes, but, after all, life is quite as safe among us as in any country I have ever visited.

As for the Church, a regard for law and order reigns to a degree not surpassed in any other country. There is no confusion of the respective rights of the ministry and people. The duties of both are well understood everywhere. . . . No one ever hears of unauthorized, unlicensed persons being allowed to speak in our meetings for public worship. Those leveling doctrines, now spreading in other countries—doctrines which would reduce the ministry to nothing, and encourage "lay-brethren" to take it upon them to preach or teach in the churches—will, I dare affirm, make small progress among us. Attempts to introduce something of this sort have often been made, but in vain. We have, indeed, our meetings in which debate is allowed, and there the laity may even take the lead, but these meetings relate to the temporal affairs of the church, or the calling of a pastor, not the public worship of God.

One of the most important and difficult duties of a minister in a revival is rightly to direct awakened souls. Alas! how often are even good men found to fail in this. Many, whom I have known, seem to me to excel in addressing unawakened sinners, and yet to fail when called to give clear, intelligible, and Scriptural directions to those who are awakened. Many, too, fail in judging of the evidences of conversion, and "heal the hurt of the people softly."

But on no point, I am convinced, from what I have seen in America, is there a greater call for the exercise of a sound prudence, than in receiving into the Church persons who entertain the belief that they have "passed from death unto life." While they may possibly be kept back too long, the great error lies on the other side. The new convert naturally desires to join himself to those whom he now considers to be the children of God. He thinks it his duty to do so, and he may be right. But the office-bearers in the Church, whose duty it is to see that none but proper persons be admitted, are no less clearly bound to a careful ascertaining of the fact, that the candidate for membership gives such evidences of piety as, on Scriptural grounds, shall be deemed satisfactory.

I consider hasty admission to our churches the greatest of all evils connected with revivals in some parts of the country, and among some denominations in particular. But this evil is not peculiar to revivals. It is quite as likely to occur when there is no revival. With all possible care it is difficult to keep a church pure. Experience shows the necessity of decided views on this subject, and of firmness in enforcing it. On this point, as well as on all others relating to the discipline and government of the Church, too much care can not be taken to avoid latitudinarian practices. The Church must be kept a living body of believers—a company of persons who have come out from the world, and are determined to adorn the profession which they have made. In their organization and action, order, which is said to be "heaven's first law," must be maintained. In this opinion, I am sure, Christians of all denominations in the United States sincerely and entirely concur.

BOOK VI

The Evangelical Churches in America

Preliminary Remarks in Reference

to This Subject

This part of our work we propose to devote to a brief notice of the doctrines, organization, and history of each of the evangelical denominations in the United States; nothing beyond a sketch of these being consistent with our limits. . . .

Numerous as are the evangelical denominations in the United States, yet when grouped in reference to doctrine on the one hand, or church government on the other, it is surprising into how small a number they may be reduced. In doctrine we have but two great divisions—the Calvinistic and the Arminian schools; the former, with its various peculiarities, comprehending the Presbyterian, usually so called, the evangelical Baptists, the Episcopalians (though they generally consider themselves intermediate between the two), the Congregationalists, the German Reformed, the Dutch Reformed, the Covenanters, the Associate and the Associate

Reformed Churches; the latter, with its variations, comprehending the Methodists of all branches, the Lutherans, the Cumberland Presbyterians, the United Brethren or Moravians, and some other small bodies.

Considered in reference to their forms of church government, they all arrange themselves in three great families. The *Episcopal,* comprehending the Protestant Episcopal Church, the Methodist Episcopal, and the Moravians; the *Presbyterian,* including the Presbyterians, usually so called, the Dutch Reformed, the German Reformed, the Lutherans, the Cumberland Presbyterians, the Protestant Methodists, the Covenanters, the Associate, and the Associate Reformed; the *Congregational* (or Independent, as it is more commonly called in England), embracing the Congregationalists and the Baptists.

But when viewed in relation to the great doctrines which are universally conceded by Protestants to be fundamental and necessary to salvation, then they all form but one body, recognizing Christ as their common Head. Then they resemble the different parts of a great temple, all constituting but one whole; or the various corps of an army, which, though ranged in various divisions, each having an organization perfect in itself, yet compose but one great host, and are under the command of one Chief.

This suggests the observation that on no one point are all these Churches more completely united, or more firmly established, than on the doctrine of the supremacy of Christ in His Church, and the unlawfulness of any interference with its doctrine, discipline, and government, on the part of the civil magistrate. There is not a single evangelical church in the United States that does not assert and maintain this glorious doctrine of the sovereignty of Christ and His Church, and that from Him alone comes all just and lawful authority in the same. . . .

CHAPTER 57

The Protestant Episcopal Church

The Protestant Episcopal Church in the United States derives its origin from the Church of England, of which it is not only an offshoot, but to which it is "indebted under God, for a long continuance of nursing care and protection."* It agrees with that Church in doctrine; and its ritual and formularies, with some variations introduced after the Revolution by which the Colonies became independent States, are the same. Unlike the mother Church, however, it is in no way connected with the State, nor do its bishops, in virtue of their office, enjoy any civil powers, immunities, or emoluments.

The chief particulars in which the Service-Book differs from that of the Church of England are as follows: 1. A shorter form of absolution is allowed to be used instead of the English, which is, however, retained, and frequently used in the public service. 2. The Athanasian creed is omitted. 3. In the administration of baptism, the sign of the cross may be dispensed with, if requested. 4. The marriage-service has been considerably abridged. 5. In the funeral-service, some expressions, considered as liable to misconstruction, have been altered or omitted. 6. There has been a change, of course, in the prayers for rulers. 7. It is allowed to omit in the communion-service the prayer called the "Oblation," and the Invocation. 8. It is permitted to change the words, "He descended into hell," which occur in the Apostles' Creed, into "He descended into the world of departed spirits," or words equivalent. The other modifications, being of less importance and chiefly verbal, need not be specified.

As in the parent Church in England, there are three ranks or

---

* Preface to the American Book of Common Prayer.

orders in the ministry, and these are believed, by its friends, to be of apostolical institution, viz., bishops, priests, and deacons. The churches choose their own pastors, but their installation, or induction, requires the consent of the bishop of the diocese. The regulation of the temporal affairs of each church is confided to a board of church-wardens, and vestry, the former of which are chosen by the communicants, the latter by the members of the parish generally. The spiritual rule rests mainly with the pastor, or rector, as he is more commonly called.

The increase and wide diffusion of the Episcopal Church in the United States has led to the determination that each State shall constitute a diocese, except when its extent, and the number of churches in it, may require its being divided, like that of New York, into two dioceses. In some instances, however, as in Virginia, where the State is extensive, and the churches not very numerous, and especially where the principal or senior bishop does not enjoy good health, an assistant bishop has been appointed.

The Episcopal was the first Protestant Church planted on the American Continent, and the reader has seen how it was the favored Church in Virginia from the earliest settlement of that State until the Revolution; how, also, it came to be established in the colonies of Maryland, New York, and the Carolinas. But, notwithstanding all the aid which it received from the civil government, its prosperity was far from commensurate with these external advantages. When the Revolution commenced, it had not more than eighty ministers in the colonies north and east of Maryland, and even these, with the exception of such as were settled in Philadelphia, New York, Newport, Boston, and a few other of the most important cities and towns, were supported by the "Society for the Propagation of the Gospel in Foreign Parts"; while in the colonies south of Virginia, viz., the Carolinas and Georgia, all the clergy taken together were but few. The number in Virginia and Maryland, amounting to about 150, greatly exceeded that of all other colonies.

The causes of this ill success during the colonial era lay, as we have stated, in the entire dependence of the Church upon England for Episcopal supervision, and, in a great degree, for a supply of ministers; in the unfitness of many that were sent over by the Bishop of London, to whose diocese the Episcopal churches in America were then attached; and the great difficulties attending the raising up of a native clergy, and sending them to England for consecration, though this had been done to a very great extent in the colony of Connecticut—and it was in that colony that the Episcopal Church had made by far the greatest advance. We have also seen how disastrous was the Revolution, with the changes it effected on the Episcopal Church in all the colonies, and particularly in Virginia, and that it was many years before it could rise from the prostration in which the return of peace in 1783 found it.

One of the first measures after that event was the formation of an ecclesiastical constitution, by a special convention of the clergy from several of the States, held in Philadelphia in 1785, for the purpose of uniting all the Episcopal churches in one body. . . . The Rev. Drs. [William] White and [Samuel] Provoost, the former of Philadelphia, and the latter of New York, were thereupon sent over to England, and received ordination to the Episcopal office from the hands of the Archbishop of Centerbury and the Archbishop of York, the Bishops of Bath and Wells, and of Peterborough assisting. Upon their return to America, Bishops White and Provoost entered upon the discharge of their Episcopal duties in their respective dioceses.

A short time before the consecration of Bishops White and Provoost, the Rev. Samuel Seabury, D.D., had gone over to England for consecration to the Episcopal office. But having abandoned all hope of success from that quarter, he went to Scotland, and was consecrated by three of the non-juring bishops of that kingdom. Upon his return he became Bishop of Connecticut. . . .

About that epoch this Church may be said to have passed its apogee of depression, occasioned by the Revolution and its effects. Its subsequent history has been marked by an ever-increasing prosperity. I have not the means of knowing what was the precise number of its clergy in 1792, but I am sure that it could not have exceeded two hundred, and its bishops were four in number. Just forty years later, in 1832, according to the Journal of the General Convention held in New York in October of that year, the number of the bishops had increased to fifteen, and that of the clergy to 583. In 1855, we find the number of bishops augmented to thirty-eight, the clergy to 1,714, while the communicants were reported to be 105,350.

Nor has the spiritual prosperity of this church been less remarkable than its external growth. It possesses a degree of life and energy throughout all its extent, and an amount of vital piety in its ministers and members, such as it never had in its colonial days. It is blessed with precious revivals, and flourishes like a tree planted by the rivers of water. And in no portions of the country does it possess more spiritual health than in the States of Virginia and Maryland, where, in the ante-revolutionary era, it was in a deplorable state as regards piety, both in its ministry and its laity. Happier days have dawned upon it in those States, and, indeed, everywhere else.

The clergy of the Episcopal Church in America, like those of the Established Church in England, are divided into two parties, the one termed "High Church" and the other "Low." Sometimes these parties are called "evangelical" and "non-evangelical," but not with accuracy, for not a few of the high-churchmen, that is, men charged with carrying their preference for Episcopacy to an extravagant length, are entirely evangelical in their doctrines and preaching. But a part of these high-churchmen are not considered evangelical—not so much because of what they do preach, as because of what they do not preach. Their sermons are of too negative a character; an efficacy unknown to the Scriptures is ascribed to ceremonies and forms; neither are the sinner's guilt and danger as fully and earnestly set forth as they should be, nor is the glorious sufficiency of Christ unfolded, and salvation by faith alone fully and clearly presented. Their preaching, consequently, does not reach the hearts of their hearers as does that of their evangelical brethren, nor does it lead the members of their churches to renounce the "world, its pomps and vanities," to as great an extent as they should. Yet they are not to be classed with the fox-hunting, theatre-going, ball-frequenting, and card-playing clergy of some other countries. They are an infinitely better class of men and ministers.

I know not the comparative numbers of the evangelical and non-evangelical clergy, but infer, from the statements of some well-informed ministers of that Church, that they are in the proportion of about two thirds of the former to one third of the latter. Of the thirty-eight bishops, more than half are considered, I believe, entirely evangelical. But all are laboriously occupied in their official work; and I believe it would be difficult to find an Episcopal body of equal number, in any other country, surpassing them in talents, zeal, and piety. To be a bishop with us is quite a different thing from holding that office where bishops live in palaces and have princely revenues. Our bishops are frequently parish priests also, and can find time to visit their diocese only by employing an assistant preacher, or rector, to fill their places when they are engaged in their visitations. Their revenues do not much exceed, in some instances do not equal, those of many of their clergy.

As for the Puseyite or Tractarian doctrines, or whatever they may be called, *three,* or perhaps *four,* of the high-church bishops are supposed to have embraced them, or at least to be favorable to them, as understood in America. But there is *not one* who adopts the extreme views put forth of late years by some advocates of this party in England, and but one who has ever declined the name of Protestant.* Among the inferior clergy it has been feared that these sentiments have made considerable progress; but those whose situation enables them to judge with a good deal of accuracy, say that this progress is much smaller than has been supposed. Among the laity there is scarcely any sympathy with these semi-popish doctrines, and I can not believe that they will make much advance in the country at large. . . .

---

* Ed.—While this individual is never named in the text, it is possible this is a reference to John Henry Hobart (1775–1830), bishop of the diocese of New York after 1815. As a leader of the High Church party, Hobart criticized the leveling tendencies in American Protestantism and tried to prevent co-operation with the voluntary societies which Baird extols in the essay on the voluntary principle. For further information, see H. S. Smith, R. T. Handy, and L. A. Loetscher (eds.), *American Christianity, An Historical Interpretation with Representative Documents* (New York: Charles Scribner's Sons, 1963), vol. II, pp. 70, 74–79.

CHAPTER 58

The Congregational Churches

The faith of the Congregational churches of America is common to the evangelical churches of both hemispheres, but their organization and discipline are, to a considerable extent, peculiar to themselves. . . .

New England is the principal seat of the Congregational churches in America. This is the region which the Puritans planted in the first half of the seventeenth century; and here they have left upon the structure and institutions of society, and upon the opinions and manners of the people, the deepest impression of their peculiar character. In all these States, with the exception of Rhode Island, the Congregationalists are more numerous than any other sect, and in Massachusetts and Connecticut they are probably more numerous than all the others united.

Out of New England the Congregationalists have not until lately been zealous to propagate their own peculiar forms and institutions. Of the vast multitudes of emigrants from New England into other States, the great majority have chosen to unite with churches of the Presbyterian connection, rather than to maintain their own peculiarities at the expense of increased division in the household of faith. In so doing, they have followed the advice and fallen in with the arrangements of the associated bodies of Congregational pastors in New England. Yet in the States of New York, Ohio, Michigan, Illinois, Wisconsin, Iowa, and California, many congregations retain the forms of administration which have descended to them from the New England fathers, and do not come into connection with any of the Presbyterian judicatories. Since the division in the Presbyterian Church in 1838, the number of such congregations is increasing.

The whole number of Congregational churches in the United

States is probably not far from 2,450, of which more than 1,200 are in New England. The number of ministers is 2,327, of whom 1,848 are pastors, and the members or communicants may be stated at 210,000. This estimate does not include those churches originally or nominally Congregational, which have rejected what are called the doctrines of the Reformation. These churches are better known by their distinctive title, Unitarian. The churches of this description are nearly all in Massachusetts; a few are in Maine, two or three in New Hampshire, one or more in Vermont, as many in Rhode Island, and one, in a state of suspended animation, in Connecticut. Out of New England there are perhaps fifteen to twenty churches of the same kind, differing very little in their principles, or in their forms, from the Unitarians of England.

The Congregationalists differ from most other communions, in that they have no common authoritative standards of faith and order, other than the Holy Scriptures. Yet their system is well known among themselves, and from the beginning they have spared no reasonable pains to make it known to others. . . .

The following outline, it is believed, will give the reader some idea of the system of New England Congregationalism as it is at this day:

1. The Congregational system recognizes no church as an organized body politic other than a congregation of believers statedly assembling for worship and religious communion. It falls back upon the original meaning of the Greek word ἐκκλησία, and of the Latin *cœtus*.

Popery claims that all Christians constitute one visible, organized body, having its officers, its centre, and its head on earth. The first Reformers seem to have supposed that each national church has its own independent existence, and is to be considered as *one* organic body, which has somewhere within itself, in the clergy, or in the people, or in the civil government of the nation, a power to regulate and govern all the parts. Congregationalism rejects both the Universal Church of the Papists, and the National Churches which the Reformation established in England, in Scotland, in certain States of Germany and Switzerland, and attempted to establish in France.

Hence the name *Congregational*. Each congregation of believers is a church; and exists not as a subordinate part, or as under the sovereignty of a National Church, nor as a part, or under the sovereignty of an organized Universal Church, but substantively and independently.

2. A church exists by the consent, expressed or implied, of its members to walk together in obedience to the principles of the Gospel, and the institutions of Christ. In other words, a church does not derive its existence and rights from some charter conceded to it by another church, or by some higher ecclesiastical judicatory. When any competent number of believers meet together in the name of Christ, and agree, either expressly or by some implication, to commune together stately in Christian worship, and in the observance of Christ's ordinances, and to perform toward one another the mutual duties of such Christian fellowship, Christ himself is present with them (Matt., xviii, 20), and they receive from Him all the powers and privileges which belong to a church of Christ.

3. The officers of a church are of two sorts—*elders* and *deacons*. When the Congregational churches of New England were first organized, two centuries ago, the plan was that each church should have two or more elders—one a pastor—another charged with similar duties under the title of a teacher—the third ordained to his office like the other two, a ruling elder, who, with his colleagues, presided over the discipline and order of the church, but took no part in the official authoritative preaching of the Word, or in the administration of Baptism and the Lord's Supper. Thus it was intended that each church should have within itself a presbytery, or clerical body, perpetuating itself by the ordination of those who should be elected to fill successive vacancies. This plan, however, soon fell into disuse; and now, except in the rare cases of colleagues in office, all the powers and duties of the eldership devolve upon one whose ordinary official title is *pastor*. The office of deacons, of whom there are from two to six in each church, is to serve at the Lord's Table, and to receive, keep, and apply the contributions which the church makes at each communion for the

expenses of the Table, and for the poor among its own members. . . .

4. Admission to membership in the church takes place as follows: The person desiring to unite himself with the church makes known his wishes to the pastor. The pastor (or in some churches the pastor and deacons, and in others, the pastor and a committee appointed for the purpose), having conversed with the candidate, and obtained by conversation and inquiry satisfactory evidence of that spiritual renovation, that inward living piety which is regarded as the condition of membership, he is publicly proposed in the congregation, on the Lord's Day, as a candidate; so that if there be any objection in any quarter, it may be seasonably made known. At the end of a week, or more, according to the particular rule of the church, a vote of the "brotherhood" (or male members) is taken on the question, "Shall this person be admitted to membership in the church?" After this, the candidate appears before the congregation, and gives his assent to a formal profession of the Christian faith read to him by the pastor, and to form a covenant, by which he engages to give himself up to God as a child and servant, and to Christ as a redeemed sinner, and binds himself to the church conscientiously to perform all the duties of Christian communion and brotherhood.

5. The censures of the church are pronounced by the pastor in accordance with a previous vote or determination of the brotherhood. The directions given by Christ in regard to the treatment of an offending brother (Matt. xviii. 15–17) are, in most churches, literally and directly adhered to in all cases. . . . If [the offender] refuses to hear the church, that is, if the admonition, after due forbearance, is unsuccessful, the brethren, by a vote, exclude him from their fellowship, and the pastor, as Christ's minister, pronounces a public sentence of excommunication.

6. The arrangements among the Congregationalists of New England for the support of public worship are in some points peculiar. The *church,* of which we have thus far spoken exclusively, is entirely a spiritual association. But it exists in an amicable connection with a civil corporation called the *parish,* or the *ecclesiastical society,* which includes the congregation at large,

or, more accurately, those adult members of the congregation who consent to be a civil society for the support of public worship. This civil corporation is the proprietor of the house of worship, of the parsonage, if there be one, and sometimes of other endowments, consisting of gifts and legacies which have from time to time been made for the uses for which the society exists. . . . It enters into a civil contract with the pastor, and becomes bound in law to render him for his services such compensation as is agreed upon between him and them.

. . . The church, then, is designed to be a purely spiritual body. The society is a secular body. The church consists only of such as profess to have some experience of spiritual religion. The society consists of all who are willing to unite in the support of public worship—it being understood only, that no person can thrust himself into its ranks, and obtain a voice in the administration of its affairs, without the express or implied consent of those who are already members. The church watches over the deportment of its members, they being all bound to help each other in the duties of the Christian life; and on proper occasions it censures or absolves from censure those under its care. The society has nothing to do with church censures. To the church belong the ordinances of Baptism and the Lord's Supper. . . .

The great advantage of this part of the system is, that it gives to every member of the congregation an interest in its prosperity, and a voice in the management of its affairs, while at the same time it gives to the church every desirable facility for keeping itself pure in doctrine and practice. There is nothing to secularize the church; no temptation to admit irreligious or unconverted men as members for the sake of causing them to take an interest in the support of public worship; and no temptation inducing such men to seek admission to the church. The pastor and the place of worship are as much theirs as if they were communicants.

7. The pastors of neighboring churches form themselves into bodies for mutual advice and aid in the work of the ministry. This body is called an association. It has its stated meetings at the house of each member in rotation. At every meeting each member is called upon to report the state of his own flock, and to propose any question on which he may desire counsel from his

brethren. In these meetings every question which relates to the work of the ministry, or the interest of the churches, is freely discussed. The associations of each State meet annually by their delegates in a General Association.

But the most important part of the duties of the association is to examine those who desire to be introduced to the work of the ministry. This is on the principle that, as lawyers are to determine who shall be admitted to practice at the bar, and physicians determine who shall be received into the ranks of their profession, so ministers are the fittest judges for the qualifications of candidates for the ministry. The candidate, therefore, who has passed through the usual course of studies, liberal* and theological, can not begin to preach—will not be recognized by any church as a candidate— till he has received from some association a certificate of approbation, recommending him to the churches, which is his license to preach the Gospel on trial. Such a certificate is not granted without a close examination, particularly in respect to his piety, soundness in the faith, and acquaintance with the system of Christian doctrines.

8. The fathers of the New England churches seem to have acknowledged no minister of the Gospel other than the pastor or teacher of some particular church. In their zeal against a hierarchy, they found no place for any minister of Christ not elected by some organized assembly of believers to the work of ruling and teaching in that congregation. The evangelist was thought by them to be, like the apostle, only for the primitive age of Christianity. Accordingly, the pastor, when dismissed from his pastoral charge, was no longer a minister of Christ, or competent to perform anywhere any function of the ministry. . . . But these views were very early superseded. The distinction is now recognized between a minister of the Gospel having a pastoral charge, and a minister who sustains no office in any church. . . .

Ministers, therefore, whether pastors or evangelists, are now ordained only by the laying on of the hands of those who are before them in the ministry; for though it belongs to the church to make a pastor, it belongs to ministers to make a minister.

---

* By the word "liberal," as applied to education, is meant that which is obtained in making the curriculum of a college. It is synonymous with "classical."

9. The reader has already learned that the American Congregational churches disavow the name *Independent*. From the beginning they have held and practiced the communion of churches. Continually, and by various acts of affection and intercourse, they recognize each other as churches of Christ, as bound to render to each other, on all proper occasions, an account of their doings. They receive each other's members to occasional communion in ordinances. Members of one church, removing their residence to another church, take from the one a letter of dismission and recommendation, and without that, are not received to membership in the other. The principle that, in matters which concern not one church alone, but all the churches of the vicinity, no one church ought to act alone, is continually regarded in practice.

Under this ecclesiastical system the churches of New England have, it is believed by many, enjoyed for two centuries and a quarter, a more continued purity of doctrine, and fidelity of discipline, and a more constant prosperity of the spiritual religion, than has been enjoyed by any other equal body of churches, for so long a time, since the days of the Apostles. No religious communion in America has done more for religion and morals among its own people, more for the advancement of learning and general education, or more for the diffusion of the Gospel at home and abroad. None has been more characterized by that large and manly spirit which values the common Christianity of all who "hold the Head," more than the peculiar forms and institutions of its own sect. . . .

CHAPTER 59

The Regular Baptist Churches

Next to the Episcopalians and the Congregationalists, the Baptists are the oldest of the various branches of the Christian Church in the United States. And if we were to include under this name all who hold that immersion is the true and only Scriptural mode of baptism, without reference to the orthodoxy of their faith, we should probably find that they are also the largest denomination in this country. But if we separate from them a portion at least of those minor bodies which, though agreeing with them on that point, differ from them on important, and, in some cases, fundamental doctrines, we shall find that they are not equal in number to the Methodists.

In their church government the Baptists of all denominations are Independents, that is, each church is wholly independent, as respects its interior government, even of those other churches with which it may be associated in ecclesiastical union. Each separate church possesses and exercises the right of licensing or granting permission to preach the Gospel, and of ordaining elders or presbyters clothed with all the functions of the ministerial office. This is the old ground at first maintained by the Independents. The Congregationalists, spoken of in the last chapter, seem to be Independents in theory, but in spirit and practice they are very nearly Presbyterians, and have often been called "Congregational Presbyterians."

Delegates from different Baptist churches hold public meetings for purposes of mutual counsel and improvement, but not for the general government of the whole body, all right of interference in the concerns of individual churches being disclaimed by these ecclesiastical assemblies. A very large majority of our evangelical Baptist churches are associated by their pastors in District Associations and State Conventions, which meet every year for promoting missions, education, and other benevolent objects. A general convention, called the "Baptist General Convention" of the United States, formerly existed and met every three years, the last always appointing the place of meeting for the next after. The General Convention was restricted by its constitution to the promotion of foreign missions. It held its first meeting in 1814. But there are now two General Conventions, one in the North, and the other in the South. Within the last ten years, a Home Missionary Society, a General Tract Society, a Bible Society, and several societies for the education of poor and pious youths having talents adapted for the ministry, have sprung up in each of the two great branches of the Baptist body, and already exert a wide and happy influence.

The Baptists, like the Congregationalists, make it a fundamental principle to adopt the Bible as their only confession of faith. Yet most, if not all, of the evangelical churches that bear the name, find it convenient in practice to have a creed or summary of doctrine, and these creeds, although they may vary in expression, all agree in the main, and, with few exceptions, among the Regular and Associated Baptists are decidedly Calvinistic.

The Baptist churches have increased in the United States with great rapidity, particularly within the last fifty or sixty years. For although they commenced their existence in the days of Roger Williams,* . . . who, having changed his sentiments on the subject of Baptism a few years after his arrival in Massachusetts Bay, was the first Baptist preacher, and founded the first Baptist church in America, at Providence, in 1639; it was long before this denomination made much progress beyond Rhode Island. This arose, it would appear, from their being violently opposed in most of the other colonies, both in the North and in the South. In Massachusetts they were at first "fined," "whipped," and "imprisoned." And though they afterward obtained liberty of worship there, they had but eighteen churches at the commencement of the Revolutionary war. In Virginia, where they also met with much opposition and bitter persecution, they had scarcely, at that epoch, obtained any footing at all. In fact, with the exception of Rhode Island, Pennsylvania, and Delaware, they almost nowhere enjoyed perfect freedom from molestation, until the country had achieved its independence by a struggle in which the Baptists took, to say the least, in proportion to their numbers, as prominent a part as any other religious body in the land.

But slow as was their progress before the Revolution, it has been much otherwise since. . . .

Above 4,500,000 souls, being between a fifth and a sixth of the entire population of the United States, and embracing a respectable share of the wealth, talent, learning, and influence of the country, are supposed to be connected with the Regular Baptists.

---

* The reader must not infer, from what is stated above, that Roger Williams is to be considered as the founder of the Baptist Church in America. His influence was mainly confined to Rhode Island. The greater part of the Baptist churches with us owe their origin to the labors of Baptist ministers who came such directly from England.

This estimate is probably too high. It would be true of the entire body of Baptists. A large and important part of their churches lies in the Southern States, and includes many slaves and slave-owners. With the exception of the Methodists, they form by far the most numerous and influential body of Christians in that section of the country.

A strong prejudice against learning in the ministry unhappily prevailed at one time in this body, particularly in the Southern States, and this we might ascribe to several causes. In the religious denomination, which in Virginia, and the other Southern colonies, they considered their greatest enemy, learning was too often associated with want of piety, and sometimes with open irreligion. The effects of this prejudice have been very injurious, and are felt to this day in the Baptist churches throughout the Southern and South-western, and to a considerable extent even in the Middle States. But a brighter day has dawned. Great efforts have been made by zealous and devoted men among them to establish colleges and theological seminaries. . . .

. . . although not a third, perhaps, of the ministers of this denomination of Christians have been educated at colleges and theological seminaries, it comprehends, nevertheless, a body of men who, in point of talent, learning, and eloquence, as well as devoted piety, have no superiors in the country. And even among those who can make no pretensions to profound learning, not a few are men of respectable general attainments, and much efficiency in their Master's work. . . .

CHAPTER 60

The Presbyterian Church

In speaking of the Congregational Churches, we entered into a full analysis of their organization, because they comprise most of the great features of all the churches founded on what are called Independent principles, forming the basis of the churches of several other denominations, particularly the Baptists. For a like reason, in speaking of the Presbyterian Church, we shall go into considerable detail in regard to its principles and church organization, so as to save repetition when we come to notice other churches having the same principles and essentially the same organization.

The Presbyterian Church is so called because it is governed by presbyters, and not by prelates. The name, therefore, applies to any church organized and governed on that principle. Usage, however, has confined it in America to one of several Churches, which agree in believing that the government of the Church belongs to its elders or presbyters. The Dutch Reformed Church, the German Reformed, and the Scotch Secession Churches, are as truly Presbyterian as that denomination to which the name is now, among us, almost exclusively applied.

Presbyterians believe that the apostles, in organizing the Church, were accustomed, in every city or place where a congregation was gathered, to appoint a number of officers for the instruction and spiritual government of the people, and for the care of the sick and poor. The former class of these officers were called presbyters, the latter deacons. Of these presbyters, some labored in word and doctrine, others in the oversight and discipline of the flock, according to their gifts, or to their designation when ordained. As the terms bishop and presbyter were indiscriminately used to designate the spiritual instructors and governors of the congregation, in every church there came to be three classes of officers, who are denominated the bishops or pastors, or teaching presbyters, the ruling presbyters, and the deacons.

The Presbyterian Churches with us are organized on this plan. Each congregation has its bishop or pastor, its ruling elders, and its deacons, except in cases where the duties of the last-mentioned class are assumed by the elders. The duty of the pastor is to preach the word, to administer the sacraments, to superintend the religious instruction of the young, and to have the general oversight of his flock as to their spiritual concerns. He is always chosen by the people over whom he is to exercise his office. . . .

. . . no man can become a pastor of a congregation under the care of a Presbytery, whom that body does not deem to be a sound and competent minister of the Gospel. And in order to enable them to judge intelligently on this point, before proceeding to his ordination they examine him "as to his acquaintance with experimental religion, as to his knowledge of philosophy, theology, ecclesiastical history, the Greek and Hebrew languages, and such other branches of learning as to the Presbytery may appear requisite, and as to his knowledge of the constitution, the rules, and discipline of the church." Should the candidate be found deficient in any of these particulars, it is the right and duty of the Presbytery to reject him. But if they are satisfied with his ministeral qualifications, they appoint a time for his ordination in the presence of the people. . . .

The elders are regarded as the representatives of the people, and are chosen by them for the discipline of the church in connection with the pastor. They must be male members of the church in full communion, and, when elected, are required to profess their faith in the Scriptures as the only infallible rule of faith and practice, their adoption of the Westminster Confession as containing the system of doctrine, and their approbation of the government and discipline of the Presbyterian Church; and the members of the church are called upon publicly to acknowledge and receive them as ruling elders, and to promise to yield them all that honor, encouragement, and obedience in the Lord, to which their office, according to the Word of God and the constitution of the Church, entitles them. The pastor and elders constitute what is called the Session, which is the governing body in each congregation. They are authorized to inquire into the knowledge and Christian conduct of the members of the church; to admit to the sacraments those whom, upon examination, they find to possess the requisite knowledge and piety; to call before them offenders, being members of their own church; to decide cases of discipline; and to suspend or excommunicate those who are judged deserving of such censure. It is their duty, also, to keep a register of marriages, of baptisms, of those admitted to the Lord's Supper, and of the death or removal of church members.

The deacons are not members of the Session, and, consequently, have no part in the government of the church. It is their duty to take charge of the poor, to receive and appropriate the moneys collected for the support or relief of the sick or needy.

A Presbyterian church, or congregation has thus a complete organization within itself, but it is not an independent body. It is part of an extended whole, living under the same ecclesiastical constitution, and, therefore, subject to the inspection and control of the Presbytery, whose business it is to see that the standards of doctrine and rules of discipline are adhered to by all the separate churches under its care.

This superior body, the Presbytery, consists of all the pastors, or ordained ministers, and one elder from each Session, within certain geographical limits. There must be at least three ministers to constitute a Presbytery, but the maximum is not fixed. Hence our Presbyteries vary from three to fifty or sixty members. It is the bond of union between the ministers and churches within its limits. Among its most important duties is the examination and ordination of candidates for the holy ministry. Every such candidate is required to place himself under the care of that Presbytery within whose bounds he ordinarily resides. . . .

It is by means of . . . examinations, and by requiring assent to the Confession of Faith, that the Presbyterian Church in America has endeavored to secure competent learning and orthodoxy in its ministry; and it is an historical fact, which ought to be gratefully acknowledged, that since the organization of the Church in this country, more than a century and a half ago, the great body of its ministers have been liberally educated men; and it is also a fact that no man who has avowedly rejected the Calvinistic system of doctrine, has been allowed to retain his standing as a minister of that Church. Its history contains not the record of even one Arminian or Pelagian, much less Socinian, as an approved or recognized minister in its connection. Some few instances have occurred of the avowal of such sentiments, but they have uniformly been followed by the ejection from the ministry of those who entertained them. And more recently, the promulgation by a part of its ministers of doctrines supposed to be at variance with its standards, though those doctrines were not considered by their advocates as involving a rejection of the Calvinistic system, was one of the principal causes of the separation of the body into two distinct organizations. . . .

With the Presbytery the organization of a Presbyterian Church is complete. So long as the number of ministers and churches is so small that they can conveniently meet at the same time and place, there is no need of any superior body. The formation of Synods and a General Assembly becomes necessary only when the Church is too large to be comprised under one Presbytery. . . . Under the present system, the Synod is a body that intervenes between the Presbytery and General Assembly. It has power to receive and determine all appeals regularly brought up from the Presbyteries; to decide all references made to them; to review the records of Presbyteries, and to approve or censure them; to redress whatever has been done by the Presbyteries contrary to order; to take effectual care that Presbyteries observe the Constitution of the Church; to erect new Presbyteries, and unite or divide those which were before erected; and, generally, to take such order with respect to the Presbyteries, Sessions, and people under their care, as may be in conformity with the Word of God and the established rules, and which tend to promote the edification of the Church; and, finally, to propose to the General Assembly, for its adoption, such measures as may be of common advantage to the whole Church.

The General Assembly is the highest judicatory of the Presbyterian Church, and the bond of union between its several parts. It is composed of an equal delegation of ministers and elders from each Presbytery. Every Presbytery sends at least one minister and one elder; if it consists of more than twenty-four members, it sends two ministers and two elders, and so on in like proportion.

The Assembly has power to determine all appeals and references regularly brought before it from inferior judicatories; to review the records of the several Synods; to give its advice and instructions in all cases submitted to it; and constitutes the bond of union, peace, correspondence, and mutual confidence among all the churches under its care. To it also belongs to decide all controversies respecting doctrines and discipline; to reprove, warn, or bear testimony against error in doctrine or immorality in practice; to erect new Synods; to superintend the whole church; to correspond with Foreign Churches; to suppress schismatical contentions and disputations; and, in general, to recommend and attempt reformation of manners, and the promotion of charity, truth, and holiness through all the churches under its care. . . .

Having given this brief exhibition of the principles of church government adopted by Presbyterians in the United States, it is necessary to advert to their doctrinal standards. The Confession of Faith and the Larger and Shorter Catechisms, prepared by the Assembly of Divines at Westminster, were, as is well known, adopted by the Church of Scotland, and the same symbols have from the beginning constituted the creed of the Presbyterian Church in this country. . . .

When the General Assembly was formed in 1787, the Confession of Faith and Catechisms were revised, and those parts which relate to the power of the magistrates modified, and ever since it has without alteration been the standard of doctrine in the Presbyterian Church, and every minister, as already stated, is required at his ordination to declare that he "sincerely receives and adopts the Confession of Faith of this Church as containing the system of doctrines in the Holy Scriptures."

. . . The first Presbytery, consisting of seven ministers, and representing about the same number of churches, was organized in Philadelphia in 1705. In 1855, the number of ministers in the two great bodies into which the Presbyterian Church in the United States was divided in 1838, was 3,828, and that of the churches 4,738. This extraordinary increase can only be explained by a reference to the settlement of the country. The New England States were settled by English Puritans, many of whom, especially those who arrived about the commencement of the Civil War in England, as well as those who came after the Restoration, were Presbyterians. New York was settled by the Dutch, who were also Presbyterians; but these classes have retained their own separate ecclesiastical organizations, though both have contributed largely to the increase of the Presbyterian Church. The Germans, also, who settled in great numbers in Pennsylvania, and in the northern portions of Virginia, have in like manner formed extended

Churches of their own; yet they also have, in many cases, contributed to swell the number of American Presbyterians. The French emigrants, who came to this country toward the close of the seventeenth century, were almost all Protestants and Presbyterians. These are the collateral sources whence the Presbyterian Church in America derived the materials of its growth. From the beginning of the last century to the Declaration of Independence, there was a constant current of emigration of Presbyterians from Scotland, and still more from the north of Ireland. These emigrants settled principally in New Jersey, Pennsylvania, in the central portions of Virginia, and in North and South Carolina. Since the commencement of the present century, the same process has been going on. The central and western portions of the State of New York, fifty years ago, were a wilderness; that region has now a population of more than 1,500,000 people of European descent. The Western States in the Valley of the Mississippi, then in the almost exclusive possession of the Indians, have now a population of more than twelve millions. The progress of the Presbyterian Church, therefore, although rapid, has not been out of proportion to the progress of the country. On the contrary, the widely-extended denominations of the Methodists and Baptists are, to a great extent, composed of persons whose ancestors belonged to Presbyterian churches.

. . . There is still one general subject which should not be passed over: it is, What has been the result of this organization, and of these means? or, What has been the character of the Presbyterian Church in the United States? Has it been a pure, enlightened, laborious, and harmonious body? . . .

Purity in a Church may be understood either in reference to orthodoxy, or adherence to the truth of God as revealed in His Word; or in reference to the manner of life of its ministers or members. In reference to the former of these views, we think it may safely be asserted that the Presbyterian Church has, by the grace of God, been preserved pure to a very uncommon degree. The correctness of this statement is to be found, not so much in the early adoption of the Westminster Confession of Faith, and the requisition of an assent to that Confession on the part of all candidates for ordination, as in the fact that there has never been any open avowal of Pelagian or Arminian doctrines in the bosom of our Church. Cases have occurred of ministers being censured, or suspended from office, for teaching such doctrines, but no case has occurred where a Presbyterian minister has avowedly rejected the Calvinistic system, and yet retained his standing in the Church as one of its authorized preachers. Of late years, indeed, there has been much discussion on doctrinal subjects, and many sentiments have been advanced, which many excellent men considered as virtually, if not formally implying the rejection of the Calvinistic doctrines of original sin, election, and efficacious grace. With regard to these controversies, however, there are two remarks to be made. The first is, that the advocates of these sentiments strenuously denied that they were inconsistent with the doctrines just mentioned; and the second is, that the oppostion made to the exercise of discipline on account of these sentiments, was the principal cause of the division of the Presbyterian Church into two portions of nearly equal size. It therefore remains true, as stated in a preceding page, that no Presbyterian minister has avowed himself either a Pelagian or Arminian, and yet been allowed to retain his standing as one of the accredited teachers of the Church. This, indeed, may be considered by many as great bigotry. But the very thing which its friends glory in is the fact that the Presbyterian Church in America, having a Calvinistic creed, has been faithful in adhering to it.

As to the other application of the word pure, it may also be safely asserted that although painful cases of immorality in ministers have occurred, yet we know of no case in which it has been overlooked; in which either drunkenness, licentiousness, or any similar offence, has been proved against any minister, or been notoriously true with regard to him, without leading to his suspension or deposition from office. . . . The cases are certainly rare in which any such offence as falsehood, drunkenness, fornication, or adultery is tolerated in any church member. Discipline is so far preserved in our churches, that it would be a matter of general reproach if any congregation allowed the name of a man of known immoral character to remain upon its list of communicants.

In answer to the question, Whether the Presbyterian Church has had a laborious and active body of clergy? it may be said that, if in this respect she has fallen behind some of her sister Churches, she has kept in advance of others. The rapid increase of the Church since its organization in 1705; the efforts she has made to found academies, colleges, and theological seminaries; the labor and money contributed to the support of foreign and domestic missions, show that, although she has come far short of her duty, she has not been entirely unmindful of her high vocation.

With regard to the last question proposed, viz., Whether the Presbyterian Church has been a harmonious body? the answer may not appear so favorable. The existence of parties seems to be an unavoidable incident of freedom. In other words, liberty gives occasion for the manifestation of that diversity of opinion, feeling, and interest, which never fails to exist in all large communities, whether civil or religious. The expression of this diversity may be prevented by the hand of power, or concealed from view by the force of counteracting motives; but where no power exists to forbid its manifestation, or where no interests are endangered by its avowal, it will not be slow in making its existence known. In the Romish Church, all expression of difference of opinion, on certain subjects, is forbidden; in all others, where there is liberty, there is conflict. . . .

Regarding [both Old and New Schools] as one whole, it were difficult to find in any part of Christendom a branch of the kingdom of Christ more distinguished than these Churches for general learning, zeal, enterprise, liberality, and soundness in all essential doctrine. Their ministers present a body of . . . men, almost without exception liberally educated, who, after all their debates, and their final separation, are more thoroughly sound Calvinists in point of doctrine than any equally numerous ministry to be found in any other country.

The question is often asked, Whether they will ever unite again? That is by no means improbable; but whether they do or not seems to be of little consequence. In their separate state they will accomplish more than if united. There will soon be, indeed there is now, the most perfect intercourse between the churches and pastors.

The energies of both find free and ample scope, which was never the case before with either, but particularly with the Old School, who never felt at ease, or secure as to the future. . . .

CHAPTER 61

The Methodist Episcopal Church

This large and influential body holds the doctrinal opinions of the Wesleyan Methodists of England, and its ecclesiastical economy is, in all important points, identical with theirs. It took its rise in 1766, when a Mr. Philip Embury, who had been a local preacher in some of Mr. Wesley's societies in the north of Ireland, and had come over to America with a few other pious persons of the same connection, began to hold meetings for exhortation and prayer in his own house at New York. A considerable society was gradually formed in that city, which at that time, it would appear, could count but a small number, comparatively, of living and zealous Christians among its inhabitants. In a few months it was found necessary to fit up a large hired room as a place of worship, and the congregation was further augmented by the preaching of a Captain [Thomas] Webb of the British army, who, having been converted under the preaching of Mr. Wesley in England, and being now stationed in Albany, paid frequent visits to the little flock at New York.

It was not long, however, before similar meetings began to be held in several places on Long Island, in Philadelphia, and at other points. In 1768, a large place of worship was erected in New York, being the first Methodist church ever built in the United States. Next year, Mr. Wesley being requested to send over two of his preachers, Messrs. Richard Boardman and Joseph Pillmore came to New York, and about the same time, Mr. Robert Strawbridge, another local preacher from Ireland, came over and settled in Frederic county, Maryland, where he held meetings at his own house, and at the houses of other pious persons in the neighbor-hood. This extension of the Methodists into the South was further promoted by a visit from Mr. Pillmore into Virginia and North Carolina.

Pressing representations of the need of help having been made to Mr. Wesley, Mr. Francis Asbury and Mr. Richard Wright were sent over from England in 1771, and under the labors, particu-larly, of the former, the work went on increasing, year after year, until the commencement of the Revolution. That event greatly retarded the progress of Methodism in some places, not only by the ever untowardly influence of present war on such undertakings, but also by the suspicions attached by the revolutionists to Mr. Asbury, and several of his fellow-preachers, as being native Eng-lishmen, who had been too short a period in the country to have its interests truly at heart.

At length, with peace came independence, and thus, greatly to the encouragement of Mr. Asbury and his fellow-laborers, a wide and effectual door for the preaching of the Gospel was opened to them. Hitherto this attempt to revive true godliness had been confined entirely to laymen of the Episcopal Church, and with it their efforts are more connected than with any other, inasmuch as none of them had at first any intention of separating from its communion. But worthy ministers of that church being hard to be found in some places, while none were to be had at all in others, both before the Revolution broke out and during its progress, Mr. Wesley was urged to send over ordained ministers, who might administer the ordinances to his followers. To this he was greatly opposed, at first, but when the Revolution was over, considering that, from the change of circumstances, he might now lawfully do what he had refused doing while the colonies were under the government of England, he sent over, as superintendent of the Methodist churches in America, the Rev. Dr. [Thomas] Coke, a presbyter of regular standing in the Established Church of Eng-land. He was accompanied by Mr. Richard Whatcoat and Mr. Thomas Vasey, whom Mr. Wesley, assisted by Dr. Coke and the Rev. Mr. [James] Creighton, had ordained presbyters or priests, just before the sailing of the three from Bristol in September, 1784. These brethren were the bearers of a letter from Mr. Wesley to the Methodist preachers and societies in America, stating his reasons for considering himself now at liberty to accede to their requests, and informing them that he had appointed Dr. Coke and Mr. Asbury to be joint superintendents of all the societies in that country founded upon his rules, and Messrs. Whatcoat and Vasey to act as elders among them, by baptizing and administering the Lord's Supper.

On the arrival of these delegates, a conference of the preachers was immediately convened at Baltimore. It was opened on the 25th of December, 1784, and was attended by sixty out of the eighty preachers then in the country. One of its first acts was the unanimous election of Dr. Coke and Mr. Asbury as superintendents, thereby confirming Mr. Wesley's appointment. Dr. Coke and the other two presbyters then ordained Mr. Asbury, first a deacon, next a presbyter, and finally, a superintendent. Thereupon the two superintendents, or bishops, as they soon began to be called, and as their successors are styled to this day, ordained twelve of the preachers then present to the office of presbyters or elders.

Thus was the Methodist Episcopal Church in the United States organized seventy-two years ago. From that epoch they formed a new and independent religious denomination, which was soon vastly to outnumber that from which they had sprung. At that "their day of small things," their ministers and lay preachers, including Dr. Coke and his co-delegates from England amounted to eighty-six, and the members, in all, to 14,986. But small as was this beginning, great and glorious has been their increase since.

The proceedings of that conference were highly important. Twenty-five articles were adopted as the Confession of Faith for the infant Church. We will give first the titles of the whole, and then a few of them at large. The titles are as follows: Of faith in the Holy Trinity; of the Word, or Son of God, who was made very man; of the resurrection of Christ; of the Holy Ghost; of the sufficiency of the Holy Scriptures for salvation; of the Old Testament; of original sin; of free-will; of the justification of man; of good works; of works of supererogation; of sin after justification; of the Church; of purgatory; of speaking in the congregation; in such a tongue as the people understand; of the sacraments; of Baptism;

of the Lord's Supper; of both kinds;* of the one oblation of Christ, finished upon the cross; of the marriage of ministers; of the rites and ceremonies of the churches; of the rulers of the United States of America; of Christian men's goods; of a Christian man's oath.

On almost all these subjects the articles express doctrines held by every enlightened Protestant. In fact, they are a selection from the Thirty-nine Articles of the Church of England, with some verbal changes, and the omission of some parts of sentences. The seventeenth article of the Church of England (on predestination and election) is, of course, omitted, the doctrine therein taught not being held by the Methodist Episcopal Church in America. Nor do we find that of the certain perseverance of saints, for neither do they hold this. But on all the great doctrines essential to salvation, nothing can be more clear, or more consistent with the Word of God, than the sense of these articles. . . .

Besides these twenty-five articles, the General Conference have adopted a system of polity† in thirty-five sections, which treat of the entire economy of their Church, the manner of life becoming its ministers and private members, the proper style of preaching, etc. In giving directions as to the manner of treating the doctrine of perfection, the twenty-second section runs as follows: "Let us strongly and explicitly exhort all believers to go on to perfection. That we may all speak the same thing, we ask, once for all, Shall we defend this perfection or give it up? We all agree to defend it, meaning thereby (as we did from the beginning), salvation from all sin by the love of God and man filling the heart. . . . We are all agreed we may be saved from all sin, properly so called, before death, *i.e.,* sinful tempers; but we can not always speak, or think, or act aright, as dwelling in houses of clay. The substance, then, is settled; but as to the circumstances, is the change gradual or instantaneous? It is both the one and the other. 'But should we, in preaching, insist both on one and the other?' Certainly we should insist on the gradual change; and that earnestly and continually. And are there not reasons why we should insist on the instantaneous

---

* Or elements—bread and wine—both to be administered to the people.
† These rules, originally drawn by Mr. Wesley, were considerably modified in America.

change? If there be such a blessed change before death, should we not encourage all believers to expect it? And the rather, because constant experience shows, the more earnestly they expect this, the more swiftly and steadily does the gradual work of God go on in their souls; the more careful are they to grow in grace; the more zealous of good works; and the more punctual in their attendance on all the ordinances of God (whereas just the contrary effects are observed whenever this expectation ceases). They are saved by hope—by this hope of a total change, with a gradually-increasing salvation. Destroy this hope, and that salvation stands still, or, rather, decreases daily. Therefore, whoever will advance the gradual change in believers, should strongly insist on the instantaneous."

[Baird then explains that, since the Methodists have constructed an "extensive, well-adjusted, and most efficient ecclesiastical system," he will define the various strata so his readers can understand how the parts function together.]

1. In the first place, there is what is called the *society,* which includes all the members of the church residing in any particular place, or connected with it.

2. Every society comprises one or more *classes,* each consisting of from twelve to twenty or more individuals, who meet once a week for mutual edification. These classes are the real normal schools, if we may so speak, of the Methodist Church.

3. The minister, under whose pastoral care the classes in a society are placed, appoints a leader to each, whose duty it is to see every member of his class once a week, to inquire how their souls prosper, and to receive what they are willing to give for the support of the church and the poor.

4. Stewards are appointed in each society by the Quarterly Conference, on the nomination of the ruling preacher. These have charge of all the moneys collected for the support of the ministry, the poor, and for sacramental occasions, and disburse it as the Discipline directs.

5. There are *trustees,* who have charge of the church property, and hold it in trust for the use of the Methodist Episcopal Church.

These are elected by the congregation in those States where the laws so provide; in other places they are appointed as the Discipline directs.

6. There are, in most societies, *exhorters,* who receive their license from the preacher in charge; but this license can not be renewed except by a vote of the Quarterly Meeting Conference; they have the privilege of holding meetings for exhortation and prayer.

7. A preacher is one who holds a license to preach, but may not administer the sacraments. He may be a traveling or a local preacher. The former devotes his whole time to the ministry, and is supported by those among whom he labors; the latter generally supports himself by some secular employment, and preaches on the Sabbath, as well as occasionally at other times, but without temporal emolument. Both receive a license, signed by a presiding elder, from a Quarterly Meeting Conference, after being recommended each by his respective class, or by a leaders' meeting. Thus the people, in those nurseries of the Church—the "classes" and "leaders' meetings"—have the initiative in bringing forward those who are to preach the Gospel. After this license from a Quarterly Meeting Conference, they may be taken into the traveling service by an Annual Conference; after two years spent in which, and pursuing at the same time a prescribed course of reading and study, they may be ordained as deacons. Then, after two years' circuit traveling as deacons, and pursuing a further course of reading and study, they may be ordained presbyters or elders. Such is the training for the ministry in the Methodist Episcopal Church, and it is much more efficient than persons not well acquainted with it would suppose.

8. A deacon holds a parchment of ordination from a bishop, and besides his duties as a preacher, he is authorized to solemnize marriages, to administer Baptism, and to assist the elder or presbyter in the administration of the Lord's Supper.

9. An elder, in addition to these functions, is authorized to administer all the ordinances of God's house.

10. A presiding elder has the charge of several circuits, collectively called a district. . . . This office arose from the necessity of always having some one to administer the ordinances throughout

the circuits, for it often happens that the traveling preachers, from their not having received ordination, as elders, can not administer the Lord's Supper; nor even Baptism, if they are not deacons.

11. A bishop is elected by the General Conference, to which body he is amenable for his official and moral conduct. It is his duty to travel through the country, to superintend the spiritual and temporal affairs of the Church, to preside in the Annual and the General Conference, to ordain such as are elected by an Annual Conference to the office of deacons and elders, and to appoint the preachers to their stations. As there are several bishops, they usually divide the country among them, each having his own field, and all meeting at the General Conference. The Episcopacy in this Church is, however, an *office,* not an *order.*

12. A *leaders' meeting* is composed of all the class leaders in any one circuit or station. . . .

13. A *Quarterly Meeting Conference* is composed of all the traveling and local preachers, exhorters, stewards, and leaders belonging to any particular station or circuit. . . .

14. An *Annual Conference* is composed of all the traveling preachers, deacons, and elders within a specified district of country. These are the executive and judicial bodies, acting under rules prescribed to them by the General Conference. . . .

15. The *General Conference* assembles once in four years, and is composed of a certain number of delegates, elected by the annual conferences. It has the power to revise any part of the Discipline not prohibited by restrictive regulations; to elect the book agents and editors, and the bishops; to hear and determine appeals of preachers from the decision of annual conferences; to review the acts of those conferences generally; to examine into the general administration of the bishops for the four preceding years; and to try, censure, acquit, or condemn a bishop if accused. This is the highest judicatory of the Church.

16. A *Love-Feast* is a meeting of the members of a society, held occasionally, in which they partake of a simple repast of bread and water, during an hour, at which such as are disposed relate what God has done for their souls. . . . Their object is to make the members better acquainted with each other, and promote brotherly love and mutual edification.

17. The salaries of the ministers are raised by various collections in the societies, and also in public meetings. Provision is made for aged and infirm ministers who have continued to exercise the duties of the ministry until incapable of further service. Omitting unnecessary details, I need only say that each traveling minister receives at present $100.00 a year for himself, the same sum for his wife, if he has one, $16.00 a year for each child under seven years of age, and $24.00 for children above that and under fourteen years. Besides, the stewards of each circuit and station are directed to provide a "parsonage," or house of residence, for the family of each married preacher on his circuit or station, and also to grant an allowance for his fuel and table expenses, which is estimated by a committee appointed by the Quarterly Meeting Conference. In these respects there is no difference between the preachers, deacons, elders, presiding elders, and bishops—all receive the same salaries; all have their traveling expenses. The widows of all the ministers receive $100.00 each.

The above is the provision fixed by the General Conference; but we believe that in many circuits the collections, etc., do not fully meet it.

No American Christian who takes a comprehensive view of the progress of religion in his country, and considers how wonderfully the means and instrumentalities employed are adapted to the extent and the wants of that country, can hesitate for a moment to bless God for having, in His mercy, provided them all. Nor will he fail to recognize in the Methodist economy, as well as in the zeal, the devoted piety, and the efficiency of its ministry, one of the most powerful elements in the religious prosperity of the United States, as well as one of the firmest pillars of their civil and political institutions. . . .

[One chapter, "The Moravian Church," followed in the original.]

Summary of the Methodist Churches in the United States in 1855

	Bishops	Presiding Elders	Effective Ministers	Membership	Missionaries Home	Missionaries For
Meth. Epis. Church	7	235	4,579	783,358	823	47
Meth. Epis. Church, South	7	131	1,942	596,852	271	34
United Brethren in Christ	4	—	250	67,000	—	—
Evangelical Association	2	—	195	21,076	—	—
African Meth. Epis. Church	3	—	300	21,237	—	—
African Meth. Epis. Zion Ch.	2	—	155	6,203	—	—
Methodist Protestant Church [sic.]	—	—	916	70,018	103	—
Wesleyan Methodist Conn.	—	—	310	23,000	—	—
Primitive Methodist Church	—	—	12	1,100	—	—
Welsh Calvinistic Meth. Ch.	—	—	81	3,950	—	—
	25	366	8,740	1,593,794	1,197	81

CHAPTER 62

Smaller Baptist Denominations

There are a few Baptist denominations in the United States not usually included with the Regular Baptists noticed in Chapter IV [59]. They are as follows:

1. THE SEVENTH DAY BAPTISTS—. . . They are quite evangelical in the doctrines that relate to the way of salvation, and are in good repute for piety and zeal. They differ from the Regular Baptists as to the day to be observed as the Christian Sabbath, maintaining, in opposition to these, that the seventh day was not only the Sabbath originally appointed by the Creator, but that that apointment remains unrepealed.

Their churches are widely scattered throughout the States. . . .

2. FREE-WILL BAPTISTS. This body dates in America from 1780, when its first church was formed in New Hampshire. In doctrine, they hold a general atonement, and reject election and the other Calvinistic points. On the subject of the Trinity, justification by faith alone, regeneration, and sanctification, they are, with some exceptions, sound.

Starting with the wrong principle that, dispensing with written creeds, covenants, rules of discipline, or articles of organization, they would make the Bible serve for all these, they were soon in great danger from Arians and Socinians creeping in among them. . . . Some of them have come to see that creeds are unavoidable, and had better be *definitely expressed* in writing than merely *understood*. They have, accordingly, introduced creeds, and in some instances, even written articles in the form of a constitution. This augurs well.

3. DISCIPLES OF CHRIST, or REFORMERS, as they call themselves, or CAMPBELLITES, as they are most commonly called by

others. It is with some hesitation that, by placing these in this connection, I rank them among evangelical Christians. I do so because their creed, taken as it stands in written terms, is not heterodox. Not only do they not deny, but in words their creed affirms the doctrine of the Trinity, of salvation by the merits of Christ, and the necessity of the regenerating and sanctifying influences of the Holy Spirit. Yet I understand that there is much about their preaching that seems to indicate that all that they consider necessary to salvation is little if any thing more than a speculative, philosophical faith, in connection with immersion as the only proper mode of baptism; so that there is little, after all, of that "repentance toward God," and "faith toward our Lord Jesus Christ," which are the indispensable terms of the Gospel.

The founder of this sect is a Dr. Alexander Campbell, a Scotchman, who, together with his father, left the Presbyterian Church in 1812, and became Baptists. Soon after this change he began to broach doctrines that can hardly be called new. . . . His views seem to be substantially as follows: "All sects and parties of the Christian world have departed, in greater or less degrees, from the simplicity of faith and manners of the first Christians." "This defection," Dr. Campbell and his followers "attribute to the great varieties of speculation, and metaphysical dogmatism of countless creeds, formularies, liturgies, and books of discipline, adopted and inculcated as bonds of union and platforms of communion in all the parties which have sprung from the Lutheran Reformation." All this has led, as they suppose, to the displacing of the style of the living oracles, and the affixing to the sacred diction ideas wholly unknown to the Apostles.

And what does Dr. Campbell propose to do? Simply "to ascertain from the Holy Scriptures, according to commonly-received and well-established rules of interpretation, the ideas attached to the leading terms and sentences found in the Holy Scriptures, and then use the words of the Holy Spirit in the apostolic acceptation of them!" . . . However plausible it may be to talk in this way, all Church History has shown that there is no more certain way of introducing all manner of heresy than by dispensing with all written creeds and formularies of doctrine, and allowing all who profess to believe in the Bible, though attaching any meaning to it they please, to become members of the Church. For awhile, possibly, this scheme may seem to work well; but, before half a century has passed, all manner of error will be found to have entered and nestled in the House of God.

"Every one who believes what the Evangelists and Apostles have testified concerning Jesus of Nazareth, and who is willing to obey Him, is a proper subject for immersion." And this is the sum and substance of what Dr. Campbell says respecting the way in which a sinner is to attain salvation. This is all well enough, if *faith* be truly explained, and the sinner does really come to Christ with that godly sorrow for sin from which saving faith is never dissevered. But if a mere general belief in what the Evangelists and Apostles have said, together with immersion, be all that is required, it is not difficult to see that churches may soon be gathered in which there will be but little true religion.

SUMMARY OF BAPTIST CHURCHES IN THE UNITED STATES. The Baptist Family of Churches in the United States in 1855 stood thus:

	Associations	Churches	Ministers	Members
Regular Baptists	523	10,488	6,887	842,660
Anti-Mission	155	1,720	825	58,000
Free-Will Baptists	—	1,173	1,107	49,809
Seventh-Day Baptists	4	71	77	6,500
Church of God, or Winebrennarians	—	168	130	17,500
Disciples of Christ or "Campbellites"	—	—	—	300,000
Tunkers	—	150	200	8,000
Mennonites	—	300	250	36,000
Total	682	14,170	9,476	1,318,469

All these Churches are supposed to hold the doctrine of "salvation through grace," or "justification by faith."

Among the "Regular Baptist" Churches, there are five associations, sixty-six churches, forty-eight ministers, and 2,375 members of German, Swedish, and Welsh people. . . .

CHAPTER 63

Smaller Presbyterian Churches
—Cumberland Presbyterians

The origin of the Cumberland Presbyterians was as follows: In the extensive and, in some respects, wonderful revival of religion that took place in Kentucky during the years 1801–3, the call for Presbyterian ministers was far beyond what could be satisfied, and in this exigency it was proposed by some of the ministers that pious laymen of promising abilities, and who seemed to have a talent for public speaking, should be encouraged to make the best preparations in their power for the ministry, and thereafter be licensed to preach.

This suggestion was carried into effect. Several such persons were licensed by the Presbytery of Transylvania; and a new Presbytery, which had been formed in the southern part of the State in 1803, and was called the Cumberland Presbytery, admitted and ordained those licentiates, and took on trial others of similar characters and attainments.

These proceedings were considered disorderly by the Synod of Kentucky, and a commission was therefore appointed to examine them, and to inquire what were the doctrines held by persons thus admitted into the ministry, in a way so foreign to the rules and practice of the Presbyterian Church. The upshot was, that the course pursued by the Cumberland Presbytery was condemned, and this sentence having been confirmed by the General Assembly of the whole Presbyterian Church, before which it had been brought by appeal, the censured Presbytery withdrew from that body, and constituted itself an independent Church in 1810, since which has been called the Cumberland Presbyterian Church.

Its doctrines occupy a sort of middle ground between Calvinism and Arminianism. It holds that the atonement was made for all mankind; it rejects the doctrine of eternal reprobation; holds a modified view of election; and maintains the perseverance of the saints; but on the other points is essentially Calvinistic.

In its ecclesiastical polity it is Presbyterian; the Session, Presbytery, Synod, and General Assembly are all constituted in the manner described at length in our notice of the Presbyterian Church. It differs, however, in one point, from all other Presbyterian Churches, by having adopted the *itinerating* system of the Methodists. By that system of circuits and stations, its ministers have been able to reach almost all parts of the Valley of the Mississippi, that being the great scene of their labors. But their Church is not confined to the Western States and Territories of the American Union—it reaches into California. . . .

[Seven chapters on "Smaller Presbyterian Churches," "Smaller German Sects," "Smaller Methodist Denominations," and "The Friends or Quakers" followed here in the original.]

Summary of the Presbyterian Churches in the United States in 1855

	Gen. Assemblies, or Gen. Synods	Synods	Presbyteries	Ministers	Licentiates	Candidates	Churches	Members
O. S. Presb.	1	30	148	2,261	237	435	3,079	231,404
N. S. Presb.	1	24	108	1,567	111	238	1,659	143,029
Associate Presb.	1	—	20	164	21	35	267	21,588
Associate Ref. Presb.	—	5	34	315	30	60	375	40,000
Ref. Presb.	—	2	13	108	15	20	160	14,000
Cumberland Presb.	1	25	90	1,000	400	80	1,200	100,000
German Ref.	1	2	23	350	25	40	1,000	110,000
Ref. Dutch	1	2	28	380	15	35	376	36,297
Total, eight branches	6	90	464	6,145	854	943	8,116	696,318

CHAPTER 64

The Summary

We have now completed our notices of the various Evangelical Churches or Denominations in the United States, and to assist the reader in taking a general view of the whole, we proceed to place the results before his eye in a tabular form, pursuing still the order of time in which each Group or Family of Churches began to appear in the country:

	Churches	Ministers	Licentiates	Members	Population
The Episcopal Church	1,300	1,714	—	105,350	1,000,000
With the Moravian	23	28	—	3,500	12,000
	1,323	1,742	—	108,850	1,012,000
Cong. Orthodox Chs.	2,450	2,327	—	210,000	2,000,000
Baptist Churches	14,070	9,476	596	1,322,469	5,000,000
Presbyterian Churches	8,116	6,145	854	716,318	3,500,000
Methodist (estimated)	14,000*	8,740	12,618†	1,593,794	5,500,000
Lutheran Church	1,900	1,000	—	225,000	750,000
Total	42,359	29,430	14,068	4,176,431	17,762,000

* The number of church-edifices and of congregations worshiping in them, belonging to to the Methodists, may be put down for at least fourteen thousand. It was 12,484 in 1850. But the number of Methodist congregations in the United States, when estimated by the places in which they meet, viz.: "meeting-houses," private houses, school-houses, etc., is probably not less than thirty-five thousand, if not forty thousand.
† Local preachers.

In this statement are included all the Evangelical Churches or Communions, excepting the Orthodox Friends, whose "Meetings" may be three hundred and fifty, but of whose membership we have no means of forming a reliable estimate.

By uniting the Presbyterians and Congregationalists, which, as they are in many important respects the same, is entirely proper, we reduce the evangelical denominations in the United States to five great families; and thus arranged, they present the following summary:

	Churches	Ministers	Members	Population
Episcopalian	1,323	1,742	108,850	1,012,000
Presbyterian	10,566	8,472	926,318	5,500,000
Baptist	14,070	9,476	1,322,469	5,000,000
Methodist	14,000	8,740	1,593,794	5,500,000
Lutheran	1,900	1,000	225,000	750,000
Total	41,859	29,430	4,176,431	17,762,000

Such an arrangement might be called a *doctrinal* one. On the question of Church government, the Lutheran Church may be ranked with the Presbyterian; and though not Calvinistic in doctrine, it may be said to sympathize considerably with the Cumberland Presbyterian Church. Withal, it maintains an intercourse with the Presbyterian Churches generally that is not only fraternal but in many cases intimate. Ranging the Lutheran Churches with the Presbyterian, we have but four great families of evangelical Churches in the United States, viz.:

	Churches	Ministers	Members	Population
Episcopalian	1,323	1,742	108,850	1,012,000
Presbyterian	12,466	9,472	1,151,318	6,250,000
Baptist	14,070	9,476	1,322,469	5,000,000
Methodist	14,000	8,740	1,593,794	5,500,000
Total	41,859	29,430	4,176,431	17,762,000

This synopsis suggests a few observations:

1. It is impossible to state the number of churches or congregations, properly so called. Those of the Episcopalians, Presbyterians, and Baptists, taken together, amount to 27,859. But those belonging to the different Methodist communions it is impossible to ascertain, no return of them having been made. There can be no doubt that they have at least 14,000 church-edifices properly so called. This, then, would make the entire number of the churches of the evangelical denominations to have been in 1855 41,859; and supposing these to contain upon an average five hundred people each, they would accommodate more than 20,729,500 of the 26,500,000, the population of the country for that year. But if we take in all the places, whether churches or not, at which the Gospel is preached, in most cases once a week at least, and others once a fortnight, seldom less often, these will be found to amount to 62,359 or at the outside 67,359.

2. The summary gives 29,430 as the number of ministers who devote themselves entirely to the work. Adding the 12,618 Methodist local preachers, we have 42,048 as the number of actual preachers of the Gospel. Even this is exclusive of the licentiates in the Baptist and Presbyterian churches, who were in 1855 estimated at more than 1,400 and who may fairly be set against the deduction to be made on account of ordained ministers employed as professors and missionaries. But taking, all things considered, the above-stated 29,430 as the number of ministers that are evangelical on all the saving doctrines of the Gospel: and dividing the population of the United States, which, in the beginning of the year 1855 could not have been more than 26,500,000, by this number, the result will be one such minister for about nine hundred souls. Now, although figures can not express moral influences, such calculations are nevertheless not without their use. A country which has an evangelical preacher on an average for every nine hundred souls, may be considered as pretty well supplied, if they be well distributed and faithful. A perfect distribution is, indeed, altogether impossible with a population rapidly diffusing itself over immense, half-cultivated regions, yet much is done to obviate the disadvantages of such a state of things. The aid rendered by the Methodist local preachers must be regarded as an important auxiliary to the more regular ministry. The general faithfulness of this ministry has already been fully discussed.

3. The members in full communion with the churches enumerated were, in 1855, 4,176,431 in number. Now, although it be very certain that all these do not live up to their profession, yet as they belong for the most part to churches that endeavor to maintain discipline, we may fairly presume that they comprehend at least as large a proportion of consistent Christians as any equal number of professors in other parts of Christendom.

4. The last column of the summary assumes 17,762,000 of the whole population as more or less under the influence of the evangelical denominations. Accuracy in such a calculation is hardly to be expected, but I have taken the best data I could find, and doubt not that the estimate I have made is not much wide of the truth. Including all the evangelical "Friends," this estimate would fall but little short of eighteen million.

CHAPTER 65

Number of Evangelical Sects

Much has been said in Europe about the multiplicity of sects in the United States, and many seem of opinion that the religious liberty enjoyed there has led to the almost indefinite creation of different religious communions. This requires a little examination.

No doubt absolute religious liberty will ever be attended with a considerable subdivision of the religious world into "branches" or sects. Men will ever differ in their views respecting doctrine and church order, and it is to be expected that such differences will result in the formation of distinct ecclesiastical communions. In the absence of religious liberty, matters may be much otherwise, but how far for the better a little consideration will show. People in that case may be constrained to acquiesce, ostensibly at least, in a certain ecclesiastical organization, and in certain modes of faith and worship sanctioned and established by law. But such acquiescence, it is well known, instead of being real and cordial, is often merely external and constrained; and if so, its worthlessness is certain and palpable.

But as respects the evangelical communions in the United States, it must have struck the reader that this multiplicity has mainly arisen, not so much from the abuse of religious liberty by the indulgence of a capricious and sectarian spirit, as from the various quarters from which the country has been colonized. Coming in large numbers, and sometimes in compact bodies, from different parts of the Old World, nothing was more natural than the desire of establishing for themselves and their posterity the same religious formularies and modes of worship, church government, and discipline which they had cherished in the lands that had given them birth, and persecution for their adherence to which had led, in many instances, to their having emigrated. . . . Indeed, there is scarcely an evangelical communion in America which is not the mere extension by emigration of a similar body in Europe. The exceptions hardly can be reckoned such, for they consist for the most part of separations from the larger bodies, not because of differences with regard to essential doctrines and forms of church government, but on points of such inferior consequence that they can scarcely be regarded as new sects at all.

In fact, if we take all the evangelical communions that have fallen under review, and contemplate the confessedly fundamental doctrines maintained by each, it is surprising to observe how nearly they are agreed. It may, we believe, be demonstrated that among the evangelical communions in the United States, numerous as they are, there is as much real harmony of doctrine, if not of church economy, as could be found in the evangelical churches of the first three centuries.

These communions, as they exist in the United States, ought to be viewed as branches of one great body, even the entire visible Church of Christ in this land. Whatever may have been the circumstances out of which they arose, they are but constituent parts of one great whole—divisions of one vast army—though each brigade, and even each regiment, may have its own banner, and its own part of the field to occupy. And although to the inexperienced eye such an army as it moves onward against the enemy may have a confused appearance, the different divisions of infantry being arranged separately, the artillery interspersed, and the cavalry sometimes in the front, sometimes in the rear, sometimes on the flank, and sometimes between the columns, yet all are in their proper places; and to the mind of Him who assigns them their places, and directs their movements, all is systematic order where the uninitiated sees nothing but confusion. Momentary collisions, it is true, may sometimes happen—there may be jostling, and some irritation occasionally—yet they fulfill their appointed parts, and discharge their appropriate duties. So is it with the "sacramental host of God's elect" with us.

Great, however, as may be the disadvantages resulting from this multiplicity of different communions, were they all reduced to one or two, we apprehend still worse evils would follow. Diversity on

non-essential points among the churches and ministers of a neighborhood often gives opportunity to those who reside in it to attend
the services and ministrations which each finds most edifying, instead of being reduced to the sad alternative of either joining in
forms of worship which they conscientiously disapprove, and of
listening to a minister whom they find unedifying, or of abstaining
from public worship altogether. Rather than this, it is surely far
better to bear the expense of having two or three churches in a
community, for which, looking only at the mere amount of population, one might suffice.

CHAPTER 66

Alleged Want of Harmony
among the Evangelical Christians
of the United States

It has been often and widely stated in Europe, on the authority
of a certain class of visitants from the Old World, who have published their "Travels," "Tours," etc., that there is much unseemly
strife among our various religious denominations. . . . There
may, indeed, be temporary cases of disagreeable collision and un-
brotherly jealousy, but ordinarily these are of short duration. The
best of men are, after all, but men. Hence even a devoted Gospel
minister, after having long had some particular neighborhood all to
himself, may dread the opening of a new place of worship of a
different communion in the vicinity of his own, lest some of his
hearers should thereby be drawn away; and such an apprehension
may, for a time, excite some not very kind feelings in his breast.
But universal experience shows that such feelings are usually
groundless, and soon cease to be indulged by any but the most
narrow-minded persons.

Notwithstanding such cases, I hesitate not to affirm that, taking the Evangelical Churches as a whole, their intercourse, in all parts of the country, manifests a remarkable degree of mutual respect and fraternal affection. While earnest in maintaining, alike from the pulpit and the press, their own views of Truth and Church order, there is rarely any thing like denunciation and unchurching other orthodox communions, but every readiness, on the contrary, to offer help when needed. . . .

This brotherly feeling widely prevails among the laity also. In all parts of the country they scruple not, when there is no service in their own places of worship, to attend others, though of another communion; and, indeed, in our cities and large towns, not a few Christians regularly attend the lectures of pastors not of their own communion, when these fall on different evenings from those of their own pastors. . . .

Taking all the professed Christians, amounting, it has been seen, to 4,127,431, in our Evangelical Churches, I hesitate not to say that far more mutual respect and brotherly love prevail among them than would were they all coerced into one denomination. The world has already seen what sort of union and brotherhood can be produced by all being brought into one immense Church, that admits of no deviation from the decrees of its councils and con-claves. There may, indeed, be external agreement, yet beneath this apparent unanimity there will be internal divisions and heart-burn-ings in abundance. There may be union against all who dare to impugn her dogmas, but who can tell the almost infernal hatred with which her Religious Orders have been found to regard each other? Compared with this, all the temporary *attritions,* together with all the controversies and exacerbations of feeling that ac-company them, that take place in our evangelical Protestant denominations, are as nothing.

Still, the question remains, Whence have foreigners, while visit-ing the United States, received the impression, which, by being promulgated in their writings, has called for these remarks? The answer is easy. While such are the prevailing respect and regard for each other among the members of our Evangelical Churches, they all unite in opposing, on the one hand, the errors of Rome, and, on the other, the heresy that denies the proper divinity and atonement of Christ, together with those other aberrations from the true Gospel which that heresy involves. Now, it is this refusal to hold fellowship with errors of vital moment, it is this earnest contending for saving truth, that leads tourists in the United States, whom chance or choice has thrown into the society of persons opposed in their religious tenets to the Evangelical Churches, to charge us with uncharitableness. *Hinc illæ lachrymæ.*

BOOK VII

Non-evangelical Denominations in America

CHAPTER 67

Introductory Remarks

Having thus reviewed, as far as the compass of our work will permit, the Evangelical Churches or Denominations in the United States of America, we come now to speak of those that are considered by Orthodox Protestants as unevangelical; and under this head we shall, for convenience' sake, range all those sects that either renounce, or fail faithfully to exhibit the fundamental and saving truths of the Gospel. Here, however, let us not be misunderstood. When we put Roman Catholics in the same category with Unitarians, we would not for a moment be supposed to place them on the same footing. The former, doubtless, as a Church, hold those doctrines on which true believers in all ages have rested their hopes for eternal life, yet these have been so buried amid the rubbish of multiplied human traditions and inventions, as to remain hid from the great mass of the people. Still, as in their doctrinal formularies they have not denied "the Lord that bought them," however much they may have multiplied other "saviours," they must not be confounded with those who have openly rejected that "sure foundation which is laid in Zion." While, therefore, we must deplore their "holding the Truth in unrighteousness," and instead of presenting through their numerous priesthood the simple and fundamental doctrines of the Gospel, their supplanting these, in a great measure, by introducing "another Gospel," we would not say that an enlightened mind may not find in their Church the way of life, obstructed though it be by innumerable obstacles.

Neither would we be thought to put the Unitarians on the same footing with the Universalists. The moral influence of the preaching of the former, and their standing in society, make them far more valuable than the latter as a component part of the general population. Nor would we put the Jews, or even the more serious part of the Universalists, on the same level with "Socialists," "Shakers," and "Mormons."

All that we mean by putting these various bodies in one category is, that they can none of them be associated with the evangelical Protestant Churches—with Churches whose religion is the Bible, the whole Bible, and nothing but the Bible—nor, indeed, do we suppose that, however much they may dislike being brought under a common designation, they would any of them choose to be associated with the evangelical Protestant communions, or challenge for themselves that appellation. . . .

CHAPTER 68

The Roman Catholic Church

Maryland, we have seen, was originally a Roman Catholic colony founded on most liberal principles, under the auspices and through the exertions of Lord Baltimore. And although Protestant Epicopacy was established in the colony under the reign of William and Mary, the laws of England against Roman Catholics being at the same time rigorously enforced, they continued, nevertheless, to form the most numerous and influential body in the province down to the American Revolution. Even to this day, though now but a small minority of the entire population, not exceeding, it is believed, 100,000 souls, and inferior in point of numbers both to the Protestant Episcopalians and Methodists, they have much influence, and are perhaps the wealthiest communion in the State.

Except in Pennsylvania and Rhode Island, I am not aware that the Roman Catholics anywhere enjoyed their share of political rights at the commencement of the war of the Revolution, but now, I believe, they are everywhere upon the same footing with others, and enjoy all the political privileges that our Constitution affords.

The acquisition of Louisiana, in 1803, of Florida, in 1821, of New Mexico and California, in 1848, very considerably increased the Roman Catholic population of the country. To this must be added an immense immigration from Europe, mainly from Ireland and Germany, during the last sixty, still more during the last twenty-five years. Their increase has been rapid since the Revolution, partly owing to the above-mentioned territorial acquisitions, partly to conversions, but most of all to immigration. According to the Metropolitan Catholic Almanac for 1856, published at Baltimore, there were in the preceding year in the United States,

41 Dioceses.
2 Apostolic Vicariates.
7 Archbishops, 33 bishops.
1,780 Priests, of whom 1,611 are employed in the ministry, and 169 as professors of colleges, etc.
1,910 Churches.
895 Other stations for preaching, where churches had yet to be built. In all, 2,805 places for preaching.
37 Ecclesiastical Seminaries.
460 Clerical students.
49 Literary institutions for young men, 26 incorporated and 9 unincorporated colleges.
236 Female religious institutions.
130 Female academies.

The assertion has often been made by the opponents of the Roman Catholics in the United States, that they never can be safe citizens of a republic, and that the predominance of their Church would involve the overthrow of our political constitution. Such an opinion must rest, I should think, on the presumed hatred of the priests to republican institutions, and the impossibility of counteracting the influence they possess over the people. However this may be, many valuable citizens and stern patriots in this country have belonged to the Roman Catholic Church, and it remains to be seen how far it is possible for the Roman Catholic priests to obtain or exercise the same influence over their followers here that they possess in some European countries. One thing is certain: the Protestant population, and the clergy in particular, are not likely to be indifferent to their movements. The last few years have witnessed a great deal of discussion in the United States on the doctrines and influence of Romanism, and much distinguished talent and deep research have been exhibited in the course of it. Neither has this discussion been confined to any particular denomination of evangelical Protestants, but it has extended almost to every pulpit in every branch of that body. Never was there so general a determination to give publicity to the opinions they entertain of the character and tendency of the Roman Catholic religion; nor have its friends and abettors been silent under these attacks.

A visitor from Europe would, on entering the Roman Catholic churches of the United States, be struck with the few pictures and other such ornaments that they exhibit. This may arise from the want of time and money required for such things. The priests, too, dress like other citizens when not engaged in their official duties. Nor will it escape a stranger from any part of Roman Catholic Europe, that processions and religious services in the streets are hardly ever seen in the United States.

By the rapid multiplication of their priests in the United States the Roman Catholics have, no doubt, checked those conversions from their Church to Protestantism which were frequent in former times. Bishop [John] England, in one of his letters to the Propaganda, stated, a few years ago, that "the Church" had lost no fewer than 50,000 of her legitimate children in his diocese by such conversions, for want of shepherds to look after them.

But whatever may be the fact in regard to the increase of the Roman Catholics in the United States, or whatever may be the zeal and activity of the Protestants to prevent that increase, there is no well-informed American who does not rejoice in the perfect religious liberty which exists for all; nor is there wanting a good degree of kindness and social intercourse among men of all religious opinions. . . .

Of all forms of error in the United States, Romanism is by far the most formidable, because of the number of its adherents, the organization, wealth, influence, and worldly and unscrupulous policy of its hierarchy. That Romanism is increasing in the United States can not be denied; but that increase is not from conversion, but from the natural increase of the population on the one hand, and from the immigration of Roman Catholics from Europe on the other. The Roman Catholic population may be reckoned at . . . 3,250,000; but nothing very definite can be asserted, for high authorities among the Romanists themselves vary in their estimates from two to four millions. . . . Still there can be no doubt that her loss has been immense. . . . The freedom of the press in the United States, the freedom of speech, the constant contact with Protestants to which young Romanists are exposed, the manifest superiority of the Protestant population in intelligence, enterprise, wealth, and general influence, all conspire to make Roman Catholic young men inquire into the nature and claims of the two systems; and inquiry leads to great results. The infidelity into which they often fall is not likely to be lasting where favorable opportunities exist for learning the truth. Thanks be to God, much is now doing by the Protestants, in a kindly way, to cause the truth to reach the minds of their Roman Catholic fellow-citizens.

Two or three things have occurred to arouse the American people in relation to Rome and her movements. 1. The simultaneous efforts which have been of late made by her hierarchy on many of the States to obtain a portion of the funds destined to the support of public schools, and employ them for the support of their own sectarian schools, in which neither the Sacred Scriptures, nor any portions of them, are read, but avowedly sectarian instruction is given; and this, not so much for the benefit of their own children, as to prosecute effectually the work of proselyting the children of Protestants. This movement has been most signally defeated in all quarters. 2. The efforts making by the hierarchy to bring all the property of the Roman Catholic Church—church edifices, especially priests' houses, cemetaries, schools, colleges, hospitals, etc., into the possession of the bishops. It is but a few years since this movement, in which Archbishop [John] Hughes has been very prominent, commenced; and already some of their bishops are possessors of an immense amount of property. But this movement has awakened an extended and triumphant opposition; and already several States have enacted laws which require that all Church property shall be held by lay-trustees appointed by each congregation, and accountable to them for the proper use of it. . . . 3. The disposition, long well known, of some of the leaders of the great political parties, to court the Romanists for their votes at the elections, and the willingness of the hierarchy to be regarded as a "great power in the State," and as, in fact, holding the "balance of power," as has been often said—this obsequious meanness on the one hand, and unbounded arrogance on the other, have led to the formation of a political party called the "American Party," which has, for the time being, exerted a powerful influence on our political institutions. All this has been eminently injurious to the interests and pretensions of the Roman Catholic Church among us.

CHAPTER 69

Unitarianism

. . . Their doctrine was, that every man's piety is to be taken for granted, unless some scandalous error of doctrine or practice proves him destitute of it. The most important characteristic—the fundamental element—of New-England Unitarianism was [by 1750] fully developed. A party was formed, the members of which condemned and avoided all solicitude concerning their own spiritual condition or that of others.

When this state of mind had been produced and confirmed, the remainder of the process was natural and easy. As in this party there was to be no strong feeling with respect to religion, except a strong unwillingness to be disturbed by the "censoriousness" of others, there could, of course, be no vigorous opposition to a change in doctrines, no vigilance against error. A system of doctrines, too, was wanted, containing nothing to alarm the fears or disturb the repose of the members of the party. The doctrines of man's apostacy from God, and dependence on mere grace for salvation, of the necessity of an atonement by the blood of the Son of God, and of regeneration by the special influence of the Holy Spirit, were felt to be alarming doctrines. They were the doctrines by which Edwards and others had filled their hearers with anxiety, and produced excitement. They were therefore laid aside; but silently and without controversy, for controversy might have produced feeling. Men were suffered to forget that the Son and the Spirit have any thing important to do in the work of man's salvation; and then it became easy to overlook their existence. In this way the Unitarian party was formed, and furnished with all its essential attributes long before Unitarian doctrines were openly avowed, and probably long before they were distinctly embraced in theory, except by a very small number.

The first congregation that became avowedly Unitarian was that at the "King's Chapel," in Boston. It was Episcopalian. Being without a pastor, they employed Mr. [James] Freeman, afterward Dr. Freeman, as reader, in 1782. In 1785 he succeeded in introducing a revised liturgy, from which the doctrine of the Trinity was struck out. He applied to several American bishops for ordination, but none would ordain him. He was, therefore, ordained by the church-wardens, in 1787. For many years he maintained a constant correspondence with the leading Unitarians in England, and was a convenient medium of communication between them and the secret adherents of the same doctrines in America.

In and around Boston no Congregational church had yet avowed itself Unitarian. Harvard College had an orthodox president and professor of theology till after the commencement of the present century. After the death of Professor Tappan, in 1804, the

Rev. Dr. Ware was elected as his successor. While the question of his election was pending, a suspicion of his Unitarianism was suggested, but it was repelled by his friends as a calumny. Even when President Kirkland was elected, in 1812, it has been said, on high Unitarian authority, that he could not have been elected if he had been known as a defender of Unitarianism.

No pastor of a Congregational church in or near Boston had yet avowed himself a Unitarian, either from the pulpit or the press. Yet the style of preaching adopted by many was such as to excite suspicion; several periodicals openly advocated Unitarianism, and Unitarian books were imported and published in considerable numbers. Orthodox ministers, when attending councils for ordaining pastors, found themselves opposed and thwarted in their attempts to ascertain the theological views of the candidates. Many other circumstances indicated the presence and secret diffusion of error; but the means were wanting of fastening the charge upon individuals. . . .

. . . Orthodox ministers, therefore, refused to exchange pulpit labors on the Sabbath with those whom they believed to be Unitarians, or to sit with them in ecclesiastical councils, or in any other way to recognize them as ministers of Christ. This practice, however, was adopted gradually. Many orthodox men were slow in believing that one and another of their neighbors was a Unitarian; and many undecided men contrived to avoid for some time a declaration in favor of either party, and to keep on good terms with both. At length, however, successive disclosures made the dividing line so visible, throughout its whole length, that every man knew his own side of it, and the parties are completely separated without any formal excommunication of one by the other. . . .

In 1825 the number of Unitarian congregations was estimated at one hundred and twenty. In 1855, they were said to amount to about 360, of which all but eighty-six were in Massachusetts. Out of New England there were but thirty-nine. There are several causes of this increase.

Unitarianism, as has been shown, originally grew out of a dislike to the practice of requiring evidence of piety in candidates for admission to the churches. There are many, in various parts of the country, in whom this fundamental feeling of the sect is very strong, but who are yet unwilling to live without some form of religion. They are easily organized into a society which requires no creed, and subjects them to no discipline. Societies thus formed, however, often vanish as easily and suddenly as they are made.

The "American Unitarian Association," formed in 1825, is their principal organization for united action. Its object is declared to be "to diffuse the knowledge and promote the interests of pure Christianity throughout our country." This association aids from ten to twenty churches, most of them in New England, and publishes a considerable series of tracts. Its receipts have been usually about $5,000 annually.

The smallness of the amount expended by Unitarians in the way of associated action is not to be ascribed to parsimony, but to religious indifference. A large part of the wealth of Boston, and of the eastern part of Massachusetts, is in their hands; and their capitalists have made many splendid donations to literary, scientific, and humane institutions.

Their churches probably contain some truly regenerate persons, who became members of them before they were avowedly Unitarian, and who remain there from reverence for ancient usages, attachment to the places where their ancestors worshiped, and other similar causes. Others of them are men of stern and almost Puritanic morality, who have had from infancy great reverence for religion in the gross, but have never seriously studied its application to themselves in the detail of its doctrines and duties, and who would have remained steadfast members of the same congregations just as quietly had those congregations remained orthodox.

In philosophy the Unitarians of New England were at first, and for some years, followers of Locke; holding that all our ideas, or, at least, the elements of which they are formed, are received through the senses. Very naturally, therefore, they built their belief of Christianity wholly on evidence addressed to the senses. . . . Many of them held that the authors of the several parts of the New Testament had no inspiration which secured them against mistakes and false reasoning; and they very generally held that strong texts in favor of the doctrine of the Trinity, the divinity of Christ, or the personality of the Holy Spirit, must be interpolations or corruptions. Their religious guide, therefore, was so much of the Bible as they judged to be true; and their religion was, in its theory, the conformity of their hearts and lives to certain external rules, which, in all probability, were originally given by God, and which have been transmitted to us in a record which is not free from error. To this, individuals among them append more or less of sentiment and imagination, according to the prompting of their own genius. A system like this can never long continue to satisfy any community. It fails to meet certain feelings of spiritual want, which are sure to spring up in many minds. Hence there has been among the more serious, ever since the separation, a gradual going over to orthodoxy, which has retarded the growth of Unitarianism. . . .

[One chapter, "The Christ-ian Connection," followed here in the original.]

CHAPTER 70

The Universalists

In our chapter on the Unitarians, we expressed our views of the moral influence of the doctrines of the Universalists. The latter were little known as a sect in America until about the middle of the last century, when a few persons of reputation partially or wholly embraced their doctrines. . . . About the year 1790, the Rev. Hosea Ballou appeared as a Universalist preacher, and taught that all punishment is in this life, and, consequently, that the souls of the righteous and the wicked alike pass immediately at death into a state of happiness—a doctrine which, being much more acceptable to the unrenewed heart, became much more popular than that of restoration. . . . In 1810 there were but twenty-two avowed Universalist preachers; they now state their numbers to be as follows: 640 preachers, 828 churches, under a General Convention, and many Associations, and 600,000 of the population under their influence. The last item, we suspect is much too high. Their congregations are mostly small, and many attend from mere curiosity.*

The doctrines of the American Universalists are well expressed in three articles adopted as a "Profession of Belief" by the General Convention of Universalists, held in 1803. It is said to be "perfectly satisfactory to the denomination," and is as follows:

1. "We believe that the Holy Scriptures of the Old and New Testaments contain a revelation of the character of God, and of the duty, interest, and final destination of mankind.

2. "We believe that there is one God, whose nature is love; revealed in one Lord Jesus Christ, by one Holy Spirit of grace, who will finally restore the whole world of mankind to holiness and happiness.

3. "We believe that holiness and true happiness are inseparably connected; and that believers ought to be careful to maintain order and practice good works; for these things are good and profitable unto men."

The only Universalists whose preaching seems to have any moral influence, are the handful of Restorationists [those who combine a view that there is punishment for sinners with a hope for their eventual restoration]—the rest are heard with delight chiefly by the irreligious, the profane, Sabbath-breakers, drunkards, and all haters of evangelical religion. Their preaching positively exercises no reforming influence on the wicked, and what worse can be said of it?†

---

* [Ed.—In the 1844 edition Baird reported their number of preachers to be 540 and their churches, 550; the total population under their influence was estimated at 600,000. In some curious fashion Baird allowed a growth in preachers and churches, while keeping the population under their influence at the same figure from 1844 to 1856.]

† On the opening of a Universalist place of worship in any of our cities and villages, it is flocked to chiefly by low, idle, and vicious persons. Curiosity sometimes attracts others of a better description for a time; but it is a remarkable fact, established by the testimony of Universalists on becoming converted to the Truth, that few can, however desirous, ever bring themselves to believe the doctrine of universal salvation. Most are like the New England farmer who, at the close of a Universalist service, went forward and thanked the preacher for his sermon, saying that he vastly liked the doctrine, and would give him five dollars if he would only make it true!

I take pleasure in stating that of late there seems to be a growing conviction among some of the leading Universalists that there must be some punishment for the wicked in the world to come.

[One chapter, "Swedenborgians and Tunkers," followed here in the original.]

CHAPTER 71

The Jews

Whatever may have been the early legislation of the Anglo-American colonies in regard to the descendants of Abraham, it is certain that the Jew now finds an asylum, and the full enjoyment of his civil rights, in all parts of the United States. Yet I know not how it has happened, unless it be owing to the distance of our country from Europe, and its presenting less scope for the petty traffic which forms their chief employment in the Old World, that it has been only at a comparatively recent period that any considerable number of Jews have found their way to our shores. So much have they increased, however, among us during the last twenty years, that it is now computed that there are no fewer than fifty thousand in the United States. They have about fifty synagogues and the same number of Rabbis. Five or six synagogues are now to be found in New York, instead of one, as a few years ago. There is one in which the service is conducted in English, at Charleston, in South Carolina, and no doubt in other cities also. A few instances of conversion to Christianity have taken place, but only a few, the attention of Christians, we may truly say, not having been sufficiently turned to that object. This may have been from the fewness of the Jews, until of late years, causing them to be overlooked, or from the want of suitable persons to devote themselves to the work. We are pleased to see that some interest has begun to be taken in this subject during the last few years.*

---

* [Ed.—This is the same paragraph, with identical statistics, that appeared in the 1844 edition of Baird's work.]

CHAPTER 72

Rappists, Shakers, Mormons, etc.

The *Rappists* are a small body of German Protestants, who came to the United States from Wurtemburg, about the year 1803, under their pastor, a Mr. George Rapp, now deceased. They settled at a place called Economy, on the Ohio, about fifteen miles below Pittsburgh. From Economy part of them, headed by Mr. Rapp, went to the Wabash River, in Indiana, and on its banks formed a new settlement, called Harmony, but this they afterward sold to the well-known Robert Owen, and returned to Economy, in Pennsylvania. Their distinguishing principle is an entire "community of goods," upon what they suppose to have been the example of the primitive Christians. The whole scheme, however, of this small community, for it comprises but a few hundred members, seems mainly of a worldly and merely economical character, though they keep up the form of religious observances and services.*

The *Shakers* are a fanatical sect of English origin. About 1747, James Wardley, originally a Quaker, imagining that he had supernatural dreams and revelations, founded a sect which, from the bodily agitations practiced in some parts of their religious services, were called Shakers, or Shaking Quakers; it is not, however, to be supposed for a moment that they are connected with the respectable people called Quakers or Friends. Ann Lee, or, rather Mrs. Standley, (for she had married a man of that name,) the daughter of a blacksmith in Manchester, England, adopted Wardley's views and the bodily exercises of his followers. From the accounts we

---

* [Ed.—The Rappites were an important component of the religio-cultural history of the early national period, and for that reason readers might wish to consult a more adequate treatment of the subject. See for example, Charles Nordhoff, *The Communistic Societies of the United States* (New York: Schocken Books, 1965) (first published in 1875), pp. 63–95; and John A. Bole, *The Harmony Society, A Chapter in German American Culture History* (Philadelphia: Americana Germanica Press, 1904.)]

have of her she must have become a thorough adept during the nine years which she spent in convulsions, fastings, etc.; for she is said to have clenched her fists in the course of her fits so as to make the blood pass through the pores of her skin, and wasted away so that at last she had to be fed like an infant. About 1770 she discovered the wickedness of marriage, and began "testifying against it." She called herself "Ann the Word," meaning that the Word dwelt in her. And to this day her followers say that "the man who was called *Jesus,* and the woman who was called *Ann,* are verily the two first pillars of the Church, the two anointed ones." In other words, they hold that, as the first Adam was accompanied by a woman, so must be the second Adam.

In May, 1774, Ann Lee, otherwise Mrs. Standley, together with three elders, and others of the sect, emigrated to America, and two years after formed a settlement at Niskayuna, a few miles from Albany, in the State of New York. From that, as from a centre, they put forth shoots, until at length there are now about fifteen Shaker settlements, or villages, in different parts of the United States, comprising some six or eight thousand souls. Their doctrines are a strange mixture of the crudest errors with some few Gospel truths, but it would be a sad misnomer to call them *Christian.* They call themselves the Millennial Church. They hold that the millennium has begun, and that they are the only true church, and have all the apostolic gifts. They insist that Baptism and the Lord's Supper ceased with the apostolic age; that the wicked will be punished for a definite period only, except such as apostatize from them, and these will be punished forever; that the judgment has already commenced; that Christ will not again appear in the world, except in the persons of his followers, that is, the Shakers; that marriage is sinful, and that "they that have wives should be as though they had none," even now, and that thus alone purity and holiness, and the consequent beatitude of the heavenly state, can be attained. . . . In their religious worship, they range themselves at intervals in rows, and then spring upward a few inches; sometimes, however, they become so excited in this exercise as to throw off their upper garments, and jump as if they would touch the ceiling—all, as they say, to express their joy in the Lord. After this they sit down and listen awhile to their preachers, and then, when tired of hearing, resume their dancing freaks.

They maintain the doctrine of a communion of goods. The men and women live apart. The children of the proselytes are instantly separated, the boys being sent into the male apartment, and the girls into the female. Of course it is only from such recruits that a community of this kind can keep up its numbers.

The Shakers have the reputation, in general, of being honest and industrious, but I have had no means of ascertaining what their interior life and conduct may be, beyond this, that no small number of their members have left them in disgust, and are far from speaking well of them. . . . Accordingly, they remain a small and quiet obscure community, that must in time utterly disappear instead of growing into something like importance, which would be the probable result if they were persecuted. . . .

The *Mormons,* or *Latter Day Saints,* as they call themselves. The annals of modern times furnish few more remarkable examples of cunning in the leaders, and delusion in their dupes, than are presented by what is called Mormonism. An ignorant but ambitious person of the name of Joseph Smith, jun., then residing in the western part of the State of New York, pretended that an angel appeared to him in 1827, and told him where he should find a stone box, containing certain golden plates, with a revelation from heaven inscribed on them. Four years after this, the plates having, of course, been found as described, the impostor set about the writing out of this revelation, and pretended, with the aid of a pair of stone spectacles, found also in the box, to read it off to a man of the name of [Martin] Harris, and afterward to one called [Oliver] Cowdery, these acting as his amanuenses. The "prophet," as he is now called, took care, of course, that neither of them, nor any one else, should see the plates, the part of the room he occupied having been partitioned off from that where they sat by a blanket. After three years spent in concocting this new revelation, the book at last was completed, and published as a 12mo volume of 588 pages, at Palmyra, in the State of New York. It is commonly called the Mormon's Bible, but more properly *The Book of Mormon,* and is divided into fifteen books or parts, each purporting to be written by the author whose name it bears. These profess to give the history of about a thousand years from the time of Zedekiah, king of Judah, to A.D. 420. The whole work claims to be an abridgment by one Moroni, the last of the Nephites, of the seed of Israel, from the records of his people. Not to trouble the reader with details respecting this most absurd of all pretended revelations from heaven, we need only say that it undertakes "to trace the history of the Aborigines of the American Continent, in all their apostacies, pilgrimages, trials, adventures, and wars from the time of their leaving Jerusalem, in the reign of Zedekiah, under one Lehi, down to their final disaster, near the hill of Camorah, in the State of New York, where Smith found his golden plates. . . .

But the *Book of Mormon,* which they do not consider so much in the light of a substitute for the Holy Scriptures as of a supplement to them, does not contain all Joseph Smith's revelations; a 12mo volume, of about 250 pages, called *"The Book of Covenants and Revelations,"* and filled with the silliest things imaginable, of all sorts, has been added to it by way of another supplement. Thoroughly to comprehend the whole system, however, one must read Mr. Parley P. Pratt's "Voice of Warning," for he is an oracle among the Mormons, and also the newspapers which they publish as an organ for the dissemination of their doctrines. We may add that, aided by his wonderful spectacles, Smith undertook to make a new translation of the Bible, although quite unacquainted with Hebrew and Greek!

The publication of his own Bible, in 1830, may be considered as the starting-point of the sect. For some years he made but few converts, but having removed to Kirtland, Ohio, he was there joined by Sidney Rigdon, formerly a heterodox Baptist preacher, who had been preparing the way for Mormonism by propagating certain doctrines of his own, and being a much better-informed man than Smith, it was chiefly under his plastic hand that the religious economy of the sect has been formed. From Ohio they began to remove, in 1834, to Jackson county, in Missouri, where they were to have their "Mount Zion," the capital and centre of their great empire. The people of Missouri, a few years after, compelled them to leave it; upon which they went to Illinois, and there they set about building the city of Nauvoo, on the left bank of the Mississippi, and thither their disciples flocked, until their numbers amounted to several thousands. Smith and Rigdon were long their chief prophets. At last Smith was killed by the hands of those whom he cruelly injured in their domestic relations, and, driven by the enraged people of Illinois, the community removed to Salt Lake, in what is now Utah, where they have founded a city and a large settlement.

For a while, they had many to sympathize with them on account of the severity with which they have been supposed to be treated in Missouri, but so much has lately come to light in proof of the inordinate ambition, and vile character and conduct of their leaders, who want to found a kind of empire in the West, that their destruction as a sect would seem inevitable. One dupe after another is leaving them, and exposing the abominations of the fraternity and its chiefs. Their leaders are evidently atrocious impostors, who have deceived a great many weak-minded persons, by holding out to them promises of great temporal advantage. But they will soon find that America is not another Arabia, nor "Joe Smith" another Mohammed; and their hope of founding a vast empire in the Western hemisphere must soon vanish away.*

It is a singular fact that so large a proportion of them are from Great Britain. But it is not difficult to account for this. Their leaders know well that there is a large population in England of a low and ignorant character, who may be readily tempted, by the prospect of bettering their fortunes, to take part in such an enterprise. They have received a good many "recruits" to their ranks from Denmark and Norway.

. . . The Government of the United States has wisely abstained from using physical force to suppress them; for, until now, this would have created sympathy for them and augmented their numbers. But the time for sympathy is passed. Should the community continue to exist till the day comes for the admission of Utah into the confederation as a State, there will be a decided crisis; for it can not for a moment be believed that it will be

---

* [Ed.—Modern readers might wish to supplement this biased account by consulting some of the following works: William A. Linn, *The Story of the Mormons* (New York: Macmillan, 1923); Joseph F. Smith, *Essentials in Church History* (Salt Lake City: Deseret Book Co., 1959); and Thomas F. O'Dea, *The Mormons* (Chicago: University of Chicago Press, 1957).]

received so long as polygamy is not only allowed, but sustained by the sanctions of a pretended revelation from heaven. For a long time the leaders held out the idea to their more serious dupes, that the book of Mormon was only a supplement to the Christian Scriptures. To the poor, especially, in the Old World, they offered great temporal advantages. But now that the true character of the whole infernal scheme is becoming well known, we have reason to hope that the evil has reached its apogee, and that the destruction of the community will, before very many years pass away, be effected by moral influences. . . .

CHAPTER 73

Atheists, Deists,

Socialists, Fourierists, etc.

These sects can hardly be placed with propriety among religious denominations of any description: the most they pretend to, being a code of morals, such as it is. The avowed Atheists are, happily, few in number, and are chiefly to be found among the frequenters of our remaining groggeries and rum-holes.

As for our Deists, including unbelievers in Christianity of all classes, there is a considerable number, especially in New York, and some of our other large cities and towns. A very large proportion of them are foreigners. The infidelity of the present times, however, in the United States, is remarkably distinguished from what was to be found there fifty or sixty years ago, when that of France, after having diffused itself in the plausible speculations of a host of popular writers, wherever the French language was known, became at length associated with the great Revolution of that country, and obtaining credit for all that was good in a work which it only corrupted and marred, became fashionable in America as well as in Europe, among the professed admirers of liberty, in what are called the highest classes of society. At the head of these, in the United States, stood Mr. Jefferson, who was President from 1801 to 1809, and who in conversation, and by his writings, did more than any other man that ever lived among us to propagate irreligion in the most influential part of the community. In the same cause, and about the same period, labored Mr. Thomas Paine, and, at a later date, Mr. Thomas Cooper, who endeavored to train to infidelity by sophistical reasoning, and still more, by contemptible sarcasms and sneers, the youth whom it was his duty to teach better things.

Now, however, it is much otherwise. When men dislike evangelical truth, they take refuge in something which, under the name of Christianity, makes a less demand on their conscience and their conduct. Open infidelity, meanwhile, has descended to the lower ranks. It now burrows in the narrow streets and lanes, and purlieus of our large cities and towns, where it finds its proper aliment—the ignorant and the vicious to mislead and to destroy.

Owenism, Socialism, and Fourierism, are of foreign origin. The first two are from England, and are but economical or political schemes, in which infidelity seeks to imbody and sustain itself. Fourierism is also an economical scheme. It is not necessarily allied to infidelity, and has had but little success in the United States, nor is it likely to have. . . .

SUMMARY OF THE NON-EVANGELICAL BODIES

It will appear from what we have just said that the number of ministers in the non-evangelical bodies, great and small, is 3,215; of organized churches, 3,643. Under this head, however, we only reckon the Romanists, Unitarians, Universalists, Christ-ians, and Swedenborgians. The rest, however—Jews, Shakers, Mormons, etc. —ought to be called non-Christian rather than non-evangelical, and take rank with Deists and other Infidels.

As to the number of members belonging to the non-evangelical bodies in the United States, it is not easy to speak with any thing like precision. We may safely say that the Unitarians, Christ-ians, Universalists, and Swedenborgians, have 125,000 members. But as to the Roman Catholics, we have no very precise information. They publish no statistics which give us any light on the subject. They include in their statistics all who are called Roman Catholics —men, women, and children—but tell us not how many are communicants. Finally, the population which is under the influence of the non-evangelical bodies, may be estimated at from four to five millions.

CHAPTER 74

General Remarks on the
State of Theological Opinion
in America

. . . it is not difficult to draw a line between the various unevangelical sects on the one hand, and those that may be classed together as evangelical denominations on the other. The chief of the former, as we have said, are the Roman Catholics, Unitarians, Christ-ians, Universalists, Hicksite Quakers, Swedenborgians, Jews, Shakers, and so on down to the Mormons, beginning with the sect that has buried the Truth amid a heap of corruptions of heathenish origin, and ending with the grossest of all the delusions that Satanic malignity or human ambition ever sought to propagate. Now it will be observed that, with the exception of the first two, these sects have few elements of stability. Their ministers are almost all men of little learning, and that little is almost all concentrated in specious endeavors to maintain their tenets, by perverting the Scriptures, by appealing to the prejudices of their hearers, and by misrepresenting and ridiculing the doctrines of opponents who meet their subtle arguments with the plain declarations of Scripture, as well as with unanswerable arguments drawn from sound reason. . . . At times a religious revival almost annihilates, in the course of a few weeks, the attempts made by some Universalist preacher to form a society of that sect, at places where the faithful herald of the Gospel has lifted up a standard for Truth. And as none of the unevangelical bodies, not even the Roman Catholics, can absolutely debar their members from attending the preaching of evangelical ministers when they come into their neighborhood, they present no insurmountable barrier to the advance of Truth.

A better and more intimate acquaintance with the state of society in the United States than foreigners can well possess, seems necessary to account for the number, variety, and numerical magnitude of some of our unevangelical sects, and thus to abate the surprise which these may occasion to many of our readers. Nevertheless, to a certain extent, this may be brought within the comprehension even of those who have never seen the country. First, then, be it observed that not only can a far larger proportion of the white inhabitants of the United States read than is to be found in almost any other country, but they actually *do* read and pursue the acquisition of knowledge in almost every possible way. Novelty, accordingly, has always great attractions for them. Next, with the exception, perhaps, of Scotland, in no other country is there so little work done on the Lord's day; not only does the law require observance, but the disposition of the people enforces it; and as they are not at all of a character that would incline them to spend the day at home in idleness, they naturally take advantage of the opportunities within reach of attending public meetings, and listening to what may be said there. And religion being a subject to which they attach more or less importance almost universally, it is what they most like to hear discussed on the Sabbath. Thirdly, where there is no evangelical preaching, vast numbers, particularly of such as have no decided religious convictions, will resort to a Universalist, or even to an Infidel preacher, if one is announced in their neighborhood, rather than go nowhere at all. No doubt curiosity leads them thither first, and perhaps for a long time afterward. Fourthly, absolute religious liberty being the principle of the government, the people may everywhere have what preaching they please, if they can find it, and choose to be at the expense of maintaining it; and, accordingly, they who dislike faithful evangelical preaching, often combine to form a congregation where some heterodox preacher may hold forth doctrines more acceptable to them. Congregations so formed, especially in cities and large towns, may last for years, or even become in some sense permanent, but in far the greater number of cases they disappear, part of their numbers removing to some other place, and others becoming converts to the orthodox creed of the surrounding evangelical churches.

Thus it will be perceived that the unevangelical sects in the United States are mainly composed of persons who, in other countries, would remain stupidly indifferent to religion, spending their Sabbaths in employments or amusements wholly secular. Even this may be thought better by some than that they should "give heed to doctrines of devils," upon the principle that no religion is better than a false one. This may be true in many cases, but hardly in all. Experience proves, I think, very decidedly in America, that persons that occupy their minds with the subject of religion, even when they doubt the Truth or embrace positive error, are more accessible to the faithful preaching of the Gospel, than others that are sunk in stupid indifference and infidelity. The forms of error in that country have, with one exception, no element of stability—no vigorous dogmatism or permanent fascinations to oppose to the solid orthodoxy of evangelical preaching. The one exception is Romanism, which presents a sort of *mosaic* of truth and error, so artfully combined as to exert a charm over the minds of those who have once received it, which it is almost impossible to dissipate.

Next to Romanism, Unitarianism is, of all forms of error that assume the title of Christian, the most stable. Its professors are chiefly to be found in the eastern parts of Massachusetts; but as those, as well as other parts of New England, are constantly sending out emigrants to the new settlements, small knots of persons with Unitarian preferences may be found in the Middle, Southern, and Western States. Still, this dispersion of Unitarianism, and its sprouting up at various points, elsewhere than in Massachusetts, has rather the appearance than the reality of increase. It may be more than doubted whether it be not positively declining in Boston and its vicinity. Except that it by no means prevails in the same proportion, it is very much in America what Rationalism is in Protestant Europe—a disease caught by the Church from the epidemic of skepticism of the eighteenth century—a skepticism which is now in both hemispheres taking the form of a mystical pantheism. . . . At all events, no one who is well informed with regard to the present aspect of things in America, can claim for Unitarianism much vigor or any greater positive increase than that of the natural increase of the population within its pale; and it may be doubted whether it is increasing even so much as that.

A certain amount of moral influence for good may fairly be attributed to some of the unevangelical sects, but this can hardly be said of the Universalists—and they comprise nearly the whole— who deny a future judgment and all punishment beyond this life; while as for the Atheists, Deists, and Socialists of every hue, it is hardly slander to say that their influence upon society is positively mischievous.

As for the Shakers, Mormons, and other such agglomerations, they may be accounted for, I apprehend, on two principles. First, the blinding nature of human depravity, which makes men prefer any thing, however absurd, that looks like religion, and suits their fancies and their passions, to retaining, or, rather, to obtaining, the true knowledge of God. Next, these bodies always hold out some temporal good—some economical advantage—which, far more than any religious consideration, tempts persons to enter them. One would suppose, for example, that a religion which, like that of the Shakers, makes the sinfulness of marriage a fundamental prin- ciple, and obliges married proselytes to live single, could never find followers. Yet, as persons sometimes grow tired of the marriage relation, or, rather, of those with whom it has bound them as husband and wife, so some may be found willing, even by becom- ing Shakers, to rid themselves of a burden they feel to be grievous. So, also, in the separation of children from their parents, and the entire breaking up of the family relationships, weak people may always be found ready to snatch at any opportunity of ridding themselves of parental responsibility, by shifting it upon other shoulders. This despicable and unmanly selfishness may be regarded as the main foundation of all the forms of Socialism.

I would remark, in conclusion, that few things in the history of the Gospel more strikingly prove its inherent life and divinity, than the extent to which it has secured and retains a hold upon the American people. Their Christianity is not the dead formalism of ecclesiastical institutions—upheld by law, tradition, or the force of fashion.* It is not a body of superstitions, lying with oppressive weight upon the common mind, and giving support to a domineering priesthood. It is not that Rationalism which, retaining little of Christianity but the name, has had a brief ascendency in some parts of Protestant Europe. It is evangelical Christianity—the Christianity of the New Testament. Wherever the stranger sees a place of worship in our cities, or in the country, the presumption is, the probability is, with few exceptions, ten to one—that there God is worshipped in the name of the one Mediator, with faith and penitence; that there pardon is offered to the guilty, freely through Christ the Lamb of God; and that there the Holy Spirit is looked for, and is given to renew the heart of the sinner, and to fill the believing soul with joy and peace. The worship may, in many instances, be such as would offend the sensibilities of certain cultivated minds—most unlike the choral pomp of old cathedrals— still, rude as it may be, it is often that only acceptable worship which is offered in spirit and in truth. The Gospel may be preached there ignorantly, and with many imperfections, still it *is* the Gospel, and often does it become "the wisdom of God, and the power of God unto salvation."

---

* Much has been said in Europe about the *tyranny of public opinion* in the United States, but I confess I never have been able to comprehend what this expression means. M. de Tocqueville employs it, but without giving any clear idea upon the subject. . . . If public opinion be strong and decided in America, it is because the character of the people makes it so. When they form an opinion, more especially on any matter in which the judgment or the conscience is concerned (and what subject of a practical kind does not involve one or other of these?) they are not willing to change it but for good reasons. And in all matters of religion, and morals especially, the Protestant Faith, which has so much influence with a large proportion of the population, concurs with the earnestness and steadiness of the Anglo-Saxon character, to make public opinion, not only strong, but right on all points upon which it has been sufficiently informed. . . .

BOOK VIII

Efforts of the American Churches for the Conversion of the World

CHAPTER 75

Introductory Remarks

We can not well close our view of the religious condition of the United States without a brief notice of what the Churches here are doing for the propagation of the Gospel in other lands. This forms a natural sequel to what has been said of their endeavors to plant and to sustain its institutions on their own soil.

Some readers, indeed, may be surprised to learn that our Churches are doing any thing at all for the spiritual welfare of other countries, while they have so much to do in their own. . . . they may be astonished that the American churches, unaided by the government in any way, receiving no tithes, taxes, or public pecuniary grants of any kind, even for the support of religion at home, do nevertheless raise large sums for sending the Gospel to the heathen. Such, however, is not the feeling of enlightened and zealous Christians in America itself. They feel that, while called upon to do their utmost for religion at home, it is at once a duty and a privilege to assist in promoting it abroad. They feel assured that he that watereth shall himself be refreshed, and that, in complying so far as they can with their Saviour's command to "preach the Gospel to every creature," they are most likely to secure the blessing of that Saviour upon their country. And facts abundantly prove that they judge rightly. . . .

CHAPTER 76

Earlier Efforts to Convert the Aborigines

Notwithstanding the common mistake at the present day, of those who conceive that religious liberty, and to some extent, also, the enjoyment of political rights, were the sole inducements that led to the original colonization of the United States, we have seen that the plantations of both Virginia and New England were designed to conduce to the spread of Christianity by the conversion of the Aborigines, as is proved both by the royal charters establishing those early colonies, and by the expressed sentiments of the Massachusetts settlers.

It is no easy task, indeed, to Christianize and civilize savages who, from times unknown, have been devoted to hunting and to war; and, when not thus occupied, lounge like their dogs about their miserable hovels and tents, clad in skins, and leaving to their women, or squaws, the drudgery of cultivating a little patch of maize or "Indian corn," making the fires, and even dressing the animals that have been slain in the chase, as well as all other domestic cares. Their aversion to the methodical labor required for the arts of civilized life, is such as none can conceive without a personal knowledge of them. Not a single noble aspiration seems ever to enter their souls, but all they care about seems to be that they may pass away their life as their fathers did, and then die amid the vague and shadowy visions of the unknown future. In short, as long as their forests last, and game can be found, they seem not to have a thought of adopting the habits of civilized life.

Some persons are forever indulging mawkish lamentations over the disappearance of the aboriginal tribes of North America, and, if one may interpret their sentimental distress on this subject, they would rather see this vast continent occupied by a few hundred thousand savages, roaming the forests, and continually at war with each other, than covered with a civilized and Christian population; either forgetting, or else never having known, that a savage state is not only wretched, but necessarily tends to annihilation.

But how civilized men are to share the same continent with the uncivilized, without the latter being supplanted and made to disappear, is a question by no means of easy solution. On the discovery of a continent of great natural resources, and possessing every thing calculated to invite civilized men to its shores, it is easy to see that the time can not be distant when civilized men, by natural increase and immigration, will crowd upon and displace the uncivilized. To save the latter from extinction, under such circumstances, one or other of two courses must be pursued: either the two races must be amalgamated, which is next to impossible while one remains uncivilized, and can only be done by reducing one of them to a species of slavery, and thus bringing them into the bosom of civilized society, as was very much the course pursued by the Spaniards in Mexico and South America; or the uncivilized race be allowed to preserve their natural existence as tribes in some distinct territory. The plan pursued by the Spaniards was revolting to the feelings of the English colonists, and they adopted, accordingly, that of letting the Indians enjoy a separate existence.

But even this, easy as it may seem at first sight, is attended with many difficulties. It would be very practicable if all men were what they ought to be; for then, after the immigrants had purchased the territory they required, the Indians would be left in undisturbed possession of what they chose to reserve to themselves, and the two races would live in each other's presence, respecting each other's rights, and each contented with its own possessions. But this, alas! is not a likely result among fallen men whom even Christianity has only partially restored. As the civilized inhabitants increased in numbers, they desired more and more territory, which the Indians did not hesitate to sell as long as their own domain seemed almost boundless, and so the white men went on pushing the red further and further toward the West. Meanwhile, the latter disappointed the expectations of those who had looked forward to their adopting the manners and customs of civilized life. Living in close proximity to the white men's settlements, they often visited these with the skins of animals or blankets thrown over their shoulders, and their extremities exposed in the coldest weather; and then, after lounging about the houses of the colonists, and taking such presents as might be offered, they returned to their comfortless wigwams without having acquired the slightest desire to exchange their wretched mode of living for the conveniences and comforts they had just witnessed. They were too fond of the habits in which they had been nurtured, and too averse to every thing like steady industry, to seek any change.

. . . The little that was done must be ascribed to the missionaries sent to them chiefly by the churches in the colonies. These succeeded, in several instances, in partially civilizing the Indians among whom they labored, and to this the still extant remnants of tribes may be said to owe their preservation to this day, inasmuch as those in which Christianity never gained any footing, and in which agriculture and the mechanical arts never made any progress, almost wholly disappeared, either by becoming extinct, or by being merged in other uncivilized and heathen tribes.

. . . But where was there a territory ample enough to be found over which no charter extended its claims? At last, by the acquisition of Louisiana, this desideratum was supplied, and men, as benevolent as America has ever possessed, soon comprehended the important use that might be made of it, and pressed it upon the attention of the government. Accordingly, the country lying between the State of Arkansas and the Great American Desert, which stretches as far west as the Oregon Mountains, was set apart for the purpose, being sufficiently large, and containing much good land, and to it the government has succeeded in removing above twenty tribes, or remnants of tribes, from its own organized States and Territories. Soon all that remain will follow, so that there will probably be an Indian population of above one hundred thousand souls on a compact territory, stretching about four or five hundred miles from north to south, and about two hundred from east to west. Thither, also, have the missionaries, who had been laboring among those tribes, gone; and though the removal of the several nations from their ancient homes, and from the graves of their forefathers, has been followed by some years of that hardship and suffering which all removals from ancient settlements, whether more or less civilized, to the denser forests must occasion, yet they are surmounting these, and gradually establishing themselves in their new homes. In process of time they will have their little farms and lots of ground cleared, comfortable houses erected, mills built, and the more necessary arts of civilized life introduced among them. . . .

CHAPTER 77

American Board of Commissioners
for Foreign Missions

With the exception of that of the United Brethren, the American Board of Commissioners for Foreign Missions is the oldest society for foreign missions in the United States. It has also the greatest number of missions and missionaries, and the largest amount of receipts. . . .

ITS ORIGIN AND CONSTITUTION.—The Board had its origin in

the following manner: Several young men, graduates of New England colleges, and preparing for the Gospel ministry at the Theological Seminary at Andover, in the State of Massachusetts, agreed, in the year 1809, to unite their efforts in establishing a mission among the heathen in some foreign land. In this they were encouraged by the Faculty of the seminary. As the General Association of Congregational Ministers in Massachusetts were to hold their annual meeting in June, 1810, these young men were advised to submit their case to that body. This was done by four of their number—Messrs. Mills, Judson, Newell, and Nott. . . .

On the 29th of June, the Association elected a Board of Commissioners for Foreign Missions, consisting of nine persons. The Board, at its first meeting, held in the following September, adopted the name of the *American Board of Commissioners for Foreign Missions,* thus recognizing its high calling to act for all in every part of the nation, who might choose to employ its agency in the work of missions among the heathen. . . .

The following is a summary view of what, through the Divine favor, has been accomplished by this Board. The amount received into the treasury of the Board during the year ending on the 31st of July, 1855, was $310,427.77; and the amount of expenditure was $318,893.18. The treasury is at present indebted to the amount of $20,507.90.

The number of missions sustained during the year was twenty-nine; connected with which are 120 stations, at which were laboring 157 ordained missionaries, seven of whom were physicians: besides seven lay physicians, seventeen other male, and 203 female assistant missionaries—making the whole number of missionary laborers sent from this country and sustained by the Board 387. If to these be added sixty-three native preachers and 229 other native helpers, the whole number of missionary laborers connected with the missions, and sustained from the treasury of the Board will be 679. Of these missionary laborers, eight ordained missionaries, one missionary physician, one male, and seven female assistant missionaries, in all seventeen, were sent forth during the last year.

Organized by these missions, and under their pastoral care, are 115 churches, to which have been received during the last year

635, and which now embrace, in regular standing, 26,806 members. . . .

THEORY OF THE MISSIONS OF THE BOARD.—The Board does not regard any of its missions as permanent institutions. Their object is, through the grace of God, to impart the spirit and plant the institutions of the Gospel where they do not exist, and then to leave them to the conservative influences that shall have been gathered about them. This is true theoretically, and it will come out in fact as soon as the means are furnished for prosecuting the work with becoming vigor. The missionary is emphatically, in the essential principle of his calling, a sojourner, pilgrim, stranger, having no continuing city.

The leading object of its missions, therefore, is the training and employment of a native ministry, as the only way in which the Gospel can soon become indigenous to the soil, and the Gospel institutions acquire a self-supporting, self-propagating energy. And the fact is important to be noted, that the elders or pastors, whom the apostles ordained over the churches they gathered among the heathen, were generally, if not always, *natives of the country*. While the apostles had not the facilities of the present day for training men for this office by education, they had not the necessity for so doing. Among their converts at Ephesus, Berea, Corinth, Rome, and elsewhere, they had no difficulty in finding men who only required some instruction in theology, and scarcely that when endowed with miraculous gifts, to be prepared for the pastoral office. How they did, or would have done, beyond the Roman Empire and the bounds of civilization, we are not informed; but in the use they made of a native ministry, we recognize one of the grand principles of their missions, and also the true theory of those missions—simple, economical, practical, Scriptural, mighty through God.

[Seven chapters, "Board of Foreign Missions of the Presbyterian Church," "American Baptist Missionary Union," "Foreign Missions of the Methodist Episcopal Church," "Board of Missions of the Protestant Episcopal Church," "Foreign Missions of Other Denominations," "American Society for Ameliorating the Condition of the Jews," and "American and Foreign Christian Union," followed here in the original.]

CHAPTER 78

American Colonization Society

. . . we propose to say a few words respecting the American
Colonization Society, because of its connection with missions in
Western Africa, and its bearing upon the general interests of
humanity.

Though originating in a sincere desire to promote the benefit of
the African race, on the part of some of the best men that America
has ever seen, this society has for many years past been much
decried in America, and misrepresented to some extent in Europe.
The three persons who may be regarded as its founders have all
passed from the present scene to their reward above. These were
the late Rev. Dr. [Robert] Finlay, of New Jersey, the Rev. Samuel
J. Mills, of Connecticut, and the Hon. Elias B. Caldwell, of
Washington city, Clerk to the Supreme Court of the United States.
The society was organized in 1817, and its objects are expressed
as follows, in the second article of its constitution: "To promote
and execute a plan of colonizing (with their consent) the free
people of color residing in our country, in Africa, or such other
place as Congress shall deem most expedient." The primary
motive of its founders was to place the colored man in circumstances in which he might acquire that real independence of station
and character and, consequently, that equality in social life which
they supposed that he can not reach in the midst of a white population.

These colonies have been of slow growth, for the society,
unaided by the General Government, has been unable to conduct
the enterprise on a large scale. Inexperience, too, led to several
blunders in the first years, to which must be added want of union
and energy on the part of the National Society, and the loss of the

confidence of part of the public, particularly of the members of the Anti-slavery and Abolition Societies. Notwithstanding all this, the society has been gradually advancing. Its yearly income has for some time past exceeded $50,000, and its colonies, now supposed to number about ten thousand emigrants, are in a tolerably thriving state. Fatal as the climate of Liberia is to white men, the colored find it so much otherwise, that the mortality among them has not been greater than was to be expected—not more than what was experienced by the first settlers in Virginia and Massachusetts. Cape Palmas, from its elevated position, has been found remarkably healthy, and not oppressive even to the missionaries, though whites.

I have remarked that the society has been much opposed, especially by the friends of the Anti-slavery Societies in the United States. This opposition has arisen from the manner in which the society has been advocated. Some of its friends have been apt to recommend it as presenting the *sole* method of ridding the United States of slavery. This is absurd. It has diverted the minds of slaveholders in the South from the duty of universally emancipating their slaves, whether they shall remain in the country or not; and in this way has done mischief. Its friends have perhaps said too much, also, about the impossibility of the colored population rising to respectability and political equality in the United States. The difficulties are indeed great, but good men should never lend their aid in fostering the unreasonable prejudices against the colored race, entertained by too large a part of our people.

Notwithstanding these and some other errors which might be mentioned, I can not but feel the deepest interest in the cause of African colonization; first, because it may be advocated even before slaveholders in such a way as to favor emancipation, a thing which can not be done at present by the agents of our "Abolition" and "Anti-slavery Societies"; secondly, because it provides slaveholders who wish to emancipate their slaves, and who, by certain State laws, are obliged to remove them out of the State when so emancipated, with an opportunity of sending them to a country which *does* afford the prospect of their rising to independence and comfort; thirdly, because the colonization of Africa, in one way or other, presents the sole effectual method of breaking up the slave-trade; and lastly, because it is the surest way of introducing civilization into Africa, and also furnishes a *point d'appui* for the prosecution of Christian missions. . . .

CHAPTER 79

The Summary

Thus it will be perceived that almost every evangelical church in the United States is doing more or less for the propagation of the Gospel in foreign, and especially in heathen lands. I know not, indeed, that there is a single exception, unless it be among some of the smaller German denominations, or some branches of the Methodist and Presbyterian Churches. Even these, however, seem almost all to contribute toward this great object through societies or boards, either belonging to other denominations, or common to several. . . .

This is a gratifying fact, whether we regard it as a sign of life, or an earnest of its still further increase in the churches. Not that these have done all that their glorious Lord may justly look for at their hands; but that what they have hitherto done is but the promise of much greater things for the future, we may reasonably infer from the comparatively recent period that either domestic or foreign missions began seriously to interest the Christian public of the United States. . . .

It is difficult to present at one view the statistics of all these missionary efforts with perfect accuracy, at least if we would include all the particulars upon which the reader may think information desirable. On the main points we may obtain pretty accurate results. Including the missions of the evangelical churches alone, and those of the others are hardly of sufficient importance to call for notice, the receipts from all sources for propagating the Gospel in foreign and chiefly heathen lands, for the year 1855 may safely be reckoned at $933,062.* This is exclusive, also, of the income of the colonization societies, amounting, say, to $80,000, these not being missionary societies.

The number of distinct missions prosecuted by the United States churches is at least eighty; that of stations and out-stations exceeds three hundred. These employed in 1855 at least 450 preaching American missionaries, who, with a few exceptions, were ordained ministers, and above seventy American laymen, chiefly physicians, printers, teachers, and catechists. The American females, chiefly wives of missionaries and teachers, amounted to five hundred, making a total of 950 persons from the United States connected with these missions, and all laboring, in one way or another, to promote the Gospel among the heathen. The natives who assist as ministers, evangelists, teachers, distributors of tracts, etc., etc., amounted at least to five hundred.

Conclusion

In the foregoing pages I had proposed to treat of the Origin, History, Economy, Action, and Influence of Religion in the United States of America, and in the execution of this task I have en-

---

* The following table gives the details on this point:

The American Board of Commissioners for Foreign Missions	$310,427
Board of Foreign Missions of the Presbyterian Church	184,074
Boards of Foreign Missions of the Baptist Churches	163,660
Foreign Missions of the Methodist Episcopal Church	128,000
Foreign Missions of the Protestant Episcopal Church	57,600
Foreign Missionary Society of the Free-Will Baptists	6,301
Foreign Missionary Society of the Lutheran Church, (about)	3,000
Foreign Missionary Society of the United Brethren, (about)	10,000
American and Foreign Christian Union (to the foreign field) about	15,000
Other Societies	5,000
Grants from American Bible Society, the American and Foreign Bible Society, and the American Tract Society, estimated to be at least	50,000
Total	$933,062

Nor does this statement include the annual grant of the general government of $10,000 for the support of schools among the Indian tribes, which is laid out through the missionary societies. I have not been able to obtain the exact amount raised by two or three of the societies; but the supposed sums can not be far from the truth.

deavored to omit nothing that seemed requisite to a full elucidation of the subject. The extent of ground necessarily traversed has rendered it indispensable that I should lay before the reader very numerous details; but these, I trust, he has found at once pertinent and interesting. Here the work properly ends; but I am desirous of recalling the attention of the reader to a few of the most important facts which it brings to light, and briefly to remark upon them, in order, if possible, to render them more useful to those who may be led to contemplate them. I wish, also, to make a reply to several charges against my country, and especially against its religious institutions, which I have heard in certain parts of Europe.

IV. THE TRUE MEANS OF SUCCESS. . . . our religious liberty, unbounded and precious as it is, is not the cause of the success which has attended the Gospel in America. It is only the *occasion,* if I may so express myself, not the *means,* by which the Church of Christ has made so great advances in the United States. It has wonderfully opened the way for this blessed prosperity: it has removed hindrances, allayed prejudices, and placed the country in a true position in regard to Christianity. It has created an open field, in which Truth may contend with Error, clad in her own panoply, and relying on her own weapons.

Much as I love the perfect liberty of conscience and of worship which we enjoy in America, there are other things which, to my mind, must be regarded as the causes of the success which has attended the efforts of God's people among us to promote his kingdom. Let us notice these for a few moments.

1. There is the grouping of our children, rich and poor, in the Sunday-schools, arranging them in small classes, and bringing their young minds and hearts into contact with the Word of God.

2. There is the continuation of this good work in the Bible-class. What a powerful means of doing good! and how well calculated to follow up, or prepare the way for the instruction around the family altar.

3. There are our societies for educating in a thorough manner young men of piety and talents for the work of preaching the Gospel. And many hundreds of young men of promise, whom

God's Spirit urges to preach salvation to their dying fellow-men, are thus every year brought forward for the work.

4. Next come the Home Missionary Societies and Boards, which send forth these young men, when prepared to preach, to the new and destitute portions of the country, and help the people to sustain them.

5. In connection with these the Maternal Associations, and other means for impressing on parents the duty of bringing up their children for the Lord, and for aiding them in the attempt, must not be overlooked; nor those efforts which are made to disseminate the Sacred Scriptures and religious tracts and books. These are silent but efficient means of co-operation in this blessed work.

6. And, lastly and chiefly, there remains the *preaching of the Word,* the most effective of all instrumentalities for the conversion and sanctification of men. There is nothing which may supplant this. And here we have abundant occasion for thankfulness. We have many thousands of pious and faithful preachers; very many of whom are able, skillful, and successful laborers in the vineyard of the Lord.

V. THE TRUE SOURCE OF ALL SUCCESS. Still, these must all be considered as only *means;* the success is of God. "It is not by might, nor by power, but by My Spirit, saith the Lord." Here is all our hope; even Truth itself is impotent to renovate the heart of man, depraved and debased as he is, without the influence of the Holy Spirit. . . .

There is no one thing which has more decidedly characterized the preaching of our best and most successful divines, or the feelings of our most devoted Christians, than the doctrine of the existence, the personality, the offices, and the saving operation of the Holy Spirit. It has been the great dominant idea, if I may so term it, which has pervaded and influenced the Church of Christ in America during the last hundred years. Hence the esteem in which revivals of religion are held.

To this great subject I can not but entreat the religious reader to direct his most serious attention. It is one of vital importance. Surely God has led His people to expect a great outpouring of His Spirit in the "latter days." And, surely, the world, as well as the

Church, has seen the need of such an influence, if it is ever to be brought under the renovating influences of the Gospel to a degree corresponding with its necessities. And whatever importance the author may attach to other portions of it which relates to Religious Revivals may be most deeply pondered by every reader.

VI. Grounds of Hope in Relation to the Churches in America. I know of nothing which is so well calculated to inspire hope in relation to our American churches as the extensive diffusion of the spirit of missions among them within the last few years, for it is the spirit of Christ. . . .

. . . It is the wide diffusion of the spirit of missions through our churches, rather than its positive and present results, which I am here holding up as a ground of hope. And in that light I am sure it may fairly be regarded. It is the best omen for good both to the Church and to the nation. It is our great palladium. It is also our best pledge, and even our most certain means, of prosperity to all the interests of Truth. As long as the spirit of missions is existent and efficient in our Churches of every name, we may venture to hope that, whatever may go wrong in our political organization, or however wickedness may augment, God will regard us in mercy, and say of us as a nation, "Spare it, for there is a blessing in it."

XVI. Misconception and Misrepresentations Abroad. To notice all the misconceptions and misrepresentations which are prevalent in some, if not in all portions of Europe, respecting the religious and moral condition of America, is wholly impossible in a work like this; we must, therefore, confine our attention to but a few of them.

1. One of the most common objections against the religious institutions of this country is, that they have not prevented the bankruptcies and other species of dishonesty which have here occurred, especially a few years since. But is it reasonable to make the religious institutions of a country responsible for the occurrence of such things? Must the churches in America be blamed for the unwise legislation of the country, as well general as local, which has been the primary cause of the overtrading and inordinate speculation which prevailed some years ago, and which was so

disastrous in its reaction? Must they be accountable for the avidity with which the *foreign* merchant, manufacturer, and money-lender encourage the adventurous American merchant and trader to purchase their goods on credit, and invest their money in American stocks, often with little or no effort to make a proper discrimination between them? Must they be expected not only to prevent our own people, whether in an individual or a corporate capacity, from committing acts of rascality, but also to exert a similar influence upon the foreign adventurers, who come among us from all parts of the Old World (and their number is not small), the real object of many of whom is to swindle the American creditor out of all they can, and then escape to Europe? Take our merchants who are engaged in foreign commerce, and I hesitate not to say that, as a body, they have acted with as much good faith as any men in similar circumstances have ever done, during the years of commercial and financial difficulty through which the country has passed. Many of them ruined themselves in endeavoring to meet their engagements abroad, by paying an exorbitant interest on the loans which they made for that purpose. I speak here of them as a *body;* that there have been instances of dishonesty among them will not be denied, nor will any one be astonished at it.

We are willing that religion should be held accountable for a great deal; but we are not willing that the Churches in America should be blamed for not preventing what the Churches in no other countries have been able to prevent. The members proper of all our Churches, evangelical and unevangelical, do not exceed a fifth part of our population; and though the influence which they exert is unquestionably as salutary as that of any other body of equal number in the world, yet it is obvious they can not control circumstances such as I have alluded to. Would the Churches in Great Britain, France, Holland, Germany, or any other country, like to be held responsible for all the acts of legislation, domestic and foreign, of their respective countries, and all the villainies which have been and are annually perpetrated in them? I think not; nor should they apply to their brethren in America a rule by which they would not like to be measured themselves.

2. The *Political* disturbances which occur in America are not unfrequently spoken of in Europe in a way that conveys a reflection upon the Churches of this land, as if they ought to prevent these things. That these disturbances do take place, no one will deny. There is not a good man in the United States who did not lament what were called the "Abolition Riots," and other disgraceful scenes which occurred there some years since. These disturbances, however, were very greatly exaggerated as to their frequency and their extent, in the reports which reached Europe. Our newsmongers, in their eagerness to concoct a piquant article of news for those for whom they cater, often give the most astounding exaggeration of what was a dispute or open quarrel between some firemen, or between the blacks and whites in the suburbs of our cities, or affrays between the "native" population and the "foreign," or the interruption which some lecturer on slavery has encountered in some of our villages.* These representations go abroad, are circulated there, and lead many people to think that our whole country is in a continual state of disorder. But every American knows how to appreciate these reports, and is no way concerned about them, except to regret their occurrence. Indeed, neither their frequency nor their nature is such as to give him any serious apprehensions. For these things are local, unfrequent, and wholly insignificant in comparison with the bruit which our newspapers make about them. And they no more affect the peace of the country than the passing cloud ruffles the bosom of our beautiful lakes.

Within the last fifteen or twenty years there have been some disgraceful instances of summary punishment, without the intervention of a proper trial before the courts of law, in the case of some gamblers, swindlers, and negroes (who had committed shocking crimes) in some of our South-western States and Territories. But these instances have hardly exceeded in number that of

---

* Much also has been said in Europe about the prejudice that exists in America against the colored people, and the difficulty of the two races living together. But it is a singular and indisputable fact, that almost all the disturbances (and these, after all, do not amount to much) that occur between the blacks and whites in the suburbs of Philadelphia, New York, and other cities, take place between the former and the Germans and the Irish who live in those districts.

the years in which they have occurred. They took place, too, in a part of the country which is new, and very thinly settled; where religious institutions have scarcely taken root, and where the forms in which the administration of justice is carried on have hardly begun to exist. However much every well-informed, good man in America must lament these things, he can not but be less astonished at their occurrence than at the infrequency of them. No man can look at the great extent of even the settled portion of the United States, the long line of sea-coast which bounds the country on the east, south, and west; of wilderness and mountain-ranges in the centre, and the forests that abound almost everywhere, furnishing innumerable facilities for the commission of crime and escape from punishment, without being surprised that we have had so few disturbances of a serious character, especially when we have had so large a foreign element, with all its concomitant evils, to augment the difficulty of our position. It would require the army of the Czar of all the Russias to keep up a strong armed police, which some upbraid us for not having, and which would be necessary, if it were not that the moral influence that pervades the country—and owes its existence to our religious institutions—furnishes a substitute infinitely better. We have had three attempts, one in Pennsylvania, one in South Carolina, and one in Rhode Island, not to overthrow the political institutions of the country, but to obtain redress of grievances, real or imaginary, in an extra-constitutional way; and yet all three were suppressed without the loss of one life taken away either in battle or by the administration of law. To what was this owing? To the patience, the conciliation, and the due use of argument which the Christianity of the country could alone inspire and teach.

There have been seasons of great excitement, when the nation was agitated to its centre. For instance, during times of unparalleled commercial distress, when so many banks, and so many of our best merchants and traders, our enterprising mechanics and manufacturers—and, indeed so many men in all the walks of industry, and in every station of life—were ruined. How was all this borne? Was there the slightest attempt to seek redress by revolution? No. The government was severely blamed; all these evils were believed, by probably a majority of the people, to have been occasioned by unwise legislation, obstinately persevered in; and yet not a gun was seized, not a sword was drawn, and not one human life was lost during the long and dreadful crisis. The only resort was to the *ballot-box,* as our elections are often termed.

3. The American people have been represented sometimes by foreigners as being an *immoral people.* Now, although I know it is not easy to reply to such charges in a satisfactory manner in the very restricted space which I must allow to them, neverthelss, I will say a few words upon this topic.

That there are vices and crimes in America, and in no inconsiderable amount, is both acknowledged and deplored. But that they exist to such an extent as to justify the assertion that the American people are, *par excellence,* an immoral nation, is denied.

It is certainly not extraordinary, as was well remarked a few years ago by a writer in the "Westminster Review," that there should be in the United States swindlers, counterfeiters, thieves, bigamists, murderers, and other criminals, since, in addition to those of indigenous growth, they receive so many from the Old World. This is a correct view of the subject. For it is a fact, that while there are cases in which foreign criminals, especially those who have committed crimes which most deeply affect the conscience and heart, who have come to our shores and changed their names, reform and do well in a land where their past history is unknown (and certainly the friends of humanity must rejoice that it is so), there are very many in which it is otherwise. A man who has been a thief, a robber, a counterfeiter, a bigamist, in Europe, is not likely to reform in America, unless arrested by God's grace. There is more hope of a man who has committed manslaughter, or even murder, than of him.

A few general statements will, however, best express all that I have to say on this subject.

Although thieves and robbers are not wanting in our large cities and towns, where, all the world over, such people most congregate and find the greatest facilities for their nefarious vocation, yet, taking the country at large, it will be difficult to name another where property is more safe, or where people live in greater security.

As to murder, the most horrible of all crimes, the most exact enumeration has seldom been able to show that more than one hundred cases have occurred (and some years not much more than one half that number), in any one year. This number is sufficient to excite deep distress in the heart of every good man; but it is less than that which takes place in many other countries between which and ours comparisons on this point as well as others are sometimes instituted. . . .

And though there is a considerable amount of prostitution in some of our large cities on the sea-board—as, for instance, New York, Philadelphia, Baltimore, and New Orleans—and something of it in the largest interior cities, yet, take the nation as a whole, there is far less of this sin than is to be found in most countries in Europe. In many of our cities and towns of ten and twenty thousand inhabitants, public prostitution is almost unknown. . . .

We may be charged, as a people, with being rude, and wanting in habitual politeness in our manners. Witlings who visit us to find subjects on which to employ their pens, and with which to garnish their worthless pages, may accomplish their ends, and carry home portfolios laden with stories respecting the oddities and awkwardness which they have remarked among certain classes; but beneath the rough and unpolished exterior of our people there will be found much sincere benevolence, as well as many of those other enduring virtues which conduce to social happiness. We are, comparatively, a new people; this is emphatically true of a large portion of our population. And notwithstanding our vices, whether of native or foreign origin, there is among us a vast amount of practical and efficient goodness. We have much to learn, but I trust we shall not be slow to imitate whatever is excellent in the manners or the deeds of other nations.

4. But the last topic which I shall mention, on which we have been the subjects of more misrepresentation and abuse than any other, is *slavery*. On this difficult and humiliating question I can not enter into detail. It would require a volume to say all that might be said about it, and even all that ought to be said, in order

to make our position fully comprehended by foreigners. I can say only a few words.

It may not be amiss for me to say, however, that this mighty task will never be effected peaceably but through the influence of Christianity. This has accomplished all that has hitherto been done—the destruction of slavery in seven States, and the prevention of its entrance into nine more, besides several Territories; the abolition of the slave-trade before any other nation had done any thing on the subject, and the declaring of it to be of the nature of piracy, and meriting the same punishment. And however desperate the struggle may prove to be, she will not shrink from it.

The example of England in abolishing slavery in her islands will not be lost upon us. It has given a great impulse to the moral movement which is steadily going on in the community. It is true that, as slavery is by our Constitution left to the government of each State in which it exists, to be managed by it alone, there can be no such action among us as that of England, by which the overthrow of slavery in her dominions was effected at a blow. It is in the midst of us; it is not at a distance. Its destruction with us can be accomplished only by those whose pecuniary interests are at stake for its maintenance. This point foreigners should well comprehend. It is the slaveholders among us, or the inhabitants of each slaveholding State, who alone can overthrow it. This it is which makes our position so difficult.

I am of opinion that it will require many years to efface this dreadful evil from the midst of us. It will require long and persevering efforts on the part of good men, and a large amount of that "wisdom which cometh down from above." But of one thing I feel very sure: it is, that although some may act rashly, and sometimes attempt to promote the cause by unwise measures; and others may be too supine, and, through fear of evil consequences, not come up to its help as they ought; although both these parties may charge each other, and perhaps justly, with so acting as to retard the work, yet there is a growing dissatisfaction with this great evil, a conviction that it should and must be terminated as speedily as possible, consistently with the true interests of all concerned, which will one day lead to its overthrow. I do not know how it will be brought about, but Christianity will effect it. God—our fathers' God—invoked more and more earnestly, as I am sure He is, will, by His providence, open the way for this great achievement.

. . . To overthrow slavery in the United States is a great work—the greatest and most difficult, I hesitate not to say, that ever man undertook to accomplish. And there is nothing but Christianity, employing its blessed influences, LIGHT and LOVE, which can effect it. A good deal of time, and a great deal of patience and prudence will also be required, if we would see this evil come to an end in a peaceful way.

God has some great and good end in view in allowing the African race to be brought to America, and placed in a state of servitude. They were regarded at first just as the aboriginal inhabitants of the country were, as barbarous heathen—very much as the Jews regarded the Canaanites, whom the Almighty allowed them to destroy or to reduce to bondage. For a long time, no laws were made for them in some of the colonies—in fact, the laws seemed not to recognize even their existence. But what did Christianity do for them, even in the portions of the country where there was the least amount of true religion? It took them up from their degradation; gave them the manners of civilized life in a good measure; made their masters, especially believing masters, to treat them with kindness; gave them one day of rest in seven; made many of them savingly acquainted with the way of life; and secured to them manifold more blessings, hard as the lot of many may have been, than they could have enjoyed in Africa. Still more, while Christianity said to them, "If you can obtain your freedom, avail yourselves of it," it also said to their masters, "If circumstances allow you to liberate these people in such a way as to secure their true and best welfare, it is your duty, in obedience to the law of Christian kindness, to let them go free." And was this influence of Christianity in vain? Whence, then, came the 54,333 free people of color that were in Virginia in the year 1850? or the 74,723 in Maryland? Whence came the 230,424 that lived in the slaveholding States in that year? These people, or their ancestors, obtained their freedom through the influence of the Gospel on the hearts of their former masters. And so, directly or indirectly, did the 204,484 who were to be found in the free States. There are nearly half a million of free colored people in the United States today, who owe their freedom to the influences of Christianity. And, in my humble judgment, if ever the three millions and a half still in bondage obtain their freedom in a peaceful manner, whether to go to Africa and carry civilization and true religion there, or to remain at home, the most effectual course to reach this great end will be, to augment the influences of the Gospel in the States where they are found, as greatly and as rapidly as possible. I am sorry to say, that this is about the last course which some men among us think of pursuing, and yet they deem themselves Christians.

It would not be difficult to show that, discouraging as some things are in relation to this most important subject, there are, on the other hand, many that are highly encouraging. One of which is, that in no State is any slave forbidden by law to buy a Bible, or receive it as a gift; and if he can read it, he may do so to his heart's content; and if he can not read it, he may hear it read; and in the ten States where it is not allowed to teach the slaves in schools, there is no law to forbid the masters or members of their families to teach them privately, or to impart the knowledge of the word of God, orally, to them in large numbers. Above all, in no State in the American Union is it forbidden by law to preach the Gospel to any man, whether he be bond or free. Shall we say, then, that nothing can be done, and sit down in despair, even although the only men who have conrol over this question are the very men who are most interested in upholding the system?

On the other hand, the anti-slavery feeling of the Northern or Free States (which now form the majority, whereas, at the outset, all of the thirteen original States were slaveholding States) has become exceedingly intense; and while there is no intention to interfere with the subject in portions of the country where, according to the Constitution, the North has no power to act, yet there is a strong determination not to allow slavery to be extended beyond its present limits. On this subject the excitement threatens to be productive of most serious consequences. Great wisdom will be requisite to carry the country safely through the difficulties which surround this great question. Our trust must be in God, that with patience and prudence, slavery will be done away in time, in a way consistent with the best interests of all concerned.

We have sometimes been not a little grieved by the severity—no doubt often inconsiderate—and the want of discrimination with which some of our Christian brethren in the Old World have spoken and written respecting the American Churches, in relation to this subject. Now I have no disposition to say that the American Churches have done all that they ought to do, that they feel all the solicitude, and distress, and sorrow, which they ought for the continued existence of this great evil. There is nothing more probable in itself than that our Churches should fail of coming up to their whole duty on this subject, more than on almost any other, when we consider how they are situated. I do not say this by way of apology, but to state the case truly. But to accuse our Churches throughout the land with *approving* of slavery, because, in some parts of the country, they think they are compelled to *tolerate* it as an evil from which circumstances do not at present allow them to extricate themselves (and this is the most which can be said against them on this point), is going beyond the bounds of Christian charity. Besides, to charge all the American Churches, as well those in the sixteen States and seven Territories in which slavery is unknown, as those in the fifteen States and one District in which it does still exist, with the sin of "robbery," "man-stealing," etc., is to be guilty of something more than a mere want of Christian charity.

But sympathy, love, prayer, and co-operation better become those who love God in all lands, than crimination and recrimination. They form one vast brotherhood, and their trials, their labors, and their hopes are common. Neither difference of language, nor separating oceans, nor diversity of government and of ecclesiastical organizations, nor variety of modes of worship, can divide them. They have their various difficulties to encounter, and their respective works to perform. And how they should delight to encourage each other in every good enterprise, rejoice in each other's success, stimulate and reprove each other (when reproof is necessary) with kindness, and not with bitterness; and thus strive to hasten the universal triumph of the kingdom of their common Lord! . . .

Selected Reading List

GENERAL WORKS ON THE PERIOD

C. Bode (ed.), *American Life in the 1840's* (New York, 1967);
M. Meyers, *The Jacksonian Persuasion; Politics and Belief*
(Stanford, 1967); R. W. B. Lewis, *The American Adam; Inno-
cence, Tragedy and Tradition in the Nineteenth Century* (Chi-
cago, 1955); H. N. Smith, *Virgin Land: The American West as
Symbol and Myth* (Cambridge, Mass., 1950); P. Miller, *The
Life of the Mind in America; From the Revolution to the Civil
War* (New York, 1965).

PRIMARY SOURCES ON RELIGION IN THE PERIOD

B. M. Cross (ed.), *The Autobiography of Lyman Beecher* (Cam-
bridge, Mass., 1961); W. P. Strickland (ed.), *Autobiography of
Peter Cartwright, the Backwoods Preacher* (New York, 1856);
C. G. Finney, *Memoirs of the Rev. Charles G. Finney, Written
by Himself* (New York, 1903); W. G. McLoughlin (ed.), *The
American Evangelicals, 1800–1900* (New York, 1968), chaps.
1–8; R. L. Ferm (ed.), *Issues in American Protestantism, A
Documentary History from the Puritans to the Present* (Garden
City, N.Y., 1969), parts IV–VII.

SECONDARY WORKS ON MAJOR RELIGIOUS TOPICS IN THE PERIOD

S. E. Ahlstrom (ed.), *Theology in America, The Major Protestant
Voices from Puritanism to Neo-Orthodoxy* (Indianapolis,
1967), parts III–IX; S. E. Mead, *The Lively Experiment, The
Shaping of Christianity in America* (New York, 1963), chaps. 2,
3, 6, 7; J. F. Wilson (ed.), *Church and State in American
History* (Boston, 1965), parts I–IV; W. G. McLoughlin, *Modern Revivalism: Charles Grandison Finney to Billy Graham*

(New York, 1959); A. F. Tyler, *Freedom's Ferment, Phases of American Social History from the Colonial Period to the Outbreak of the Civil War* (Minneapolis, 1944); T. L. Smith, *Revivalism and Social Reform in Mid-Nineteenth Century America* (Nashville, Tenn., 1957); W. R. Cross, *The Burned-Over District, The Social and Intellectual History of Enthusiastic Religion in Western New York, 1800–1850* (Ithaca, N.Y., 1950); T. S. Miyakawa, *Protestants and Pioneers, Individualism and Conformity on the American Frontier* (Chicago, 1964); C. C. Cole, Jr., *The Social Ideas of the Northern Evangelists, 1826–1860* (New York, 1954); C. S. Griffin, *Their Brothers' Keepers, Moral Stewardship in the United States, 1800–1865* (New Brunswick, N.J., 1960); C. I. Foster, *An Errand of Mercy; the Evangelical United Front, 1790–1837* (Chapel Hill, N.C., 1960); W. Smith, *Professors and Public Ethics; Studies of Moral Philosophers before the Civil War* (Ithaca, N.Y., 1956); R. A. Billington, *The Protestant Crusade, 1800–1860, A Study of the Origins of American Nativism* (New York, 1938); O. Handlin, *Race and Nationality in American Life* (Boston, 1957); R. F. Berkhofer, Jr., *Salvation and the Savage; An Analysis of Protestant Missions and American Indian Response, 1787–1862* (Lexington, Ky., 1965); O. W. Elsbree, *The Rise of the Missionary Spirit in America, 1780–1815* (Williamsport, Pa., 1928); C. B. Goodykoontz, *Home Missions on the American Frontier* (Caldwell, Ind., 1939); G. H. Barnes, *The Anti-Slavery Impulse, 1830–1844* (New York, 1933); D. G. Mathews, *Slavery and Methodism; A Chapter in American Morality, 1780–1845* (Princeton, N.J., 1965); E. F. Frazier, *The Negro Church in America* (Liverpool, 1964); C. G. Woodson, *History of the Negro Church* (Washington, D.C., 1921).

BIBLIOGRAPHICAL AND RESEARCH AIDS

E. S. Gaustad, *Historical Atlas of Religion in America* (New York, 1962), parts I, II; N. R. Burr, *A Critical Bibliography of Religion in America* (Princeton, N.J., 1961); H. S. Smith, R. T. Handy and L. A. Loetscher (eds.), *American Christianity, An Historical Interpretation with Representative Documents* (New York, 1960 and 1963).

Index